ON FREEDOM AND REVOLT:
A COMPARATIVE INVESTIGATION

Carl E. Moyler

ON FREEDOM AND REVOLT:
A COMPARATIVE INVESTIGATION

ReadersMagnet, LLC

Published in the United States of America
ISBN Paperback: 978-1-949981-08-7
ISBN Hardback: 978-1-949981-09-4
ISBN eBook: 978-1-949981-10-0

ReadersMagnet, LLC
10620 Treena Street, Suite 230 | San Diego, California, 92131 USA
1.619. 354. 2643 | www.readersmagnet.com

Book design copyright © 2019 by ReadersMagnet, LLC. All rights reserved.
Cover design by Ericka Walker
Interior design by Shemaryl Evans

PREFACE

THIS PROJECT DEMONSTRATING EXCELLENCE IS DEDICATED TO ALL those heroes and heroines who have seen and will see life as a daring adventure to be given in the name of service to humanity, to justice, and to freedom. We know a few of them, but many others are lost among the nameless crowd. Albert Camus and Martin Luther King Jr. were first class role models who lived out their passions for justice and freedom and are among the heroes who are well remembered around the world. The following words seem appropriate to reflect what they stood for:

"For all who have sought to make a difference in the lives of men by their service, life, and to lighten the dark places of the earth." (Source: inscription on the wall of the Civil Rights Museum, 16th Street, Birmingham, Alabama (author unknown).

No man is an island, no man stands alone.

Each man's joy is joy to me;
Each man's grief is my own.
We need one another;

So, I must defend each man as my brother,
Each man as my friend.
(John Donne)

Translations for this project: All citations for Albert Camus are the published translations of the referenced texts.

I wish to give thanks and express my gratitude to my First Core, Dr. Sylvia Hill, my Adjuncts, Dr. Rob Robison and Dr. Peter Rose, my Peers Dr. Joseph Lewis and Dr. Elma Lee Moore, and my Second Core, Dr. Joseph Meeker. These wonderful people have provided me with unselfish assistance and encouragement as I have gone through the challenging labors of this doctoral project.

CONTENTS

Chapter One

Chapter Two

Chapter Three

Chapter Four

Chapter Five

Chapter Six

CHAPTER ONE

INTRODUCTORY CHAPTER AND CONTEXT

THE IDEA OF REVOLT AND FREEDOM FROM OPPRESSION and tyranny are as old as the Bible. Moses was sent to Egypt by God on a mission of revolt to bring freedom to the Jews who were being dominated and held in slavery by the Egyptians (Exodus, Chapters 5-14). The Jewish revolt for freedom and a Promised Land did not take place until the powers of Pharaoh, the oppressor, were assaulted by ten plagues and their devastating consequences. Then, through miraculous and divine intervention, the Jews received their release from captivity and made their exodus to freedom.

In the United States, both the Revolutionary War (1775-1783) and the Civil War (1861-1865) were fought over issues dealing with justice and freedom. Indeed, the concept of being endowed with "life, liberty and the pursuit of happiness" by our Creator is written into the Bill of Rights of the Declaration of Independence. The idea of the founding of America was based on a quest for freedom. The first settlers came to American shores in search of relief from religious and economic persecution. They were willing to suffer and sacrifice for a better life.

According to the *World Book Encyclopedia* (1999), for years people from all over the world have come to America through New York Harbor past the Statue of Liberty. This great monument dedicated to freedom and the overthrow of tyranny was given to the United States by France in 1844. Its proper name is "Liberty Enlightening the World." Words from the poem, "A New Colossus" (1903), by Emma Lazarus are inscribed on the pedestal: "Give me your tired your poor, Your huddled masses yearning to breathe free, The wretched refuse of your teeming shore. Send these, the homeless, tempest-toss to me, I lift my lamp beside the golden door!" (873). So, America has always been perceived as the land of the free where opportunity beckons the people of the world. However, blacks were brought to this country as slaves, in chains, and were kept in a state of servitude for 250 years. This glaring contradiction between promise and practice was one of the major platforms for revolt pursued by Dr. Martin Luther King, Jr. during his Civil Rights leadership campaign.

In a similar manner, the motto of the Republic of France since the French Revolution of 1789 has been "Liberty, Equality and Brotherhood." No doubt, Albert Camus remembered this motto as he attempted to understand the age into which he was born. His meager and impoverished beginnings in Algeria, North Africa, surely helped to sensitize him to the sufferings of Europeans between 1922 and 1947. During that time, some 70 million men, women and children were displaced, sent to another country or killed (Cruickshank 1978).

In connection with the above, Cruickshank informs us that:

It is within this context that Camus created his work as a writer. This is the background of events which he witnessed, which we have witnessed and which he approached with a questioning urgency. It is the subject of human suffering in our time. Faced with such a spectacle, Camus felt humility and inadequacy, but he was not prepared to close his eyes to it. We all know, at least second hand, of torture and brainwashing, mass deportations and scientifically controlled destruction, racial hatred and the summary judgments of "people's courts." What is so particularly alarming is that all these things have been defended at one time or another, in the name of ideologies claiming as their ultimate goal the greater happiness of human kind? The age for which Camus wrote is thus one of moral and intellectual confusion and convulsion. The same values have been invoked on behalf of so many conflicting causes that these values have lost all meaning. The story of our century has been the story of increasingly terrible blows dealt against the traditional humanist assumptions (ix).

There appears to be little question that the flight from oppression in search of a better life and world is a natural desire of human nature. Viewing the world from the perspective of an Afro American clergyman, Dr. Martin Luther King, Jr. answered the call of conscience to enter the struggle of revolt and freedom from injustice and oppression as a goal. Historically, Negroes had survived two hundred fifty years of slavery and even with the Emancipation Proclamation of 1863, they were still treated as second class citizens, outcasts, and with few rights. Thus, they were segregated and discriminated against socially, educationally, economically and politically.

Camus and King were born, reared and lived as personal witnesses to the social and political ravages of their time and place. Neither man was willing to stand in the presence of the evils of oppression and do nothing. They entered the struggle as full participants, one an agnostic humanist and the other a seminary trained Christian. Not surprisingly, it appears that there are parallels in their search for solutions to the most perplexing human problems of our times, such as: tyranny, oppression, racism, exploitation, murder, and war. Both men were world leaders in their vocations and were Nobel Prize winners. What can we learn from them that will improve the civilization of our times as we move into the twenty-first century? What were they telling us to do? Let us take a closer look.

Sales data from Gallimard Publishing, Paris, the publisher of Camus' works, indicates that his publications continue to appear at the top of sales lists. (Interview with Catherine Camus, the daughter, 1995). To enlarge on this point, these data indicate, further, that they are read by persons of all races, sexes, ages, classes and persuasions. What is it about Camus' writings that give them such broad range audience appeal? Perhaps the answer can be found in a piece of research from an Internet source entitled *Discovering Authors Module—Most Studied Authors on CD-ROM*, Gale Research (1996). The research stated that "he was a moral conscience of thousands of young people in Europe and the United States, as he is still today." It is obvious, then, that Camus was able to impart to generations, past and present, a voice of hope and optimism that relieved fear and uncertainty (Todd 1996).

On the other hand, what is it about the power, life, witness and role model of Dr. Martin Luther King, Jr. that has lifted both his life and writings to world prominence? What has his legacy of civil rights struggle and nonviolent revolt left as a message for todays and future generations? John Hope Franklin in Albert and Hoffman, eds. (1990). *We Shall Overcome*, informs us that it is, indeed, Dr. King's determined philosophy of militant nonviolent revolt in the face of overwhelming violence against himself and his followers that has set him apart in giving generations yet to come a new power that is infused with hope, justice and love.

How, then, and at what points, do these men's lives and thoughts cross, parallel, illumine and find common ground with one another? Those are the relevant questions in this research. Using a comparative approach, I will endeavor to investigate, and see if there are answers that will provide a different perspective on the concepts of freedom and revolt, as perceived by Camus and King. It is important to point out that, within the parameters of comparative literature, this comparison is being made between a professional writer and a seminary trained pastor who was also a gifted writer.

STATEMENT OF THE PROBLEM

A COMPARISON OF THE CONCEPTS OF REVOLT AND FREEDOM IN THE THINKING OF ALBERT CAMUS AND DR. MARTIN LUTHER KING, JR.

The concepts of revolt and freedom are key words and points of reference in the works and thought of Albert Camus and Dr. Martin Luther King, Jr. Both men chose to answer the call, within the context of their vocations, to address the needs of human beings who were suffering, exploited, dehumanized and oppressed. Individual and collective strategies founded upon revolt and protest for freedom became their agenda for involvement, leadership, and writing.

However, at what points do their lives parallel one another? What comparisons and commonalties are evident in their work? For certain, they were both agents for change who lived courageous, and at times, threatened lives. While both met premature deaths at the very pinnacle of their careers, Camus in 1960 at age 46, and King in 1968 at age 39. They, nonetheless, appear to have left a message for human beings that is still bearing the burden of truth, example, and direction for a better world and a more hopeful future (Lottman 1979; Oates 1982).

PURPOSE OF THE STUDY

The purpose of this qualitative study will be to present and comparatively examine the ideas and visions of two highly acclaimed human rights champions whose lives, work and thoughts were worthy enough for both of them to be awarded a Nobel Prize. Their impact on "Making a Difference" (Brée 1964; Bennett 1968) for the good of humanity and the world we live in is still undetermined. It is my desire to research and discover their individual message for today's generations. In addition, I believe their **combined message** has implications and directions that will provide the foundation for plans of action that will assist with the development of the **moral courage** for positive changes among people living in a civilized society. Further, they seem to provide answers to the problems of oppression, tyranny, racism, injustice and war. These destructive problems hinder human progress and productivity and prevent human beings from being their best. The two writers urged every human being to be actively involved in answering the challenges presented in this undertaking. In so doing, everyone can join the ranks of Camus and King in helping to bring about reconciliation among all people and the lessening of suffering for all. In brief, then, what are an agnostic and a Christian telling us to do to civilize and humanize the world for now and the future?

Studies of Camus have situated him at different times as a twentieth century writer of the absurd, existentialism, anti-Christian sentiment, revolt and freedom. Studies of King have situated him as a civil rights fighter, social/political activist, theologian/intellectual and leader for revolt and freedom for oppressed people. A comparative study of the thought of these two men has not yet been undertaken by scholars. The current study proposes to address this gap in our knowledge and to further the impact of their thought upon ongoing attempts to resolve the problems of freedom and justice.

This comparison is being made between an agnostic humanist and a staunch God-fearing seminary trained theologian. Camus, on the one hand, embraced a humanism that called upon human beings to care and show compassion to each other. There was no omnipotent being to help fight battles or remove obstacles. The struggle was in the hands, individually and collectively, of human beings willing to join the team. Dr. King, on the other hand was a Baptist preacher, a graduate of Crozer Theological Seminary who had earned a Ph.D. in Systematic Theology from Boston University. He believed in the Creator and omnipotent God of the Bible who offered sufficient grace for every struggle to those who believed in Him. (Oates 1982; Cone 1991).

IMPORTANCE OF THE STUDY

The writings of Albert Camus addressed the problems of his time and ours that weigh negatively on the lives and consciences of humankind. His view was that the prose writer had a specific job and calling to accomplish. The writer must confront and engage an audience or reading public with a writing ethic that calls for revolt against any of the various faces of tyranny, be it injustice, oppression, racism, war, persecution, greed, or holocaust (Brée 1964; Lottman 1978). For Camus, while each individual is called to stand up to oppression, it is the power and impact found in the solidarity of collective or group revolt that most effectively addresses the problem of our inhumanity to one another (Cruickshank 1978).

Camus participated in the French Resistance against Nazi occupation in France. This underground organization of freedom fighters represented for him both the social and the political will of a people who had mustered the courage to stand up to the evils of totalitarianism. Further, this individual and collective revolt against tyranny and injustice are evident in two of his major works, *The Plague* and *The Just Assassins*. Both of these literary pieces are presented and explained in depth in Chapter Two of this document. Let us now take a look at Dr. King and his early involvement with oppression and injustice.

Dr. King led The Montgomery (Alabama) Improvement Association boycott of segregated busing in that city. The protest against inhumane, indignant and disrespectful treatment given to blacks on public transportation in that city gave rise to the call for revolt. A master plan of **militant nonviolence** was organized and implemented that began the civil rights movement of the 50's and 60's in the United States (Oates 1982). This master plan is presented in much more detail in a discussion of Dr. King's book *Stride Toward Freedom* in Chapter Two of this document. The meaning and impact of the Montgomery movement has literally touched the lives, in some manner or other, of every American (and people worldwide) during the last five years. Dr. King, motivated by his hunger for justice and freedom, created the vehicle of revolt that included such strategies as marches, sit-ins, wade-ins, kneel-ins, demonstrations, boycotts and peaceful confrontation. These strategies (combined with some borrowed from other places) have been adopted around the world by groups seeking redress to grievances and injustices.

Dr. King's writings, from his first book, *Stride Toward Freedom* (1958) to his last book *The Trumpet of Conscience* (1968) document with passionate eloquence the yearning of the Negro people for freedom from generations of unspeakable oppression (1619-1968) which demanded revolt. Writing in the *Trumpet of Conscience* Dr. King adds:

> The blanket of fear was lifted by Negro youth. When they took their struggle to the streets, a new spirit of resistance was born. Inspired by the boldness and ingenuity of Negroes, white youth stirred into action and formed an alliance that aroused the conscience of the nation. (45).

Looking at the importance of this study from another point of view, neither Camus nor Dr. King believed in violence as a means of settling discord, disagreements, grievances and arguments –between persons, between institutions, between ethnic groups, or between nations. Nonviolence was identified as a strategy of protest when human freedom was being oppressed. Here in the United States, *what if* the statutes, strategies, and principles of nonviolence had been taught to the persons who have committed senseless, multiple shootings and murder in Paducah, Kentucky; Jonesboro, Arkansas; Littleton, Colorado; Skokie/Chicago, Illinois; and Sidney, Ohio? The most recent carnages have been in Atlanta, Georgia, and at a Jewish synagogue in Los Angeles, California.

There are other incidents of multiple shootings and murder of innocent victims that are not included in the listing above. However, all of these atrocities have resulted from a disregard for human life, ethnic hate/racism, a loss of hope, and a nihilistic disposition towards life's difficulties, rejections, and shattered dreams. If the statutes, strategies, and principles of nonviolence had been taught to these individuals, what would have been the difference? What would have happened if the assailants had at their disposal better coping mechanisms to utilize when the disappointments of life became severe? Was no reconciliation possible? Will there be others who will follow these patterns? Is there no solution available, or will all Americans, at any time and place, continue to be at risk? Hopefully, this research will provide some answers.

Moving now from the national to the worldwide domain, what could have served as a deterrent to the war of ethnic cleansing and the grievously inhumane atrocities and, murders that took place in Kosovo, Yugoslavia? There is civil war currently going on among ethnic groups in Africa–Angola, Sierra Leone as well as in Sri Lanka and Indonesia. Is the utter destruction, disruption, and terrors of war the best means to solve differences between ethnic groups and nations? Is a solution possible? I believe Camus and King will have some thoughts to compare on these questions.

BASIC ASSUMPTIONS

Assumptions are stated here in order that the reader will connect the various issues clearly. While assumptions are self-evident, many researcher include them "so that those inspecting the research procedure may see every component and evaluate accordingly" (Leedy 1995: 8)

1. Camus' and King's works mutually illuminate each other.

2. Parallel events in their lives regarding revolt and freedom impacted them in similar ways.

3. The difference in their religious beliefs explains significant differences in their thought and their life decisions.

4. Their opposition to oppression unifies their thought and provides direction for modern society.

DELIMITATIONS

1. The purpose of these research delimitations is to establish, as precisely as possible; the parameters that will be addressed and will not be addressed (Leedy 1995: 59). Ten common grounds will be the basis of comparison for this study. While there are other areas that could be included in this investigation, the ten areas chosen appear adequate for this comparative study. These common grounds are listed in Chapter Three.

2. At least two common grounds will be the basis of contrast for this study. The same rationale given above applies here.

3. Freedom and revolt will be the focus around which the Project Demonstrating Excellence (PDE) or dissertation will evolve and will comprise the major part of the text.

4. The data collected for this study is qualitative in nature. No attempt was made to collect quantitative data for statistical analysis due to the comparative literature format of the investigation.

DEFINITION OF TERMS

The writer has developed the following working definitions for this study with reference to the *World Book Encyclopedia Dictionary* (1999). The purpose of these definitions is to assure that the readers will interpret these often used words with the same understanding as the researcher.

1. **Revolt**—resistance against any unjust power or restriction. An act or condition of rebelling. To turn against a leader or condition. To cause to feel disgust concerning a condition. To disobey unjust legal authority.

2. **Freedom**—the state or condition of being free. Not being under another person's control, the power to do, say or think as one pleases, liberty, free movement or action of one's person; the right to aspire to fulfill one's goals with equal opportunity.

3. **Nihilism**—the rejection of established beliefs, such as in religion, morals, government, family and laws; the denial of all existence; rejection of objective morality or the basis of objective morality; the use of violence and terrorism as a means to achieve social and political ends.

4. **Metaphysical**—the study of the nature of things, knowledge and reality, the abstract study of humans' relation to one another, to the created world, and, to the laws of the universe.

5. **Agape Love**—the love and care of another person because that person is human and made in the image and likeness of God; the expectation of nothing in return for this caring and love; love in return for evil and abuse.

6. **Absurdity**—a negative view of life that manifests itself in an attitude of estrangement and detachment from hope and optimism.

7. **Solidarity**—a commitment to a cause that is characterized by unity, team work, common goals, interests, caring, and service. It is looking beyond self with an attitude of giving to others. It is taking a stand against tyranny and oppression; and it is a concerted effort to obtain justice and freedom.

SUMMARY OF CHAPTER ONE

Chapter One of this dissertation has covered the following content:

1. **The Introduction** which established the historical as well as the current context of the study.

2. **The Statement of the Problem** which identified revolt and freedom as the defining comparative literature concepts through which the works of Camus and King would be interpreted.

3. **The Purpose of the Study** is to present and comparatively examine the ideas and visions of two highly acclaimed human rights champions whose lives, work and thoughts were worthy of Nobel Prize awards. This particular comparative study of the thought of these two men has not yet been undertaken by scholars in the field. The current study proposes to address this gap in our knowledge.

4. **The Importance of the Study** will be to examine and interpret the messages that Camus and King brought forth in addressing the human condition problems of their times and ours–These problems weigh negatively on the lives and consciences of humankind. These problems include oppression, tyranny, injustice, murder, racism, war, persecution, greed or holocaust.

5. **The Basic Assumptions** of the study have addressed the axioms that propose to synthesize the major issues in a manner that adds clarity for the reader. Four basic assumptions were given.

6. **The Delimitations** have been presented in order to provide the particular parameters that will guide and control the investigation. This is necessary inasmuch as numerous studies have been written on both men and a beginning and ending point had to be established.

7. **The Definition of Terms** has been provided in order to define frequently used terms in the study. These definitions give consistent interpretations to key words and concepts for the readers.

OVERVIEW OF THE ORGANIZATION FOR THE REMAINDER OF THE STUDY

The remainder of this study will be recorded as follows:

Chapter 2:   **The Review of Literature**
Chapter 3:   **The Research Methodology**
Chapter 4:   **The Findings and Results**
Chapter 5:   **The Summary of Findings and Conclusions**
Chapter 6:   **The Recommendations**

CHAPTER TWO

LITERATURE REVIEW

THE REVIEW OF LITERATURE HAS BEEN ORGANIZED INTO sections according to the focus of this study. These sections will include: (1). A comparative analysis of revolt and freedom in the key works of Albert Camus and Dr. Martin Luther King, Jr. Both primary and secondary sources will be used to interpret these concepts. (2). A comparative critique of the Nobel Prize acceptance speeches of Albert Camus and Dr. Martin Luther King, Jr. The Nobel Prize speeches are a primary source of information that reflects several important points of view regarding the thoughts of these two men.

A COMPARATIVE ANALYSIS OF REVOLT AND FREEDOM AS THEY APPEAR IN THE KEY WORKS OF ALBERT CAMUS AND DR. MARTIN LUTHER KING, JR.

It would be difficult to discuss the work of Albert Camus or Dr. Martin Luther King, Jr. without coming to grips with two concepts that are focal in their messages to humankind: **Revolt and Freedom.** A close examination of the works of both men reveal that these words have a special meaning that encapsulates humankind's most promising hope for a more rational order where justice and happiness might reign. My procedure in this section of the literature review will be: 1.)—to present an analysis of each writer as he addresses revolt and freedom individually and 2.)–to provide critical interpretation of key passages from secondary sources that address revolt and freedom in their work, then, 3.)–to summarize the literature review using a comparative discussion format.

REVOLT AND FREEDOM IN THE WORKS OF ALBERT CAMUS

According to Germaine Brée (1964), a writer's background and maturation experiences often play a key role in what is written and how it is written. Albert Camus was born November 7, 1913, in Mondavi, Algeria, North Africa. His father, Lucien, was a day laborer who taught himself to read at age twenty. He was called into military service during the First World War and died of a wound suffered at the battle of the Marne in France. Albert was one year old at the time. This left Catherine Camus, his mother, with the responsibility of providing for the family on cleaning woman's wages. Catherine was illiterate, hard of hearing and suffered a speech impediment. Due to meager finances, the family was forced to move into a small three room apartment with Catherine's mother, Catherine Sintes, two brothers, Joseph and Etienne and a paralyzed uncle, in the blue collar section of Algeria known as Belcourt. There was no running water or bathroom. An oil lamp provided the only artificial light. The grandmother was stern, unloving and overbearing. She suffered from liver disease. The whole family, including young Albert Camus, lived an impoverished life. Camus spent the first seventeen years of his life living under these circumstances. According to Brée (1964), Camus would say later in life that," Each artist preserves deep down a unique spring which, throughout his life, feeds what he is and what he says. I know that for me this spring is in the world of poverty and light I lived in for a long time (5).

Along the same line of thought, concerning his literary values, Ellison (1990) tells us that:

Because Camus grew up among simple people, many of whom were illiterate, and because he witnessed their enduring dignity through periods of material hardship, hunger, and physical suffering, he retained throughout his career a strong sense of empathy for those people whose lives were consumed by unremitting labor, whose aspirations rarely were fulfilled. This empathy underlies his political positions and informs substantial parts of his literary works (5).

Thus, Camus never forgets who he is, his humble origins, and how he had seen severe hardship in the lives of his fellow Algerians, and why he as an artist must bear witness to the truth in deploring injustice, poverty, and the oppression of political ideologies.

Brée (1964; Thody 1989; and Todd 1996), inform us that at the age of seventeen, in 1930, he contacted and fought a life-threatening battle with tuberculosis, which began in his right lung and then spread to the left. This illness was to be a burden through out his life. He, thus learned at an early age the agony and suffering of a serious illness and a confrontation with his own mortality. In the thirties and forties, tuberculosis was a deadly disease. Initially, it prevented Camus from entering university teaching because he could not pass the physical. Later, it prevented him from serving in the military. However, he states some years later that his meager and difficult beginnings developed in him an appreciation for hard and honest work as well as a caring and loving attitude towards poverty, hardship, and suffering. Further, his working class background gave him a strong sense of responsibility in the face of social injustice. However, the oppression of poverty and the confrontation with his own mortality, due to his illness, did not make him bitter, because he still enjoyed the liberation given to him by the beauty of nature found in the North African landscape. Algeria and North Africa provided the seed of Camus' thought and spiritual landscape. The sun, sea, sky, wind, and climate inspired his values as a person and as a writer. Camus was a great lover of the gorgeous outdoors found in the Mediterranean world. According to Mairowitz and Korkos (1998), Algeria took on the personage of a main character in several of Camus' works: *The Stranger* (1942), *The Plague* (1947), *The Inside and the Outside* (1937), *Nuptials* (1938), *The First Man* (1994). These works owe their distinct originality and setting to Camus' strong desire to convey the quality and meaning of his native country, its people, climate, and landscape. His native background experiences influenced him in a way that gave his language and writing a power and brilliance that set him apart from other French writers of his times who were from mainland France (Brée 1964). According to Wyatt (1998), "Camus was born into poverty, raised by a widowed, nearly-deaf mother... Experiences produce biases—and Camus' biases were rooted in poverty and suffering... Human rights and equality preoccupied Camus" (3).

Camus was a bright student and attended secondary school on a full government scholarship. He received early mentoring and encouragement from Professor Louis Germain who recognized in the young man the capacity of original thinking and creative expression. Professor Germain was instrumental in persuading the family to allow Camus to prepare for the university. Germain allowed Camus to use books from his library and continued to give him private tutoring. Camus was a scholar of superior quality in all of his studies. Also, during his teen years, Camus developed into an excellent athlete, becoming an accomplished swimmer and soccer player. After successfully completing secondary school, Camus attendyd the University of Algiers, from 1932 to 1936. He studied philosophy, poetry, Greek and the general classics required by his course of study. His university studies were accomplished under the tutelage of Professor Jean Grenier, another personal mentor. Camus graduated with the equivalent of a Masters Degree in philosophy in 1936. He wanted to teach at the university level, but because of poor health and the inability to pass the necessary physical tests, he did not meet teacher qualifications. Consequently, he began to pursue a career in journalism. During this time (1934), Camus had his first marriage with Simone Hie, which ended in divorce one year later. In 1940, he married Francine Faure. In 1945 twins were born to this second marriage, a girl and a boy, Catherine and Jean (Brée 1964; Lottman 1979; Todd 1996).

Before he graduated from the University of Algiers, Camus had already given evidence of a burning passion in search of truth by writing essays. These essays were to become parts of his two earliest works, *Betwixt and Between* (1937) and *Revolt in the Asturias* (1937). This was the generation of the 1930s and Camus had already declared himself an artist with a responsibility to humankind. By 1941 Camus had moved to Paris and was able to personally witness the atrocities of Nazism. He became active in the French Resistance and the editor of the underground tabloid *Combat.* He continued to write as well as work as a professional reader for Gallimard Publishing. As noted in his Nobel acceptance speech in 1957, Camus states that "art is not a solitary pleasure. It is a means of moving the greatest number of people by offering them a privileged image of common sufferings and common joys." Extending this line of reasoning to an earlier date, Thody (1961), states that Camus' perception of his art was "the role of the artist and intellectual was not for him to take part in politics at the everyday level of argument, controversy, negotiation, and compromise. But to tell the truth on those occasions when the threat to freedom existed beyond all possible doubt" (202). Camus states further in Todd (1996) concerning political party involvement that: "To create a party takes all of a man's time and energy, and I don't believe I am that man. I'm already serving politics, history, and man in my way, which is a double way. First, I fight as a basic militant; second I use language to define what I think is right... I know my limits" (248). Thus, while Camus is steering clear of involvement with the starting of any political party, he is nonetheless choosing his own weapons to address militancy, politics, and his definitions of what is right.

Cruickshank (1978) informs us that among the post 1900 generation of Sartre, Malraux, Camus, and Anouilh—absolute revolt often seemed an inevitable attitude. These writers had "witnessed at a crucial stage in their emotional and intellectual development the failure of progress, of science, of democracy, of reason and finally the failure of man." (Cruickshank: 6). Consequently, there was a loss of faith in traditional Christian beliefs, which relied on a transcendental being. Thus, the literature of revolt helped to turn from the worship of God to the worship of human beings carving out their own uncertain destinies vis-a-vis human condition circumstances. Camus believed that the job of the writer was to be a witness of the times in search of freedom and justice in the midst of chaos. Therefore, as an artist and moralist, Camus succeeded in being able to expound the moral conscience of modern human beings as his works penetrated relevant questions concerning revolt, justice, freedom, human suffering, and the meaning of life as it is threatened by death. Ellison (1990) takes the point of view that one of Camus' truly great gifts was his unique ability to write about serious ethical issues in manner that was realistic to the reader. As a reflection of his impressive talent and versatility, Camus presented his works to the reader using the novel, short story, philosophical essay, essay, and the play. Each of these genre was used in a particular manner to convey the concepts of revolt and freedom. Literary products representing each of these genre will be included in this research report.

In the evolution of Camus' works, we can see two distinct types of revolt (Br e 1964: 224–230). The first is metaphysical revolt or revolt against life conditions, reality and the nature of existence vis-a-vis God and the world. Stated further, in the words of Camus: "Metaphysical rebellion is a claim, motivated by the concept of complete unity, against the suffering of life and death and a protest against the human condition both for its incompleteness, thanks to death, and its wastefulness thanks to evil." *(The Rebel* 1956: 24). The second is historical or collective revolt or the revolt against the injustices and oppression meted out by other human beings. For a discussion of the former, we will return to the generation of the forties and his work, *The Stranger.*

THE STRANGER

The Stranger (1942), was written in Algeria in 1939 and 1940. It was the first work of Camus to achieve prominence in French literary circles. For Europe, this was the middle of World War II. The moral and universal vision of Camus was evident in the book. Symbolically, he was portraying the uncertain and death threatening atmosphere of the times. The main character, Meursault seems to have been driven to commit an avoidable murder for reasons beyond his control. How could this act of violence have been reconciled for a better end? This is the major question around which the idea of the absurd flows in and out of the novel.

Camus tells us that, "In a world suddenly stripped of dreams and hope, man feels like a stranger. This exile is without memories of a lost homeland or of the hope of a Promised Land. This divorce between man and life, the actor and his background is in truth the feeling of absurdity." *(The Myth of Sisyphus:* 5). It appears that this feeling of estrangement and detachment from life and meaning were a common life style during the generation of the forties.

The character of Meursault in *The Stranger* embodies the concept of exile to which Camus refers. Meursault's life is devoid of any meaning with the exception of physical sensations. He is detached and insensitive to all that would have a bearing upon his life. He is unconcerned about his mother's death, job advancement, meaningful love of a woman, his friends, or an Arab that he nonchalantly kills on a beach. Meursault is a man of his times who has lived a life of relative values. The evidence presented at Meursault's murder trial recounts a long history of an uncaring and unfocused life. He never asks questions about anything and his answers to questions are cold and indifferent. At the murder trial, the prosecuting attorney and the jury found Meursault's attitude obnoxious, detached, and rude. Wyatt (1998) sees Meursault "as an anti-hero, at best. His only redeeming quality is his honesty, no matter how absurd" (4). Hopkins (1969) views Meursault as an individual who only attaches importance to the tangible—the things that he can experience as concrete realities. Thus, Meursault is sentenced to death more for his flagrant abuse of societal norms than for shooting the Arab four times. In Algerian courts of law at that time, due to racism, the murder of an Arab by a Frenchman was not a capital offense (O'Brien: 22). However, Meursault does nothing to save his life. Finally, it is Meursault's own impending execution and loss of life, which causes him, at the end of the novel, to realize that life, does have meaning just within itself. He concludes that, "I am aware for the first time of the tender indifference of the world" (153). He realizes, thus, that he had been happy and would like to live life all over again. He has lost his penchant for indifference. For him, the inevitability of death intensifies and gives value to life. Therefore, for Camus, it appears that Meursualt's voice and life were reflections of a universal human condition.

"Meursault doesn't play the game. He refuses to lie… He refuses to disguise his feelings and immediately society feels threatened. He is asked, for example, to say that he regrets his crime according to the ritual formula. He replies that he feels about it more annoyance than real regret, and this shade of meaning condemns him." (O'Brien 1970:19). It would appear that Meursault's alienation from his world of people and circumstances make him a stranger. In a quote from Jean-Paul Sartre in *Most Studied Authors on CD-ROM*, Gale Research: 1996), the point is made: "And now we fully understand the title of Camus' novel. The stranger he wants to portray is precisely one of those terrible innocents who shock society by not accepting the rules of its game. He lives among outsiders, but to them, too, he is a stranger… And we ourselves, who, on opening the book are not yet familiar with the feeling of the absurd, vainly try to judge him according to our usual standards. For us, too, he is a stranger" (9).

At the time, *The Stranger* was written in 1942, Meursault's voice for Camus was that of a living man, and his life was symbolic of the general human condition of that time. The world was bleak and hostile. Europeans had gone through two world wars. And above all, due to the devastation in every direction due to war, humans were just trying to survive and were certainly aware of their own mortality. Meursault's exile was their exile, detachment, and estrangement. Concerning Meursault, Germaine Brée (1964), points out that Meursault loses because he refused to revolt against an absurd life and to seek the freedom he so desperately wanted:

> The very essence of *the absurd* in his case is that out of indifference, he linked forces with violence and death, not with love and life… In *The Stranger* Camus thus suggests that in the face of the absurd no man can afford passively just to exist. To fail to question the meaning of the spectacle of life is to condemn both ourselves as individuals and the whole world to nothingness (117).

Thus, In *The Stranger,* Camus puts into place a plot that unleashes a chain of events that destroys freedom and that destroys the person who pursues life along this course of absurdity. Thus, as Sartre has commented, Meursault is indeed a stranger, very different, and most normal readers would probably find him a somewhat pitiful personality trying to find his way.

Murchland (1962) in G. Brée, eds., *Camus: A Collection of Critical Essays* states that the meaning of the absurd is "infirmity, ignorance, irrationality, nostalgia, the impossibility of distinguishing the true from the false, our radical inability to know ourselves or others, the implacable mystery of the world" (61). This seems to be a good description of Meursault. So, the fact of the absurd is a given and it is a challenge to freedom, but it must be faced with courage and understanding and overcome with constant commitment, revolt, and dedication to a more positive response to life's dilemmas. Meursault did none of these things in a search for his freedom. Consequently, his life did not succeed. What could he have done? Due to his indifference, was he manipulated by the law? Let us now take a look at another of Camus' popular works to find an answer to these questions.

THE MYTH OF SISYPHUS

In response to Meursault, *The Myth of Sisyphus* (1942) offers a provisional attitude to be adopted towards life's metaphysical dilemma. It is Camus' own and is addressed to all those whose acts lose their significance due to the lack of any system to which they can be related. Camus finds in Sisyphus the symbolic champion of man's ability to deal with life in its most profound emptiness, bordering on the brink of death. Germaine Brée, *Camus* (1964), concludes that, "our only certainty is our life. Logically, it is precisely because our life has no meaning beyond itself that we must violently reject any thought of coming to terms with death. Revolt against death is the only possible human attitude" (203). Brand (1987) concludes in Frank Magill, eds., *The Nobel Prize Winners-Literature* (1987) that "the absurd is the void between man's need for a universe that is coherent, lucid and rational, and the universe's refusal to reveal itself in this manner, instead showing itself to be largely incoherent, meaningless, and irrational" (637). Thus, *The Myth of Sisyphus* takes on twentieth century relevance.

The Myth of Sisyphus is a philosophical essay that had its origin in the wartime personal experiences of Camus just as does *The Stranger*. The essay offers a symbolic answer to the absurd. Stories from antiquity have it that Sisyphus was a wise and prudent man. He made the mistake, however, of defying the power and patience of the gods. His resulting punishment was with malice and extreme cruelty. He was condemned to roll a huge rock up a steep mountain; once the rock reached the top, he was to watch as he allowed it to roll back down to the starting point. He then started the task all over again. This was to go on for the rest of his life (O'Brien 1970; Ellison 1990). The work of laboriously pushing the rock to the top of the mountain accomplished nothing and has become the symbol of useless work, done under duress, and undertaken in despair.

The first idea raised by *The Myth of Sisyphus* is the question of whether it is worth living since it is so empty of meaning. Why not commit suicide? That is a choice available to those persons who feel that being dead is more valuable than being alive. But Camus questions this solution: "Does the absurd demand that I should kill myself?" *(The Rebel:* 1). Therefore, the question as to whether we should be alive at all must be answered before life can be seen as a negative or positive value. Following this line of reasoning, Camus tells us that we are all assaulted by conditions that can render life absurd in some manner or other. The unexpected loss of a loved one, the loss of a job and livelihood, a disastrous marriage, a debilitating injury, the sudden loss of health, general racial injustice, or an oppressive existence. What is the answer?

To pierce the invisible curtain of the infinite with our human and finite minds has always been a dilemma (Brée 1964; Thody 1989). Camus' answer to this enigma is to be found in the idea of *The Myth of Sisyphus*. Sisyphus could be the person of any time or place who had goals, projects, hopes, freedom and ambitions for his life and for his future. But all of this is lost in one sudden moment of life circumstance, and he ends up being faced with death (Ellison1990; Todd 1996). How does one live through it all?

Camus, through Sisyphus' attitude, puts forth a possible answer as Sisyphus returns to the bottom of his mountain:

"It is during this return, this pause that Sisyphus interests me. This hour which is like a welcome breathing and which comes back as surely as his misfortune, this hour is that of consciousness... Sisyphus, proletarian of the gods, impotent and rebellious, knows the extent of his miserable condition: It is on this condition that he reflects during his descent. The clairvoyance that was intended as his torment simultaneously serves his triumph. Camus concludes: "There is no fate that cannot be surmounted by scorn." (90).

Apparently, it is this scorn that was Sisyphus' revolt and his freedom from absurdity. Therefore, Sisyphus is confronted with a lifetime absurd condition. The question that is raised by Sisyphus' eternal condition is "what is more degrading than work that is both useless and without hope?" (164). But human beings need not succumb to this condition. Look at Sisyphus: "Each time that he leaves the top of the hill and slowly returns to the bottom, he is superior to his life sentence. He is stronger than his rock" (89). Sisyphus is victorious because, he: "Powerless and in revolt understands completely the extent of his miserable condition: that is what he meditates about during his descent. The clairvoyance, which ought to cause his torment, accounts at the same time for his victory (90). Sisyphus is telling us that it is the mindset and attitude concerning the condition that determines victory or defeat.

Two of Camus' characters, therefore, Meursault and Sisyphus, both faced with similar absurd life conditions—make a response. One is a loser and one is a winner. One is swallowed up in disaster. One is walking in victory. Life, after all, according to Camus, abounds in the incomprehensible, unpredictable, incongruous, and the purposeless. Notwithstanding, it is valuable and must be preserved at all costs to the bitter end. It is Sisyphus' compassionate commitment to this principle that underlines his success. The struggle of life itself gives him joy and in the final analysis, as stated in the essay, "We have to conclude that Sisyphus is happy" (91). In fact, "Sisyphus is a call to happiness in the midst of chaos." (Brée 1964: 211).

The burden of this metaphysical revolt and the opportunity for victory are placed squarely on the shoulders of human beings. It seems that Camus is saying to us that reliance on doctrines, religious or otherwise, just as often as not, causes inertia and superstition, and that he alone must bear the burden and responsibility for his life. For O'Brien (1970), the central message is that the true revolt against absurdity of existence consists not in suicide but in continuing to live. It appears, then, that the metaphysical revolt in *The Myth of Sisyphus* is a personal defiance in the face of death, since death by whatever causes, including suicide, brings to a close a beautiful and valuable life, and for Camus, every life is valuable.

However, after 1944, the idea of revolt evolves into the idea of a total force, as total group effort towards a more just order. It originated in the primitive feeling of human solidarity and dignity. This is historical or collective revolt. He is concerned with oppression, the inhumanity of war, intolerance, and any of the other faces of tyranny that are used to afflict suffering upon human beings. The ravages of World War II and German atrocities appear to be uppermost in his thought.

Thomas Hanna (1962) in G. Brée, eds. *Camus: A Collection of Critical Essays,* offers the view of this type of revolt as "nothing more or less than a call to create, to transform the inhumanity of the world into the image of man, to humanize what is inhuman–in short, to civilize" (58). Brand (1987) in Magill, eds., *The Nobel Prize Winners–Literature,* states that "in the face of nihilism's enormous temptations, Camus pledged himself to distill a literature of dignity and courage from a century often at war, beset by self-doubts, and threatened by disintegration" (634). Camus' characters are asking the question: "How can I find a meaningful existence in a meaningless universe?" (639).

Through Sisyphus' attitude towards the absurd, Camus identifies a route to victory. Sisyphus is alive with hope even though his miserable condition will not change. Humanly outward, there was darkness. But, humanly inward, there was light. Camus concludes for the people or his time and for all time that it is attitude, revolt, and struggle that turn the idea of the absurd into a modest triumph (Ellison 1990).

In 1960, the last year of his life, Camus tells us that there were two places that he had been supremely happy. One was on stage; he loved the theatre. The other place was a newspaper composing room. In each case, a team effort and specific goal were involved (Brée 1964). The evolution of his work shows much evidence of his confidence in the effectiveness of the team spirit and solidarity. This was later translated into collective revolt, which had as its objective the bringing about of a positive change in regards to suffering and oppression in the world. He goes farther with the idea of collective revolt in his next book.

THE PLAGUE

Camus pursues the discussion of this idea of collective struggle and revolt in The Plague (1947). The book recounts the moral and physical consequences of an epidemic of the plague in Oran, Algeria, Camus' country of birth. More precisely, the novel is an allegory of, and bears similarities to, the German Occupation of France, 1940-1944, and the attendant Nazi nightmare. The struggle by a group of dedicated men against the devastation of the plague suggests that of the French Resistance movement against the Nazis and the movement's eventual success. Camus addresses the issue of Nazi injustices and atrocities in *letters to a german friend* (On Freedom and Revolt: A Comparative Investigation), which were written between 1943 and 1944: "I cannot allow these letters to be reprinted without saying what they are. They were written and published in the clandestine press. They had a purpose, which was to throw some light on our blind struggle and to make our fight more effective" (Lottman 1979: 289). Camus deplored the tortures, executions and concentration camps that had snuffed out the lives of so many Europeans by the Nazis. One of Camus' closest friends in the struggle was executed. And working with the French Underground. Camus was at risk of being caught and executed himself. These were the types of atrocities that incited the writing of The Plague (1947).

In a general sense, *The Plague* is symbolic of the human collective struggle against war, illness, tyranny, colonialism, exploitation, injustice, or whatever conditions the world bring, to bear upon the lives of human beings. In the world of health and medicine, the plague is pestilence, disease and fear at their worse. At this particular moment, Camus finds that the plague reflects life itself and that it represents the undeserved oppression and sufferings that would cause the strongest religious faith to question and to waver.

One finds in *The Plague* a miniature world of different types of human beings making their different responses to life whether it is revolt, escape, indifference, collaboration, extraordinary courage, resignation, or defeat. We are being told that this response, whichever it may be, will determine victory or defeat. There must be a choice. For one also chooses when one does nothing, and Camus deplored acquiescence.

Oran, a city in Algeria, is the routine banality of any city anywhere in the world whose people are overnight isolated from the world and exiled into a symbolic struggle to the death. The enemy, this time, is the plague that would conquer them, demoralize them, cause grievous suffering to them, persecute them, terrorize them, dehumanize them, and even for many, kill them. The people hold on to a few memories of past happiness. Their foe leaves a bleak and seemingly hopeless future. This is the threat. How will it be met? This is the uncertainty of the human condition. How can one accept it? This could be gross tyranny and injustice. How would one overthrow it?

Camus makes the statement with *The Plague* that it is through the humanism of collective revolt that we prevail. Thus, the main characters, Rieux, Tarrou, Grand, Rambert, Cottard, Othon and Father Paneloux, whose interests run from those of a dedicated doctor, to those of a would be agnostic saint, to those of an obscure clerk, to those of an indifferent, "This isn't my fight," to an unstable mercenary, to a stoic, to a devout Christian. These persons forge their courage, compassion, endurance, unity, and charity to slug it out with their common enemy.

Because, according to Camus, tyranny affects everybody. Indeed, as pointed out by Germaine Brée (1964), the plague "symbolizes any force which cuts off human beings from the living breath of life: The physical joy of moving freely on this earth, the inner joy of love, the freedom to plan our tomorrows" (128).

One of the principal characters, the medical doctor, Dr. Rieux observes that the people of Oran are out of touch with reality. They cannot clearly distinguish between good and evil.

This is a perfect environment for the spread of plague disease. So, without any real obstacles, the plague brings together, according to Brée (1964), all that is evil into a fine tuned system. "It kills hope and joy, the sense of duration, faith in the future, the value of human life." (124). Likewise, it undermines or destroys all that is good: "Freedom, hope and, most particularly, love" (118).

However, while suffering and death will bring assault upon human beings as to the why, who, what and where, and will leave much unexplained, Camus feels that it is the solidarity of revolt that puts to flight the plagues of the world, whatever type it might be, and replaces it with a relative freedom, justice and a semblance of order and happiness—provisional though they may be. For one can never know if the day might come again: "For man's misfortune and instruction, the plague will awaken its rats and send them to die in a happy city" (287). Rhein states that Camus has concluded that revolt in its true meaning is the only course in a world that has shown clear evidence of the lack of religious faith. "Revolt protests against the suffering and injustices of an absurd world and in itself creates a moral value based on the idea of moderation" (1989:16). In conclusion, then, It is revolt that makes a people equal the task of overcoming and offers to them a cautious reason to hope. Let us now examine Camus' work from a different perspective.

THE REBEL

Looking again at the evolution of Camus' writing, *The Rebel* (1951) is a synthesis of his second period (1950-1960) philosophical attitude, just as Sisyphus was of his first period (1937-1949). *The Rebel* is a treatise on rebellion viewed from the perspective of philosophical theory and political systems. Further, it is a penetrating essay on human rights, ideological oppression, and the meanings of freedom and revolt. From this perspective, Camus gives his thoughts on rebellion from a metaphysical, historical, and artistic point of view. Concerning politics, Camus was not a politician and "political problems were of interest only in so far as they touched one of his major preoccupations, that is, the daily life of human beings, their freedom and the human justice meted out to them on this earth." (Brée: 8). Evidently, Camus felt strongly that the role of the artist was to be a witness and combatant for freedom, even though to fulfill this role, he realized that the costs at times would be heavy. A discussion of *The Rebel* attitude, with comments, follows here.

Camus explained that if people cannot refer to a common value recognized by all as existing in each other, then they are incomprehensible to each other (23). Revolt on the part of the rebel is a demand for clarity and justice because "theoretical equality conceals great factual inequalities" (20). Any rebellion expresses, in principle, the aspiration to make the world fair and just. As Camus sees it, the rebel "opposes the principle of justice which he sees in himself to that of injustice which he sees being applied in the world" (24). Rebellion refutes the idea that one person is superior over another. The true rebel for justice will not tolerate racism or ethnic cleansing because these contradict a fundamental premise of rebellion, which declares that all humanity should have equality and freedom (14).

We return to the question: What is a rebel? The answer is that s/he is a person who calls a halt to the limits to which s/he will allow his/her humanity to be oppressed and transgressed upon. For Camus, "It is a claim motivated by the concept of a complete unity against the suffering of life and death and a protest against the human condition both for its incompleteness, thanks to death, and its wastefulness thanks to evil" (24). This rebellion insists upon certain absolute rights. It cannot exist otherwise. The rebel insists on loyalty to certain aspects of himself and he is willing to support these aspects to the death (15). And what are these aspects as seen by Camus?

When the rebel's silence is broken, which heretofore could be compared to the tranquillity of galley slaves, opposition to oppression crops up. The slave begins to evaluate, to judge and to desire. His act of rebellion invokes value (14). A reaction to everything he previously accepted takes place. "The very moment that the slave refuses to obey the humiliating orders of the master, he simultaneously rejects the condition of slavery. The act of rebellion carries him far beyond the point he had reached by simply refusing. He now demands to be treated equal" (14) Camus claims, "The man's obstinate resistance becomes the whole man–who is identified with and summed up in this resistance." (15). He places the value of this new sought freedom above life itself. It is for him the supreme good. For the slave this rebellion speaks to the fact that a human nature does exist and that there is something permanent in oneself worth preserving (15). This rebellion is for the sake of everyone in the world. It is common ground where all men, even the man who insults and oppresses, have a natural community. (16). Camus goes further to define revolt as a force that drives people to defend what is right and just for every human being and "the malady experienced by a single man becomes a mass plague… It finds its first value on the whole human race. I rebel—therefore we exist." (22).

Therefore, according to Camus, true revolt, as it progresses, involves three participants: there is the master, the revolting slave, and the person observing the slave who feels a common humanity with his suffering. Solidarity enters between the observer and the slave and revolt, thus, becomes a collective experience. The revolt of this observer is just as authentic as the slave, if not more so. This duality of rebellion establishes the "We," brotherhood, and solidarity. Camus notes that "man's solidarity is founded upon rebellion, and rebellion, in its turn, can only find its justification in this solidarity" (22).

Camus returns one hundred fifty years into history to 1789, the French Revolution, and the revolt of the masses against the divine right of kings to document the nuances, achievements and failures of revolt (113). After this inquiry, he concludes that one always finds "the same desperate and bloody effort to affirm the dignity of man in defiance of the things that deny its existence" (116). According to Cruickshank, "The concept of revolt provides a key both to Camus' ideas themselves and to his significance for his times"(1978: 5). Cruickshank continues: "Revolt is not a nihilism that keeps humans in a constant state of lamentation about how bad things are; Yes, agreed, things are terrible, unjust, oppressive, demeaning and often times fatal. But the revolt that Camus espouses is one based on values and ideals that are basically humane, uplifting, moral and looking to optimism" (222).

Protest against evil is the very basis of revolt *(The Rebel:* 23). There could be no revolt if the justice promised to all, in theory, did not manifest itself to be grave injustice in practice (24). The rebel is constantly seeking absolute clarity as to the why of suffering, pain, and the unexplainable of the human condition. Without knowing it, he is in quest of a moral ethic based upon true justice, which he, himself, must define. And as Camus' works appear to state, God does not help to get the job done (24). So, while the acts of revolt are at times ignoble, the basic aims of revolt are always noble (101).

Camus points out to us, however, there are two means by which revolt can destroy. The first by deifying through total rejection and absolute negation that which exists (suicide) (101). The second is by accepting what exists and giving voice to absolute assent (murder) (101). In both cases, revolt ends in murder and no longer has the right to be called rebellion. Camus' thought on this point is that "Even though he is faced with mutilated justice, the rebel can never be an ally to generalized injustice" (102). It is at this point that reason and limits become madness. Being thus, it was nihilism and not revolt that illuminated the world of Camus' era.

Camus believed that Nazism and Marxism/Communism were the main perpetrators of this near absolute destruction. Historically, nihilism had its beginnings in Russia in the mid–1 800s and advocated the elimination of opposition by violence and terrorism (151). On the other hand, the nihilism found in the literature of Camus' generation advocated the general rejection of customary beliefs in morality, religion, truth, and hope based on a transcendental God.

Nihilism, then, was possible due to human beings arrival at that place in history where they were confronted with the injustice being done to man rebuked God thus, according to Camus: "Even if you exist, you do not deserve to exist." Therefore, "You do not exist" (102). So with God murdered and human beings having deified themselves, they can find justification for anything, and from that day to the present, man without God has progressively wielded more power, brutality and tyranny (102). The total deification and awesome brutality of his crimes culminated with Auschwitz, Belsen and Dachau, concentration and slave labor camps–the introduction of reasoned and legalized murder. This is revolt gone mad; and Camus tells us that, "On the day when crime dons the apparel of innocence, through curious transposition to our times, it is innocence that is called upon to justify itself" (4).

While *The Rebel* spoke from a point of view that reflected the times and experience of Camus, he knew that if human beings opposed the kingdom of grace, they must find a new kingdom: the kingdom of justice: "And the human community must be reunited among the debris of the fallen city of God, where absolute freedom or nihilism becomes a prison of absolute duties, a collective asceticism" (103). Therefore, the rebel must not forget his original quest was the mastery of his own condition and its maintenance in the face of God, because if God does not exist mankind does (103). Nihilism must not smother the force of a new creation, which is the final end of all revolt (102). This new creation affirms an intense hunger for freedom. It seems that this is what Camus was saying in the introduction to *The Rebel* when he stated that "Man is the only creature who refuses to be what he is" (11). The implication is that human beings are creatures created to aspire to brotherhood, caring, freedom, and peace–not to destroy one another.

Camus concludes this episode with hope and the call to become a creative force being forever vigilant against nihilism and the false gods of life. Just as men rallied to a collective revolt against *The Plague*, Camus calls us all to be partners in the stubborn weary, unglamorous struggle of mankind and to respond to the "inner flame" of comradeship in the service of human survival that will mark the limits of the plague's dehumanizing power. This vital force of solidarity, finally, is humankind's brightest ray for the kingdom of justice and freedom that Camus would have become a reality.

The struggle for freedom has always been costly. The French Revolution has already been cited. The French Underground freedom fighters during World War II paid in blood. The fight against French colonialism in Algeria cost many lives. But people are still willing to die for freedom. Let us give freedom a definition: According to the World Book Encyclopedia (1978: 849), freedom means being free–not being under another's control and the power to do, say or think, as one pleases. To have equal opportunity; to be treated equal to others; to be treated equally before the law; to have the free will to pursue life, liberty and happiness, according to one's talents and means.

Writing in The Rebel, Camus states:

> No doubt the rebel demands a certain freedom for himself; but in no circumstances does he demand, if he is consistent, the right to destroy the person and freedom of someone else. He degrades no one. The freedom which he demands he claims for everybody; that which he rejects, he forbids all others to exercise. He is not simply a slave opposing his master but a man opposing the world of master and slave (113).

In both periods of Camus' works, the idea of limits to freedom is maintained. The first concerns limits to metaphysical freedom. The second concerns the limits to historical freedom. We will now examine four of his works for signs of these manifestations: *Caligula* (1938-1944), a play, *The Stranger* (1941), a novel, *The Misunderstanding* (1942-1943), a play, *The Just Assassins (1950). a play.*

CALIGULA

The emperor Caligula has lost his sister and mistress Drusilla and is suddenly confronted with the finality and inevitability of death. He revolts. To him life is a fraud. Men are not happy living and they are not happy dying. Everything is an incoherent state of affairs. The possible offers no reward. Caligula will seek to find coherence in the impossible. He states: "All of a sudden, I feel the need of the impossible. Things don't satisfy me the way they are." He continues that the world is unbearable and that he has: "Need of the moon or happiness or immorta lity, the need of something that might be insane perhaps but which is not of this world" (36).

It follows, then, that Caligula unleashes three years of holocaust and perversion upon his subjects through such acts as: wanton murder without reason, making his senators do his slaves tasks, emptying the state treasury, addressing grown men as "My darling and my pretty one" (55). At dinner, he spits olive pits into others' plates (61). He takes a man's wife from his side and to the man's shock, goes to bed with her in the next room (64). He closes the public granary–threatening famine. He gives decorations to those who have most often frequented his prostitution houses (71). At the same time, he threatens to exile or execute those who do not attend them at least once per year. He forces the father of a close friend to drink poison (71). He even acquiesces in the plot against his own life when he learns of it.

All of these excesses and others are an affirmation of the absolute freedom that Caligula seeks. He is "God." He impersonates his idea of God: the cruel, derisive force that has taken his sister and that destroys human security.

Caligula, thus, kills, perverts, destroys, humiliates and deifies his person. Total freedom and seeking after the absolute Camus tells us, will always lead to destruction—of others and of self. During Camus times, Franco, Hitler, Mussolini, and Stalin were examples of ruthless leaders who were in search of the impossible (Ellison 1990).

It appears that Camus is also saying that we all have some absurd in us. But even though humans may carry potential devastation within that could amount to crimes and ravages, they must dispute, protest and control them in themselves and in others. Absurdity in the search of absolute freedom breeds Caligulas. Caligula will meet the limits imposed upon his acts by universal reason and the oppressed. Listen to this exchange of conversation between him and Cherea.

CHEREA

"I consider you to be noxious. I have the feeling and need of security. Most people are like me. They are unable to live in a world where the most bizarre thought can in the matter of seconds become reality—and most of the time, it enters like a dagger in your heart" (112).

CALIGULA

"Security and logic don't go together."

CHEREA:

"That is true. That is not logical but it makes common sense."

CALIGULA: "CONTINUE." CHEREA:

"I don't have anything else to say. I don't want to become a part of your logic. I have another idea of my duties as a man... You are destructive to everybody. It is natural for you to die."

People want to live and be happy, Cherea tells Caligula. Nothing will survive, however, "By pushing the absurd to the most extreme consequences" (113).

At the beginning, as is often the case, Caligula's revolt and anxiety over the uncertainty of his condition were sincere. However, his means in arriving at a solution lead him to fatalistic nihilism and he becomes guilty of doing, in attempting to be coherent, all the things that Camus tells that revolt cannot be without confronting itself with contradiction. Caligula, thus, negates himself and desires despair in his passion for an absolute. This despair reaches an absolute when Caligula exalts in bliss as he slowly snuffs out the life of Caesonia, the only person who has caused him to experience any kind of affection during his lifetime. Caligula's sterile "freedom" is now complete (152).

In the end, Caligula finds that man, within himself, can only have a limited freedom. Even though he wants to be God, thus ordering the world after his own values, each time he stands before the mirror, (which Caligula does often to admire himself and his greatness) he realizes that he is only another human being, finite, limited, and that the impossible is an illusion. Therefore, there are limits to the freedom that will be tolerated. Caligula realizes this as he is about to be slain by the masses: "I have not followed the life style that I ought to have. I am ending up with nothing. My freedom has no meaning" (154). Caligula's life is saying that even though we all carry within ourselves the potential to commit outrageous acts against others and against society, we must fight to keep self-control and civilized conduct in command. A comparison can be made between the nihilism of Caligula and Meursault in *The Stranger*. This latter was commented on previously.

Meursault, the main character in the novel, seems little conscious of the fact that there are limits to what one may do and have accepted by his contemporaries. One of the implications of the story is the dangerous inadequacy of his attitude as a way of life. It is impossible to live a life without values, when to live is in itself a value judgment. Translated into action or expression, Meursault is inconceivable as to what life ought to be. Life confronts him with the limits to a freedom that brings about his demise. Thus, it is apparent that Camus was weary of both extremes of the absolute. Persons can no more do everything *(Caligula)*, in the name of freedom and revolt, than they can do nothing (Meursault).

Germaine Brée (1964) has said that Camus saw in the modern human the restless, impatient surge to transcend human limitation where the irrational prevails. We have seen this desire to transcend human limitations destroy Caligula, where on one hand he wanted to pierce the absurd and on the other his confrontation with its impossibility. In trying to bridge the two, he ends up as an "impossible character." O'Brien (1970), adds that "in Caligula the idea of carrying truth of feeling—the artist's truth—to its extreme limits is shown as hideously inhuman (30). Freeman (1971), points out that "for the audiences of 1945 there was the ghoulish and macabre fascination of the hero himself at a time when Europe and particularly France were emerging from the chaos created by Hitler and Mussolini, two imperial megalomaniacs whose personalities bore many superficial likeness to that of Caligula (36). But, let us take yet another look at the concept of freedom and its limits.

THE MISUNDERSTANDING

The Misunderstanding (1945) will present through an "impossible situation" a similar desire to transcend limits to freedom. Martha, twenty years old, and her mother are the proprietors of an inn in Bohemia (Czechoslovakia). It is secluded and off the beaten track. The women have become weary of a boring and depressing existence that, according to them, offers little for the present or future. Martha, the young daughter, feels bogged down and lost in a forgotten country. She dreams of, "This other country where summers are superbly beautiful, where the rains of winter wash down the cities, and where, finally, things are as they ought to be" (211). In a revolt against the absurdity, boredom and meager existence of their present state, and in order to get to this romantic country of bright lights, they decide to murder and rob the customers who stop at their inn. They revolt to deadly nihilism as a means to find solutions to their dilemma.

A son, Jan, who has been missing for twenty years, shows up one day. They do not recognize him. In his absence, he has become wealthy and happy. Having learned of the destitute situation of his mother and sister, he has returned to share some of his good fortune with them and to take them, for that matter, to the very country of their dreams. He does not reveal hi:-. identify, however. That night, he is drugged, robbed, and murdered. The son's identity is learned when his mother and sister see his passport. The mother commits suicide out of love for her son, the added meaninglessness of her own life, and the realization of her own sordid conduct. The daughter commits suicide protesting an absurd, hopeless and cruel world.

The impossible situation is created through Jan and Martha. They both want to bring happiness to the inn situation. They differ, of course as to means. Jan makes the fatal mistake of relying on fate to work things out and be recognized by his mother because, "a mother always recognizes her son" (172). Thus, he walks innocently into Martha's desperation. She tells him as much: "What is human about me is what I desire, and to obtain what I desire, I believe that I would crush anything that is in my way" (212). For her, the ends justify the means. Therefore, she feels complete justification in this enterprise of murder for happiness and freedom. Martha speaks to her mother of the now dead Jan: "But he spoke to me about the places that I have been dreaming about, and knowing how to reach me, he gave me weapons against himself. This is the way that innocence is rewarded" (227). So, irrationally, Martha does not really take responsibility for killing her brother. She blames him for causing his own murder. Thus, the circumstances, where mother, sister and brother remain unknown to each other, render the situation impossible. Everyone fails. No one ever sees the identity of the other, even though there are suspicions on both sides. Jan dies due to his innocence. Martha and her mother die due to their violence. All three characters end up in a state of absurdity and solitude. They never connect by communicating and finding the freedom they all so desperately seek.

The absurdity of life itself puts the first limit on their freedom. They revolt for a new quantity in life. It is this quantity instead of quality that Martha seeks. Murder is not the means though. Camus presents in young Martha a cold-blooded killer who affirms her right to murder for prosperity—even her brother whom she disclaims. Martha is a supreme example of a revolting person gone out of control and beyond limits of the possible. She portrays her warped personality to the fullest at the end of the play in a revealing dialog with her dead brother's widow who has come to meet her husband at the inn. Martha is adamantly defensive and never gives a hint at accepting responsibility for her murders. Thus, Marth, I goes to her death (suicide) unrepentant, estranged, fault finding, vindictive, and wrapped in a cloak of self-pity and self-righteousness. Camus shows her, then, as a rebel whose means of rebellion have caused her to self-destruct. She has done all that a true rebel can never do in the name of her freedom.

The irony of *The Misunderstanding*, of course, is that the possibility of freedom and happiness is always just a word or an explanation away. The course of circumstances could have been altered had Jan revealed his identity. However, the conclusion seems to say that chance does not solve problems or bring freedom. Neither is God willing to solve problems. The old servant who has been mute and impersonal throughout the play is symbolic of God giving answers to human supplications. At the end of the play, he enters the room where Jan's wife Maria cries out, "Oh God I can't live in this terrible place. It is to you that I will speak and will know how to find words… Have pity on me. Tum and look on me… Have pity and consent to help me (253). "The old servant answers in an even voice, "No," and walks away (254).

It is revolt to nihilism itself, which imposes limits upon Martha and her mother. The mother sums it up, "I suppose that a time comes when all murderers are like me, empty on the inside, sterile and without a possible future." She adds a moment later. That's why people suppress them. They are good for nothing." She then adds, "I have lost my freedom. It is hell that has begun" (235). So, freedom within the confines of human limits must be accepted. Any response to man's condition must be within the realm of human rationality. The personality types that address life as Caligula, Martha, and her mother do not survive. Freeman (1971), in examining *The Misunderstanding* concludes that the play is an excellent representation of a human condition that reflects sterility, exile, and death in an absurd world that is overwhelmed with uncontrollable circumstances. Hopkins' (1969) point of view is that Camus' message found in *Caligula* and *The Misunderstanding* is that absolute freedom, which goes beyond human limitations, ends in nihilism and destructiveness. Camus now moves us to revolutionary historical revolt.

THE JUST ASSASSINS

The Just Assassins (1949) adds another dimension to the concepts of revolt, freedom and limits. The play is based on a true historical event concerning a small group of revolutionaries who in 1905 assassinated the Grand Duke Sergei, Russian Minister of Justice. Camus dramatizes this event because he felt it would provide the most realistic circumstances to project the ideas of historical revolt with all of its nuances and contradictions.

Conor Cruise O'Brien (1970) puts forth the view that *The Just Assassins* is a critique of *revolutionary* violence and—most especially—of violence legitimized by the ethos of past revolution. The emphasis falls heavily on the question of the morality of violence being used to secure social and political change.

It appears that Camus intends for this play to be an answer to rebels' questions of today. The following basic questions are raised in the play:

1. Is it right to kill for justice?

2. Should ones means to the end have measure or limits?

3. What are the limits of loyalty to revolt?

4. What are the rewards of revolt?

In **The Plague** (1947), Tarrou said that a man has no right to kill another, whatever the reason. This is no longer the case in *The Just Assassins* (1949). The idea here is that when one kills a tyrant, he is neither a murderer nor an assassin but a "just man" or "lover of justice" (85), committing an act in the name of, and for the good of the people. Kaliayev, who throws the bomb, tells fellow revolutionaries how he feels about killing the Duke: "It is not him that I am killing. I am killing despotism" (55). He gives a similar answer to Skouratov, the chief of police, in their prison conversation: "I threw the bomb on your tyranny not on a man" (154). He doesn't even recognize it to be a crime, as he answers the Grand Duchesses (the Duke's widow) interrogation: "What crime? I only remember an act of justice" (164). He refuses her offer of God's grace and forgiveness. Murder is justified then, on the grounds that it has the establishing of justice as its aim. There are limits even here though, according to Camus' revolutionaries, because violence can only be an extreme limit to combat another form of violence, and when this violence ends in murder, the rebel must, just as Kaliayev, be willing to pay with his own life (91).

"Mesure' or limits must be honored at all times while moving from means to end. This point is brought out through opposing ideologies of revolt as seen in Stepan in contrast to the other members of the group. The first confrontation is whether the grandchildren of the Duke should have been spared, they by chance having been along at a moment when the Duke was due for assassination. Stepan says no. The others say yes (80-85). Here is a portion of their gripping conversation:

DORA

"Open your eyes and understand that the organization would lose its power and its influence if it tolerated, for a single moment, that children be blown up by our bombs" (80).

STEPAN

"I don't want to hear such nonsense. When we decide to forget children, that is the day that we will be masters of the world and the revolution will triumph" (80).

FOKA

"That day, the revolution will be hated by all humanity" (80).

To all of this, Stepan replies angrily, there are no limits. The end justifies the means (p. 82). So, "What does the deaths of two children matter?" (85). Kaliayev gives the final answer to Stepan: "I accept killing to overthrow despotism. But behind what you are saying, I see a despotism coming about that if it ever takes place, would make of me an executioner while I am trying to be a "just man" (85). The point is that Stepan's revolt has lost its origins of freedom and brotherhood. He would let injustice serve justice. He would let means to ends be inhuman. His revolt has evolved into hate. And Dora tells him so: "Love does not have this appearance" (81). It appears that Stepan would desire total freedom in revolt, when it can never be more than relative. One can conclude from Stepan's actions that he would lie. He would sacrifice others when he can only give his own life. By killing innocent children, he would ignore the honor code of revolt. In this respect, he is nihilist. Stepan is ardent, revolutionary, and willing to die. It is all out of hatred though. A true rebel sacrifices and is inspired out of 'love.' Stepan has become a false rebel, even though he is not willing to accept it.

The rebels, each in his own way answers the third question:

VOINOV

"I understood that it is not enough to denounce injustice. One must give one's life to fight against it. Now, I am happy" (28).

KALIAYEV

"To die for the idea, that is the only way to be in full compliance with the idea. That is proof." (48).

ANNENKOV

When asked when he has last loved responds, "Four years." asked further, his length of service as chief of the Organization, he responds: "Four years... Now it is the Organization that I love" (196).

In regards to the rewards of revolt, the dialogue continues:

> Dora—speaking of Kaliayev's execution: "Don't cry. No, no, don't cry. You see it's the day of proof. Something is rising up at this hour that is testimony to all us other rebels… There is a return to the joy of childhood" (209-210). This childhood joy, it appears, is symbolic of the hoped for freedom and innocence that will be the result of the rebel's struggle.

Camus' book, *The Rebel* (1956) informs us that the rebel's commitment to the revolt for freedom consumes the whole person and the Organization becomes his life and his life is identified with the purposes of the Organization. There is no goal that is held in higher esteem. This is a fitting description, it seems, for *The Just Assassins*. However, the rewards of revolt leave some ambiguity. It is not a question of the portion of freedom that would be achieved for the masses. It is a question of the effect that dedication-to-the-death idealism has upon the lives of those who are caught up in revolt's drama. Kaliayev and Dora, who are lovers in the play are good examples.

The play defines two types of love: first of all, there is love of an idea, 'a monologue' characterized by "a flame and revolt." Then, there is love of a person characterized by 'tenderness,' which is dialogue. Annenkov has told us that love of the first will cause one to abandon thought of the second. There doesn't seem to be enough room in the heart for both to co-exist. The Organization is always first. Dora Tells Kaliayev. "There is too much blood, too much violence. Those who truly love justice don't have the right to love. Love turns your head, Yanek. We, We have a stiff neck" (117). Kaliayev's answer to Dora's question whether he loves her more than justice or the Organization is: "I do not separate you the Organization and justice" (120). This does not seem to be an answer that would flatter most females. Finally, Dora admits despairingly: "We are not of this world, we are the just. There is a warmth that is not for us. Oh! pity on the just!" (123).

Even though Kaliayev and Dora love each other passionately, they can only find in death the peace and unity that they desire. They will both die in order to gain life and freedom. According to Camus, this is consistent with rebel thinking that individuals, from antiquity to the present, have been willing to die for the sake of freedom. They do not die wholly, thus; but they achieve a rebel's freedom from their own death. And this freedom from their own death causes their ideas to live on to be renewed again and again by new generations.

The epigraph from Romeo and Juliet is recalled, "O love! 0 life! not life but love in death!" (Act 4, Scene 5). This is the implication for Dora and Kaliayev and it is not clear at the end of the play if rebel happiness is compatible with this life, or, if it must be forsaken in the name of the tension and sacrifice that are part of the rebel lifestyle.

SUMMARY AND INTERPRETATION

In conclusion, let us now take a closer look at Camus' works from the view of literary form and content. I have researched and presented the conception of freedom and revolt as seen in his works. He has shown impressive literary versatility in revealing these concepts to the reader. The Nobel Prize was awarded to Camus in 1957 for his work that, according to the Nobel Committee, "brings to light the problems, which weigh on the consciences of men during our times." Camus' work is always most relevant to the moment that it was written—from the late 1930s to the late 1950s. During these years, his literary values were a protest for a more meaningful, fulfilled, and just human experience.

During the first period of his writing, (1937-1945), he witnessed the absurd and nihilism in human existence. Unlike other authors, however, he was not concerned with a philosophy of the absurd. He was not satisfied that human beings, the apex of creation, could be relegated to an existence amounting to a big question mark of uncertainty. Granting the absurd, Camus was concerned with how profitably to live with it while transforming it into a positive, lucid and creative force through revolt in search of freedom. He has shown that there must be moral limits.

During the second period of his writing, 1946-1958, Camus' writing ethic called for a revolt that would bring the outrage against humanity to an end so that justice could prevail. His general label for these outrages against humanity was the plague. The solidarity of rebel revolt could bring an end to the plague. Historically, justice and freedom have always been the main preoccupation of the rebel. Camus is, thus, what he felt the artist must be himself—a rebel, of the highest order, in search of liberation for an oppressed people. We are reminded again of the powerfully metaphorical definition of the plague given by Brée (1964) when she writes that "The plague… symbolizes any force which systematically cuts human beings off from the living breath of life: the physical joy of moving freely on this earth, the inner joy of love, the freedom to plan our tomorrows. In a general way it is death, and, in human terms, all that enters into complicity with death" (128). It seems to me that this definition captures the meaning of plague as applied in the writings of Camus.

During both periods, Camus is a moralist in search of a truth that leads to freedom. Again, Brée points out that "freedom was what Camus as an artist most needed, that freedom which is the leitmotiv of his work: freedom in respect to himself and to his age, freedom in respect to his art and to other human beings, a freedom which, at the time of his death, he was just beginning to enjoy" (252). Finding a relief for suffering humanity seemed to be a watchword of his work. And, he holds the individual accountable and responsible, throughout, for the transgressions that he will allow to be perpetrated against humanity. He refuses religion, philosophy and history the right to usurp this right from human beings. In this regard, the values of revolt must be honed out of the conditions of the times. He goes on to say that these values, while lacking perfection, provide the best opportunity for victory when combined with the limits of the possible. An example of this individual and collective revolt in struggling against the symbolic tyrannies of life is found in the solidarity and team effort demonstrated by several of *The Plague's* main characters as they joined forces in fighting the ravages of the plague epidemic. This team included Rieux, Tarrou, Grand, Rambert, Othon, and Father Paneloux.

Freeman's (1971), point of view on revolt is that it is "two things at the same time: a rejection of existing values and the discovery of new ones… a discovery and preservation of new values as much as, if not more than, the rejection and destruction of existing (unjust) values (30). Camus used his art and the power of his unique literary perception concerning the value of life and human existence to chart a course for all people that called for the liberation of the oppressed and the presence of freedom.

In addressing the themes of revolt and freedom, Camus' writings covered a broad range of literary form and content that included narrative fiction, drama, and non-fiction prose. Writings that are included In the category of narrative fiction include: *The Stranger, The Plague, The Fall, The Exile and Kingdom,* and *The Myth of Sisyphus.* Writings that fall within the domain of drama include: *Revolt in the Asturias, The Misunderstanding, Caligula, The Just,* and *State of Siege.* Writings that are included in the non-fiction prose domain include: *Nuptials, The Inside and the Outside, letters to a german friend, Political Articles I & II, The Rebel,* and *Summer.* Some of these titles are not included in this study due to their content; however, they are given here to show the range of Camus' artistry.

The themes of several of Camus' key writings include:

The Stranger (1942)—Indifference, the absurd, alienation, guilt, freedom, responsibility, revolt;

The Myth of Sisyphus (1942)—Oppression, measure, the absurd, suicide, freedom, revolt;

Caligula (1944)—Oppression, the absurd, freedom, revolt;

The Misunderstanding (1944)—The absurd, freedom, revolt;

The Plague (1947)—Oppression,.solidarity, the absurd, freedom, revolt;

The Just Assassins (1950)—Oppression, revolt, freedom;

The Rebel (1951)—Tyranny, revolt, freedom, moderation, betrayal, human value.

We have seen in these works the different approaches to the ideas or concepts of revolt and freedom used by Camus. In the case of *The Stranger*, the protagonist's revolt led to alienation, indifference, and the search for freedom through nihilism and the absurd. Thus, he negated self, family, others, career, and society. The consequences were predictable. His life was a failure and he suffered a tragic demise.

The Myth of Sisyphus also confronts the protagonist with the choice to pursue revolt and freedom through nihilism and absurdity. However, Sisyphus makes the choice to struggle against the chaos of nihilism and absurdity. He revolts in his mind and attitude and through the power of his intellect finds freedom and a life of value and happiness within the most debilitating circumstances.

Caligula seeks after something that is "not of this world" in his quest for a solution to the absurd. In his revolt for freedom, he crosses the line of limits into the domain of excess in search of the absolute. His goal is the unattainable infinite. Thus, in this play, Caligula becomes a brutal tyrant who destroys, maims, degrades, and kills. He violates every premise of legitimate revolt, and the people, the masses whom he has violated and whose freedom he has trampled, in the end, come to bring an end to his perversion and to his life.

The Plague is symbolic of all the things that hinder the freedom, happiness, and peace of human beings. The names of the plague are war, illness, tyranny, murder, colonialism, racism, injustice, poverty or whatever conditions the world brings that adversely affect the lives of human beings. The solidarity of collective revolt is a solution to this problem, and it is through the humanism of this revolt that human beings prevail.

The Rebel is a far reaching essay on human rights, systemic oppression, freedom and revolt. This book is a treatise on rebellion written from the perspective of philosophical theory, political ideologies, and political systems. It is Camus' attempt to historically clarify the meaning of rebellion and freedom, the value of life, justice and injustice, protest against evil, limits, and the absolute human rights that should be available to every human being.

The Misunderstanding, another of Camus' plays, presents freedom and revolt with yet another approach. It presents two women inn keepers who revolt against their boring life style by murdering and then robbing their customers in order to get money to escape to freedom and happiness. To their unknowing, they end up murdering their own son and brother who does not reveal his identity. The story is telling us that revolt for freedom using nihilistic means, such as murder, is doomed to failure. Life is to be valued, and murder does not produce freedom. Another point is the misunderstanding that takes place when people don't reveal who they are. This pertains to the long absent son Jan. Freedom and happiness may be just a word or an explanation away, and chance does not solve human problems or bring solutions. Humans, themselves, with no help from any other quarter, are responsible for generating optimism, hope, and freedom. We hide our identities at the risk of provoking absurd consequences.

Finally, the ideas of freedom and revolt are dramatized by Camus in the play, *The Just Assassins*. Camus' purpose with this play was to use a true event to provide a realistic setting for historical revolt. He wanted to operationalize the issue of the morality of violence (assassination) to secure a social and political change that would alleviate oppression and bring about a measure of freedom. The dilemma for the small group of revolting revolutionaries centered around the plot of how to go about their task. The questions were raised: Is killing for justice a truly civilized act? Should means and ends have limits? Is loyalty unqualified? Is personal identity lost to that of the organization? The answers to these questions rest with the level of commitment of the individual rebel... with the ultimate question being, "Am I willing to die as a freedom fighter for the cause that I live for?"

Camus' methodology in putting together structure and style was done with the care of painting a masterpiece. It appears that his style was driven by his "role of the artist" point of view. That is to say, the role of the prose writer was to engage the readers and move them to action. His genius enabled him to do successful writing in several different genres. These have been cited in this research. In viewing the panorama of Camus' writings, he chose a structure and style depending on the message and impression he wanted to present. For example, *The Stranger, The Myth of Sisyphus* and *Caligula* all reflect the theme of the absurd of the early forties. Revolt and freedom are also included as themes in these works. However, one is a novel, one is a philosophical essay and the other a play. The plot and ideas of each of these literary products have determined their structure in order for Camus to effectively relay his message to the reader. (Note: See discussion and analysis of these three writings which were given earlier.) Therefore, the broad experimentation and boldness that Camus brought to his art enabled him to be creative with a style and technique that he was always in the process of developing.

Let us now move to another great champion of human rights who made a difference and whose life left a role model for all who believe in freedom and justice.

DR. MARTIN LUTHER KING JR.: A BRIEF SUMMARY OF HIS LIFE

Dr. Martin Luther King, Jr. was born on January 15, 1929 in Atlanta Georgia. He was the second of three children born to The Reverend Martin Luther King, Sr. and Mrs. Alberta Williams King. The other two children were Christine, the oldest, and Alfred Daniel, the youngest. Mrs. Alberta King had been a teacher before becoming a homemaker. King's elementary schooling was received in the public school system of Atlanta and his high school education was received at the Atlanta University Laboratory High School and Booker T. Washington High School, also in Atlanta. King was a bright and ambitious high school student who was able to skip both the 9th and 12th grades (Bennett 1968; Oates 1982).

Consequently, in 1944, he entered Morehouse College at the age of fifteen. According to Bennett and Oates, King's original educational plan was to be a doctor or lawyer. However, in 1947 after much soul searching, he announced that he would become a preacher and was ordained at the Ebenezer Baptist church where his father had held the pastorate since 1931. Socially and economically, the King family was black middle class and according to former Morehouse classmate, Lerone Bennett (1968), they were highly respected in the black community.

According to Farris (1986-Martin's sister), King was greatly influenced by his father, the Reverend King Sr. The father was both a theologian and a social activist. He was active in the NAACP and Atlanta Negro Voters League. He helped to organize picketing against "white" and "colored" facilities in city hall and led a black teachers fight for equal compensation for professional services.

Another key person of influence in the life of Martin King, Jr. was Dr. Benjamin Mays, the president of Morehouse College, (Oates 1982; Farris 1986). Besides encouraging Martin to follow his father into the ministry, Dr. Mays also spoke to Martin about striving for excellence in the academic world and the need to fight for equality on behalf of Negroes. Dr. Mays, himself, a seminary trained theologian, was one of Martin's favorite role models because he addressed socially relevant issues and because of his stimulating and intellectual speaking style. From his father and Dr. Mays, Martin learned early lessons about the importance of protest for civil rights and justice. He also learned to use his intellectual gifts in concert with the power of words and ideas.

King graduated from Morehouse in June 1948, at the age of nineteen, with a degree in sociology. In September 1948, King entered Crozer Theological Seminary, Chester, Pennsylvania as a full time student in theology. From indications, the Crozer experience was a very academically stimulating one for King. The Crozer experience also provided Martin with his first serious encounter with the Gandhian technique of nonviolent civil disobedience (Oates 1982). The occasion was from a 1950 series of lectures delivered by Modecai Johnson, the president of Howard University, Washington, D.C., after he had returned from a trip to India. After the Johnson series of lectures, Martin began to study in depth everything that he could get his hands on that would provide further enlightenment concerning Gandhi. The key to nonviolent and civil disobedience according to Bennett (1968), "Was soul force or *Satyagraha...* the power of truth" (29). He continues: "It is the vindication of truth not by infliction of suffering on the opponent but on one's self." Thus, "Suffering and sacrifice were at the heart of Gandhi's philosophy... He urged his followers to forswear violence and to work for ultimate reconciliation with their opponents by returning good for evil and by openly breaking unjust laws and willingly paying the penalty" (29). At the time that King contemplated the philosophy of nonviolence, he did not know how central it would become to the main thrust of his own future struggle into the world of civil rights, protest, and revolt.

King graduated from Crozer as president of the senior class, received the outstanding student award and a $1200 graduate study award; this award was the J. Lewis Crozer Fellowship, which was to be used wherever he chose to continue his education (Bennett 1968:30). He decided to remain in the East for further study.

In September of 1951, King enrolled at the Boston University Graduate School to begin work on the Ph.D. Degree in the field of Systematic Theology. While at Boston, he was also enrolled as a special student in classes in philosophy at Harvard University. Also, while at Boston, in 1952, he met and dated Coretta Scott who was a student at the New England Conservatory of Music. A year later, in 1953, they were married in Heiberger, Alabama, the home of Coretta. To this union would be born four children: Yolanda, November 1955; Martin Luther King, III, October, 1957; Dexter Scott, May 1961 and Bernice Albertine, March 1963 (Oates 1982; Garrow 1986).

In April of 1954, King accepted the call to pastor the Dexter Avenue Baptist Church in Montgomery, Alabama. In June of 1955, King was awarded the Ph.D. degree in Systematic Theology from Boston University. While King and Coretta had debated the pros and cons of returning to the South versus remaining in the North to teach or accepting a pulpit, they eventually decided to return home to their roots. Certainly, the existing segregation displeased both Martin and Coretta. Her career as a singer would have limited opportunity below the Mason-Dixon Line. Nonetheless, they felt a moral obligation to return to the South, at least for a period of years, to help with "the struggle" (Bennett 1968; Oates 1982). The move to Montgomery provides the background and context for his first book in this struggle.

STRIDE TOWARD FREEDOM

In his first book, *Stride Toward Freedom* (1958), King records the Montgomery bus boycott story, December 1955–December 1956. In addition, he also recounts his beginnings at the Dexter Avenue Baptist Church. Upon assuming the pastorate of the Dexter Avenue Baptist Church, King began in earnest to go about the business of organizing for effective spiritual, social and political action and making recommendations according to his view of how this particular church should function in the Montgomery community (King 1958). Little did he know that he was preparing for a date with destiny that would impact and lead to revolt and a fight for freedom for Negroes in the South, in other parts of the United States, and, indeed, people in bondage throughout the world (Bennett 1968; Coretta King 1969; Oates 1982; Branch 1988; Garrow 1986 and 1989).

Stride Toward Freedom is a personal, detailed, first-person documentary. The book is written in a direct, interpretive, easy to read essay prose. It is recorded in eleven brief chapters that provide the structure and carry the story of the essay from the beginning of the boycott to its conclusion three hundred eighty-two (382) days later. King's writing style is evident in the naming of chapter titles. These titles record and document the major events of the boycott.

Further, the progression of chapters was revealing in that they not only addressed the evolution of the story, but they also recorded the mindset and growth of Dr. King's own personal evolution towards revolt and fight for freedom, using the strategy of nonviolence. The book has served as a handbook for many later civil rights campaigns (Washington 1986). Expanding on this point concerning public transportation discrimination, Fairclough (1995), contends that :

> Few practices evoked such bitter resentment among African Americans in the South as segregation in public transportation. In theory, the system embodied the principle of "separate but equal," the rule laid down by the Supreme Court in 1896 to square state segregation laws with the ban on racial discrimination contained in the Fourteenth Amendment of the Constitution, passed in 1867. In fact, segregation meant separate and unequal (17).

When they arrived in Montgomery, the Kings found a city of complete segregation, which was instituted by custom and law (King 1958). The schools, transportation, work, social life, economics, living patterns, voting rights, the courts system and justice, etc. all adhered to rigid and unyielding segregation and inequality. Negroes appeared to be complacent and indifferent concerning existing conditions. There was lack of unity among Negro organizations. With most Negroes being employed by Whites, there were fears of reprisals for getting out of "their place" (12-13). So, what was the role of the church and religion in this environment of oppression?

According to young preacher King, a religion that is worthy to be called religion is concerned with the total person–both religious and social, "both earth and heaven, both time and eternity" (21). Further, King states: "Any religion that professes to be concerned with the souls of men and is not concerned with the slums that damn them, the economic conditions that strangle them and the social conditions that cripple them is a dry-as-dust religion" (21). King goes on to say that, "The ultimate tragedy of segregation is that it not only harms one physically but injures one spiritually. It scars the soul and degrades the personality. It inflicts the segregated with a false sense of inferiority, while confirming the segregator in a false estimate of his own superiority" (22). Therefore, since the human spirit is created to breathe free, segregation is a prelude to revolt in any society at any time. Dr. King would soon have an opportunity to see his views concerning this injustice come to confrontation.

On the evening of December 1, 1955, Mrs. Rosa Parks, a Negro seamstress and secretary of the Montgomery NAACP, who was weary after a long day of work and shopping, refused to give up her seat to a white man after demands by the bus driver. Had she given up her seat on the now crowded bus, she would have had to stand while the man took her seat. She was arrested and taken to the city courthouse and booked for violating the city's segregation ordinances. This indignant arrest (heaped upon all the other historical racial insults suffered by Negroes of a defenseless, caring, and highly regarded woman, who had been ordered to give up her seat to a man, was the catalyst that began the Negro revolt in the South (Bennett 1968; Oates 1982; Farris 1986; Branch 1986; Garrow 1986 and 1989; Cone 1991, et al). Led by Jo Ann Robinson, the Women's Political Council rallied around Parks and helped launch the Montgomery boycott for December 5. This group distributed thousands of leaflets and encouraged the NAACP, churches, and other civil rights organizations to lend their support in the boycott (Source: *Monday Matters!* (tabloid), Wilberforce University Counseling Services Center. Volume 9, Issue 9. November 16-22, 1998: 2). A one-day boycott was put into effect by the Negro community, which comprised 80% of the users of public transportation. The public transportation system was an ongoing major insult and humiliation for Negro customers, with their having to get up and surrender their seats to white passengers as well as stand over unoccupied "white only" seats when there was not a single white passenger on the bus (25). Negroes who did not comply were arrested and taken to jail. Many Negroes showed their protest by refusing to ride the buses. As a result of the boycott, The Montgomery Improvement Association (MIA) was born on December 5, 1955. The young (26 years old) articulate and charismatic preacher named Dr. Martin Luther King, Jr. was elected as president to organize and strategize the boycott and give leadership to the conditions of protest (42).

The Negro revolt caused by the refusal of Rosa Parks to give up her seat on that decisive day was saying in essence, "I have had enough." Rosa Parks was making a statement of protest fo;: herself as well as for all Negroes who had suffered the humiliation of historical racist indignities. For Dr. King, "She was a victim of both the forces of history and the forces of destiny. She had been tracked down by *Zeitgeist*–the spirit of the time" (29). She was in a state of revolt and non-cooperation against an oppressive and evil system (Garrow 1986: 12, et al).

Looking at the protest from a vision that combined the historical, the philosophical and the divine, Dr. King states in his unique style of writing:

There is something about the protest that is supraratational; it cannot be explained without a divine dimension. Some may call it a principle of concretion, with Alfred N. Whitehead; or a process of integration, with Henry N. Wieman; or Being-itself with Paul Tillich; or a personal God. Whatever the name, some extra-human force labors to create a harmony out of the discords of the universe. There is a creative power that works to pull down mountains of evil and level hilltops of injustice. God still works through history His wonders to perform. It seems as though God had decided to use Montgomery as the proving ground for the struggle and triumph of freedom and justice in America (51).

In a broader sense, the boycott was gathering momentum and cooperation from a large cross section of persons representing the full range and strata of the socio-economic spectrum–from yard men and domestics to businessmen, doctors, lawyers, preachers and college professors. Collaboration and teamwork were the order of the day. The boycott was successful beyond anyone's wildest dreams. On the first day of the boycott, the buses were empty of Negro passengers. Success was in the 100% range. Only a few white passengers were on the buses. Negroes were walking, riding in taxis, riding bicycles, hitch hiking, riding mules or in wagons. It was a mass demonstration of some 50,000 persons willing to sacrifice and suffer for their freedom and dignity (40). It was a mass demonstration of the solidarity that is a by-product of revolt in search of freedom Bennett 1968; Oates 1982; Branch 1988; Garrow 1986, 1989, et al).

The Montgomery Improvement Association (MIA) was organized for the purpose of coordinating the boycott movement. It was important for Dr. King to come forth with a strategy that embraced both the sentiments of the militancy and moderation. This was necessary to get the participation and support of diverse civil rights groups.

The Christian focus of love was chosen as the reconciling factor to cement the foundation of revolt. Dr. King admonished the activists to, "Love your enemies, bless them that curse you and pray for them that despitefully use you" (Luke 6:27-28). To understand the leadership style and focus of Dr. King, it is important to understand first and foremost that he was a Baptist preacher. Further, he was a preacher whose father, grandfather and great grandfather were preachers. He had been reared in a parsonage and began preaching at the age of eighteen. Much of his living and formal education had been in theology and the life of the Holy Spirit. His Ph.D. was in Systematic Theology and dealt with the concept of God. His vision of the world, therefore, spiritually, socially, politically, and economically were inspired and directed by a godly point of view. His style of Christian leadership inspired hope and courage that would be called upon again and again as the Montgomery boycott continued. Cornell West in Albert and Hoffman, eds. *We Shall Overcome* (1990), speaks of the driving forces behind Kings ' leadership style:

1. The prophetic black church tradition.

2. The prophetic liberal education in Christianity received in higher education.

3. The prophetic Gandhian method of nonviolent social change.

4. The prophetic American civil religion, which fuses secular and sacred history and combines Christian themes of deliverance and salvation with political ideals of democracy, freedom and equality (116).

West continues: "King was a religious intellectual who put his message on the level of the masses and became a part of their world... It was the particular conditions after World War II in America with its world power status, its unprecedented economic boom and its apartheid like structures of racial domination in the South–that set the stage for the moral vision, personal courage, and political determination of King and those who struggled alongside him" (116).

Morris reasons in Albert and Hoffman (1990), eds., that when King arrived in the early fifties•:

He possessed all the qualities needed to become a leader of the black movement. These included oratorical skills, knowledge of nonviolent mass civil disobedience, a philosophy that wedded him to the masses, an understanding of the black protest tradition, knowledge of the changes occurring in the Third World, and the kind of personal leadership style that would attract the media. Further, he headed a mass based institution within the black religious community (58).

It appears, thus, that the needs of an historical time and the particular preparation and visions of a certain individual (Dr. King) came together to create a new dynamic that brought to the world stage a revolting struggle for freedom that was unprecedented in America. It started in Montgomery, Alabama with the Rosa Parks arrest on December 1, 1955–almost one hundred years after the Emancipation Proclamation had declared freedom for Negroes (Miller 1968; Oates 1982; Branch 1988, et al).

What, then, is the meaning of the Montgomery story? The thinking of Dr. King was that Montgomery was beyond human comprehension. He felt that, "The Montgomery story would have taken place if the leaders of the protest had never been born" (51). For America, Montgomery was one of the proving grounds for revolt. Symbolically, what better place for it to happen than the heart of the "Old South and Confederacy?" What an irony that one of the most segregated and racist cities in the world would become the birthplace of "freedom and justice" (52).

As the boycott protest gathered momentum, effective systems of daily operational organization and transportation were essential to success. The best minds came together as volunteers to drive passengers, to do clerical work, to answer telephones, or to do whatever was needed in order to be a participant in this massive struggle for freedom. Walking, especially, was seen as a means of personal liberation and revolt for self and others. According to Dr. King, if a motto could have been chosen for the attitude of the boycott, It would have been the scripture from the Book of Zechariah 4:8: "Not by might, nor by power, but by my spirit saith the Lord" (64). In other words, it was King's belief that God was on the side of justice and right, and the power of his Holy Spirit would sustain and deliver his people to freedom when other means would fail.

The matter of being on the side of justice and right prompted people from around the world to send telegrams supporting the boycott struggle. Many others sent financial support to underwrite the many costs involved as the protest continued (62). As to the participants, themselves, more and more they came to the realization that the nonviolence "pep talks" delivered by Dr. King and other leaders at weekly meetings were the way to victory. Again, love and forgiveness were the cornerstones of personal attitudes. Participants were strengthened and sustained by references from scripture such as: "And now abideth faith, hope, love these three; but the greatest of these is love." 1 Corinthians 13:13. So, while on the very front lines of revolt, the Negro masses were able to maintain an attitude of physical and emotional nonviolence against racism. Calmness and self-control were the orders of the day that got the best results during the protest. Many admitted that it was difficult but necessary (68-70). Historian, John Hope Franklin, writing in Albert and Hoffman (1990) eds., gives a rationale for King's position on violence: "The courageous efforts of our own insurrectionist brothers, such as Denmark Vesey and Nat Turner should be eternal reminders to us that violent rebellion is doomed from the start... Beyond the pragmatic invalidity of violence is its inability to appeal to conscience" (100).

It is natural for human beings to strike back physically or emotionally at forces that are subjecting them to the faces of oppression and inequality. Therefore, growth in non-violence is a slow and calculated journey that requires daily effort and perseverance. As a youth Dr. King had witnessed or heard of racism, lynchings, Ku Klux Klan night rides, police brutality and economic injustice (Branch 1988). While in high school, he had been a victim of racism on buses as well as in the workplace. However, the weapon of nonviolence did not begin to take root as a moral philosophy until his days at Morehouse and Crozer. By the time he enrolled at Morehouse, he was already keenly interested in racial justice. Thoreau's *Essay on Civil Disobedience* provided the first insights into the need to refuse to cooperate with systemic injustice (Smith and Zepp 1986). Later, at Crozer, the quest continued or enlighten ment on social and ethical theories with readings from Plato, Aristotle, Rauschenbusch, Rousseau, Hobbes, Bentham, Mill, Locke Nietzsche and Niebuhr (Oates 1982). Explorations were also made into the works of Marx and Lenin. And, then, there was the pivotal occasion of listening to a speech by Dr. Modecai Johnson, president of Howard University, Washington, D.C., on Mahatma Gandhi. (Bennett 1968; Branch 1988). After studying Gandhi more closely, King recognized the power of love as a viable force for social reform and large scale societal transformation that transcended just individual one on one. In Dr. King's words:

It was in this Gandhian emphasis on love and nonviolence that I discovered the method for social reform that I had been seeking for so many months. The intellectual and moral satisfaction I failed to gain from the utilitarianism of Bentham and Mill, and the revolutionary methods of Marx and Lenin, the social contracts theory of Hobbes the "back to nature" optimism of Rousseau and the superman philosophy of Nietzsche, I found in the nonviolent resistance philosophy of Gandhi. I came to feel that this was the only morally and practically sound method open to oppressed people in the struggle for freedom (79).

As stated earlier, little did Dr. King know that Gandhian style nonviolence would be lived out in real action when he got to Montgomery–that it would, indeed, become a way of life for participants in the boycott revolt.

The effective use of nonviolence, according to Dr. King, is predicated upon six philosophical foundations, namely:

+ The method is passive physically, but strongly active spiritually. It is not passive non-resistance to evil; it is active nonviolent resistance to evil.

+ It does not seek to defeat or humiliate the opponent, but to win his friendship and understanding.

+ The attack is directed against institutional forces of evil rather than against persons who happen to be doing the evil. These forces of evil are contained in unjust courts of law, government discrimination at all levels, unfair labor practices, unequal access to public facilities, school segregation, unfair housing, etc.

+ A willingness to accept suffering without retaliation.

• An avoidance of not only external physical violence but also internal violence of the spirit.

• Nonviolence is based on the conviction that the universe is on the side of justice (83-88).

Dr. King believed that these six foundations needed to be carried out by a community of revolting persons inspired by love and hoping in a future that was yet to become a reality. This solidarity of committed people working together, as community, for the common causes of justice and truth would prevail.

King's conviction about good, truth and justice, however, flew in the face of the segregationists' belief that these were already in place, that things as they were, were right. From indications, most white persons from Montgomery felt that Negroes already had good, truth and justice working on their behalf.

Smith and Zepp (1986) offered the view that King saw a fusion of the Montgomery boycott and the subsequent unfolding civil rights movement. The two complemented each other in a continuing historical process that had freedom and justice as its vision. Therefore, the opposition to the boycott was intense and bitter. In an initial negotiation session with key city officials, the three MIA proposals met with stem objection. These proposals were:

- A guarantee of courteous treatment when using public transportation.

- Passengers to be seated on a first-come, first-served basis on public transportation.

- Employment of Negro bus operators on predominantly Negro routes.

The meeting made no progress, according to King, because white privileges are not relinquished without strong opposition. Further, it was evident that the purposes of segregation were to keep Negroes in a status of inequality and exploitation. There was no compromise. So, the boycott continued (94). According to Smith and Zepp (1986), King was seeking out ·a position where the best points would be taken from both sides, and, further to avoid unrealistic positions of either side. It is evident that reconciliation was King's ultimate goal, but negotiation tactics of city hall were made in bad faith.

A tactic used by the white city fathers was to divide and conquer. Rumors were spread that the Negro leaders were getting rich, buying new cars and property, etc. while the masses walked or found other means of transportation. Seeds of dissension were planted among th Negro leaders, themselves, as to who should be leaders and who should be followers (103). Dr. King, especially, came under severe attack as not really representing the old order Negro leadership of Montgomery. And then, there was the hoax of a settlement between the city fathers and "three prominent" Negro clergy that would end the boycott (105). No one knew who these three clergy were. The so called agreement was later repudiated by the three ministers. This defeat brought about the last strategy of the city fathers, which was a "get tough" policy.

This last get-tough policy involved the city fathers asking white employers to stop going to pick up their Negro help. Traffic tickets were given for just about any cause. Car pool drivers were stopped on every comer for checks. Even hitchhikers were threatened with arrest for vagrancy (107). While these get-tough tactics caused some to defect from the movement, in general, it made the majority more determined and committed to stay the course of revolt. Freedom costs and it was not going to be denied.

The get-tough tactics turned to violence on the night of January 30, with the bombing of Dr. King's home. His wife, daughter and a church friend were home at the time but escaped injury. As a consequence, a riot and violence seemed imminent.

However, Dr. King spoke to the crowd in careful words, "We must love our white brothers... this is what we must live by... no matter what they do to us, we must make them know that we love them. We must meet hate with love" (117). This stance of *agape* love was central and foundational to Dr. King's Christian beliefs. He defines *agape* love as the "Understanding and redeeming good will for all men" (86). It is a love that is disinterested. He continues: "Consequently, the best way to assure oneself that love is disinterested is to have love for the enemy-neighbor from whom you can expect no good in return, but, only hostility and persecution" (86).

Therefore, following this line of reasoning, it appears that Dr. King was also saying that humans must reflect who God is and what God is like in dealing with each other. This is what Dr. King was saying to the crowd that was gathered at his home that night–ready to do violence. Upon seeing the non-retaliatory stance of their leader, the crowd slowly dispersed. Thus, Dr. King had raised the love ethic to a new level as a result of the bombing. Love, itself, had become a dimension of revolt and freedom. More explicitly, the power of love enabled, simultaneously, a revolt and freedom that cleansed and liberated the emotions and attitudes from meanness, hate, spitefulness, resentment and revenge. One concludes, then, that the power to choose to love your enemy is a means of liberation of the highest order–spiritually, emotionally, and metaphysically.

This liberation was the beginning of an unstoppable and unbreakable chain of unity that was hard for the opposition to understand. Every effort of the opposition to disunite only served to strengthen the bond, solidify the courage, and raise the tolerance level for suffering. Fear was no longer a hindrance because a new persona had emerged. The old person had passed away and a new person had emerged (87). Things could never be the same again. A liberating human transformation had taken place.

As a result of the Montgomery boycott protest and subsequent filing of litigation by the NAACP, on Tuesday, November 13, 1956, The Supreme Court of the United States handed down the judgment that segregation on public transportation was unconstitutional (King 1958). Bus segregation in Montgomery came to an official end on December 21, 1956. This was 382 days after the boycott had begun in 1955. The revolt and protest for freedom from oppression had borne results. Montgomery would see a new day.

The Montgomery from December 21, 1956 on was a new story. On the buses, Negro and whites could take any seat that was unoccupied. Drivers received training on how to be courteous and civil to all passengers. All signs denoting segregation were removed from the buses. The bus company agreed to take applications from Negro driver applicants. Negroes were advised to continue nonviolence in every situation, whatever the provocation. There was to be no retaliation. There were to be no verbal confrontations about winners and losers. It was a time for racial reconciliation and harmony (145). The bloodbath that had been predicted and feared by white segregationists and others never took place. The racial environment in all domains became better in Montgomery. Many whites openly confessed admiration that Negroes had stood up for their rights, freedom, and change. The victory that was won for both Negroes and whites with the Montgomery boycott was that major social change can be accomplished without violence and that militant nonviolent revolt and protest works (151). Therefore, Montgomery became the symbol of a better future of racial understanding where some semblance of Dr. King's vision of a "**Beloved Community**" (196) which is characterized by harmony, trust, peace, and good will would began to become a reality (Smith and Zepp 1986).

But in a larger sense, the Montgomery story reached beyond the city limits and the state of Alabama. The meaning of Montgomery is the Negro willingness to struggle and sacrifice, in whatever place and time, for first class citizenship, dignity and freedom from oppression. Further, Montgomery has confronted white Americans with the flagrant hypocrisy and racial injustice that do not represent democracy. The dilemma of race exists in all corners of America. Dr. King stressed that racism is basically sinful and evil and has no place in the brotherhood of human beings because it stifles self-esteem, diminishes personality and hinders a people from aspiring to be the best with their talents. Then, due to fear and stereotyping, racism lessens the freedom of both the oppressed and the oppressor.

Dr. King, considered what must be done for future generations in order to prevent protest and to guarantee freedom and justice for all? The following issues were identified:

+ Local, state and federal governments must play a decisive role in making changes for justice and equality for all Americans (175).

+ Southerners, both white and black, "The Native Sons and Daughters," were best equipped to solve the problems of racist oppression in the South (179).

+ American labor must provide equal training and job opportunity for all employees. Economic inequality keeps the Negro in second place (180).

The church must accept its role and responsibility of leadership. Dr. King points out that "In the final analysis, racism is not a political but a moral issue." Racism denies the meaning of Christianity and oneness in Christ. The matter of one person being superior and another being inferior because of race is contrary to biblical teaching and doctrine. He adds that we belong to each other and when we harm others, we harm ourselves (182-186).

In order to achieve integration and continue to press for equality, Negroes must organize themselves into a militant and nonviolent mass movement. On a smaller scale, and where the masses are not possible, ten committed men and women can get the job done. For Twelve Apostles of Jesus, zealous champions, inspired into boldness by faith in a cause, literally turned the world upside down for Christianity. And two thousand years later, it is still going as strong as ever as a result of their work (187).

Negroes, with their historical capacity for suffering, for Christian love, understanding and good will, may be God's instrument and role model to bring about peace and survival for Western civilization and the nations of the world. To take a fresh look at the philosophy of nonviolence as a means of avoiding war, destruction and self-annihilation may be a worthwhile avenue to pursue. What is there to lose? Who will be the winners in another world war? With the threat of nuclear contamination, will the world be fit to live in afterwards? These questions can also be addressed from the perspective of revolt and freedom but on the world scale (200-201).

And on the world scale, Dr. King wanted to begin with the meaning of America, which he felt was essentially a dream—a dream of freedom. Smith and Zepp (1986) address this point.:

It is a dream of a land where men of all races, of all nationalities, and of all creeds can live together as brothers. The substance of the dream is expressed in these sublime words, words lifted to cosmic proportions: "We hold these truths to be self-evident—that all men are created equal: that they are endowed by their creator with certain inalienable rights that among these are life, liberty and the pursuit of happiness." This is the dream (127).

But beyond America, Dr. King envisioned a universal human inclusiveness of all classes, races, religions, the haves, and the have-nots, where the secular and the spiritual would come together to carry out the dream of international brotherhood. It appears that he did not see this as happening in the apocalyptic and futuristic millennial, but within the historical time frame of now (174). The bus boycott in Montgomery was a beginning chapter in this quest for liberation.

The sermons preached by Dr. King on Sunday mornings and at other times carried prophetic words of his vision of what the world ought to be like when these changes became a reality. That brings us to another of his books, *Strength to Love*.

STRENGTH TO LOVE

Strength to Love (1963) is a book of fifteen selected sermons of Dr. King, which contain his penetrating and theologically inspired beliefs concerning justice, goodness, human equality and the elimination of social evils. Further, the sermons contain the basic tenets of his thoughts on revolt, nonviolence and freedom. His firm belief, it seems, was that theology must walk step by step with social change. Otherwise, the institution of the church is not doing the job that it was put on earth to do. The ultimate goal of both theology and the church was the redemption and reconciliation of all human beings into Dr. King's envisioned **"Beloved Community"** or transformed society where harmony, trust, peace, justice, and good will would be lived out in the lives of people on a daily basis (Smith and Zepp 1986)

Fifteen selected sermons taken from fifteen different Bible texts make up the content of *Strength to Love*. It seems that Dr. King went to great lengths in researching and preparing his sermons. These sermons are essays that were delivered orally to primarily a black audience. These sermons were preached in the context of the crisis of Negro freedom in the 50's and 60's as their foundation. They were written to inform, inspire, persuade, and give hope. Since a sermon is normally preached for hearing, these principles and ideas were put into writing so that readers from all ethnic groups, places, and walks of life would be able to share and reflect on Dr. King 's thinking. As m the case of the great "I Have a Dream" speech of 1963, Dr. King's sermon oratory appeals to all people because of the power and truth of his words, his rich metaphorical style and vocabulary, his skillful voice inflections, and his repetitive use of word and phrase nuances to drive home his points. Some of these principles, ideas, and view points have been excerpted and paraphrased with analysis, where possible:

> Love is the *internal* principle that is the ultimate reality of life and existence for
> all the human race, and nonviolent protest is its *external* worldly counterpart
> (5-6). The success, survival, and freedom of the human race are caught up and
> forever bound to the fact that we are our brother's keeper. "We are tied in a single

garment of destiny" and we have been ordained, all of us, from the beginning of creation, to love one another (70).

Certainly, Dr. King realized that true Christian love is costly, because loving your enemies is a task that most peoples find impossible. However, the admonition of Jesus from the Book of Matthew 5: 43-45 states:

Ye have heard that it hath been said. Thou shalt love thy neighbor and hate thine enemy. But I Say unto you, love your enemies, bless them that curse you, do good to them that hate you, and pray for them which despitefully use you, and persecute you that you may be children of your Father which is in heaven (47).

There is no problem loving those who love you. But, to love those who wish to harm, who oppress you, and who will obstruct every road to progress that you may pursue? This is asking for a dimension of love that is unknown to most human beings. According to Dr. King, this is the love that is revolt against and a conqueror of hate. A vengeful "Eye for an eye, tooth for a tooth" life style will leave all human beings maimed or dead. The hate has to stop someplace and Jesus shows us the way. It seems that Dr. King is saying here that the responsibility of Christians is to live out this command in their daily lives. In so doing they choose the freedom to love, to forgive, to see the good in people and not the bad, to seek not to defeat or humiliate but to reconcile. Finally, humans are made in the image and likeness of God. God loves everybody, saints and sinners. We are called to do the same. Constant love changes enemies into friends and results in a measure of freedom for both.

Revolt against oppression obliges us to struggle, suffer, and, if necessary, to die for the freedom that ought to be the opportunity and God given right of every human being Christians are called by God, just as he called the Twelve Apostles, "To eliminate the world's evils—evils so flagrant and self-evident that they glare at us from every ghetto street and rural hovel… by reaching into and beyond ourselves and tapping the moral ethic of love" (6).

Protagonists in the struggle for freedom must be able to bring together into a successful working unit different personality types (10-12). King identifies four types: the tough minded, the tenderhearted, the hardhearted and the softminded. The tough-minded is firm dedicated, dependable and committed. The tenderhearted is easily influenced by the media, half-truths, prejudices and propaganda. The hardhearted would inflict violence and hatred upon the opponent. The softminded would bow to oppression by willfully tolerating it. The tough-minded person is the freedom fighter who persists and perseveres to the end as the most staunch advocate of freedom. King goes on to say that Hitler, writing in *Mein Kampf,* realized that softmindedness was so prevalent among his followers that he asserted: By means of shrewd lies, unremittingly repeated, it is possible to make people believe that heaven is hell—and hell, heaven… The greater the lie, the more readily will it be believed (12).

Therefore, softmindedness is a breeding ground for racism and violence. But then, there are the individuals who have the characteristics of the hardhearted. These are individuals who would inflict physical violence and hatred upon the opponent. Dr. King states in strong terms that while violence may win a skirmish, it will fail to win the battle:

> Violence only brings temporary victories; violence by creating many more social problems than it solves, never brings permanent peace. I am convinced that if we succumb to the temptation to use violence in our struggle for freedom, unborn generations will be the recipients of a long and desolate night of bitterness, and our legacy to them will be a never-ending reign of chaos. A voice echoing through the corridors of time, says to every intemperate Peter, "Put up thy sword." (Matthew 26:52). History is cluttered with the wreckage of nations that failed to follow Christ's command (14-15).

Hardhearted violence, then, is not the answer. Finally, there is the type of individual who is without outward courage or inward fortitude. These are the softminded Negroes who bow to oppression by willfully tolerating it. They prefer to do nothing to disturb the evil status quo and, therefore, allow themselves to remain oppressed. King says that this disposition toward oppression is cowardly, a sellout to an unjust system, and, consequently, a collaborator in its evil (11-12).

The true Christian, just as Jesus, is a nonconformist. That is to say, the Christian must be willing to stand alone and take up the voice and company of the minority of three or four against the majority of a hundred or more. Consequently, Christians will often be standing alone, ostracized and talked about. Nonconformity in the pursuit of justice is another name for revolt. (19).

The historical American church has too often forsaken its brotherhood and oneness of humanity mandates from God in order to sanction the evils of segregation, war, slavery, economic oppression, and discrimination. The church has, thus, become an instrument of man and not of its Creator. While the church in America had originally been founded as an escape from oppression to freedom, conformity has put it out of touch with its origins. Indeed, the church in America was, and still is, one of the most racially exclusive institutions in existence (141-142).

What is the role of the church in providing hope, leadership and light in a world encompassed with despair, misdirection, fear and chaos? It appears that Dr. King is saying that the role of the church must be a clear call for freedom and order. Therefore, the church, itself, would become an active agent of protest for justice, goodness, freedom, and the other rights of human beings that set their minds and hearts free to become all that they can (59-64). Humans must see the promise in church practices, amidst the difficulties of their existence, the hope that "weeping may endure for a night, but joy cometh in the morning (Psalms 30:5) (66).

In all circumstances, we must see each other as human beings first, with race, sex, origin, religion, economic status, and etc. a distant second. Otherwise, humans become "things" that are depersonalized and valued as needing less freedom because of what they have, who they are and, most preferentially, what they look like (28-29). In the struggle for freedom and justice, the question to ask is: How can I make a difference? and, Who will help if I do not do it? (31).

Our pious sayings and our actions must become one. To forgive those who have oppressed and transgressed upon our humanity is the purest test of Christian love. This is what Jesus did at His agonizing Crucifixion, "Father, forgive them for they know not what they do." (Luke 23:24) Forgiveness is an ongoing attitude that gives freedom of spirit, response, and feeling to the Christian. It has no limit as to how often it should be done (38).

Generally, individuals and society do not forgive, eventhough both profess Christian love. Capital punishment is the final chapter and testimony of a societal unforgiving spirit. The law of revenge hinders freedom in society (39).

Moral blindness and the lack of enlightenment cause people to commit atrocious acts of inhumanity against others in the misuse of freedom... Historical manifestations of this legacy include: war with its threat of nuclear annihilation, slavery in America, the legend of racial superiority and the use of the Bible, science and philosophy to justify it, unjust and discriminatory laws, segregation based on race, and concentration camps. The Bible was written to teach against moral and intellectual blindness. The church and Christians are responsible for the continual enlightenment that comes from the study of the Word of God. This study becomes, in essence, a revolt against ignorance, prejudice and propaganda. There is freedom in knowing the truth (44-45).

The social order of the world is confronted with times as dark as midnight. **Externally,** the universe and the people that inhabit it are at risk. Science was the answer to problems in the past; however, in a generation where two world wars have been fought, with yet another on the horizon, science has become the ally that has brought on the weapons and instruments that will bring about global destruction. So, there is no longer an answer found in science. **Internally,** the human condition is also at risk and finds people looking for a peace and a freedom of existence that will rest their weariness, uncertainty, and agitation. The appointment calendar for psychoanalysts is booked up six months in advance. Some of the most popular books on the bestseller list, according to Dr. King, are such titles as, Man *Against Himself, The Neurotic Personality of Our Times,* and Modem *Man in Search of A Soul.* And in religion, bestseller titles are *Peace of Mind and Peace of Soul.* Then, in the world of morality, the important place of absolutes—what is right or what is wrong in any situation, has been replaced by situational ethics which may change depending on place or circumstance or be determined, consensually, by what most others are doing, or further, what one can get by with. The new standard of personal behavior, therefore, has made right wrong and wrong right. A new slogan appears to be, "the survival of the slickest" (58)

Being wealthy is no more evil than being poor is dignified and noble. What counts is how wealth is used globally, by every nation, to alleviate the suffering and violence often associated with a life of poverty. The need is overwhelming "to Feed the poor, clothe the naked, heal the sick" and provide shelter for the homeless (70). It is clear that Dr. King is saying here that wealth can be used as another instrument of revolt in freeing humans from the oppression of poverty and suffering.

Dr. King goes on to affirm that "All life is interrelated. All men are caught in an inescapable network of mutuality, tied in a single garment of destiny. Whatever affects one directly affects all indirectly. I can never be what I ought to be until you are what you ought to be, and you can never be what you ought to be until I am what I ought to be. This is the interrelated structure of reality" (70). Everyone, therefore, is a freedom provider to each other.

Evil is as present in the world as good. Examples of evil are: lust, selfishness, greed, lying, social injustice, racism, war and economic exploitation. The history of man is the story of the struggle between good and evil. But, ultimately, good will overcome evil because God is good and His truths have endured the test of time; and it is these truths, in the final analysis, that will give humankind freedom (77).

It is apparent, therefore, that the symbolic death of evil has been demonstrated in numerous historical events. Namely, in the Bible with the defeat and death of Pharaoh's army at the Red Sea, the defeat of the British Empire and colonialism by Mahatma Gandhi in Asia and Africa, the winning of independence and freedom by the many African nations from colonial despots, during the 20th Century, and in America, the freedom of Negroes from slavery by the Emancipation Proclamation. In each case, there was the presence of a zealous champion (Moses, Gandhi, Frederick Douglass, Sojourner Truth, Harriet Tubman, Abraham Lincoln, Dr. Martin Luther King, Jr., Kwame Nkrumah) fighting for the freedom of oppressed people. Even though there was confrontation and casualties in each case, freedom was pursued, demanded, or promised, and, in each case, it became a reality.

Caution must be taken against false optimism. Evil is persistent. When one oppression is overcome, another comes on the scene. The forces for all the things that are good and right and just must vigilantly maintain a continual revolt and demand for freedom. Dr. King tells those in the struggle that the attitude of *"not yet"* must be the stay alert reality of the freedom fighter (82).

God is with us and for us in the many hardships and difficulties of life. His promise has been never to leave or forsake those who surrender their lives to His protection and guidance. The Holy Spirit, or God with us, empowers people to overcome and press on to freedom and be victorious in seemingly impossible circumstances (83-84).

Shattered dreams are a part of every life. The relevant question is, "How does one cope with shattered dreams?" Is bitterness and negativeness the answer? Is emotional seclusion and withdrawal the answer? Will fatalism and pre-ordination that leave no opportunity for freedom of choice provide the answer? (all forms of nihilism). One may conclude that none of the above will heal shattered dreams; rather, the answer lies in finding ways and solutions that convert hardships, difficulties and disappointments into gain (revolt). King is saying that it is the stormy weather and disappointments of life rather than the continual days of sunshine, trouble free living and bliss that would determine the true quality, character, and integrity of a person. Anyone can smile when all is going well, but where are the smiles when one is faced with or living in debilitating circumstances. A People's most long lasting freedom, fortitude, and power could come from their deepest suffering (92).

The Negro will not solve the racism dilemma by resorting to bitterness and cynicism. Negative emotions will only offer negative results, which can destroy or scourge personalities as well as the best of efforts. To the contrary, the Negro must stand determined to overcome obstacles and oppression and hold on to hope in a God who has always heard the cries of innocent suffering and has delivered His people.

The righteous and innocent suffering of Negroes is redemptive, and, according to Dr. King, "May well offer to Western civilization, the kind of spiritual dynamic so desperately needed for survival" (92).

The doctrine of Communism as a way of life is basically diametrically opposed to Christianity, and the two cannot be made to agree for purposes of mutual accord. Communism views God and religion as manifestations of uncertainty, fright and desperation. Communism views the final voice in the world as that of material things. Communism views the church as an institution designed by leaders to rule and manipulate the common people. Communism is anti-God and proposes the atheistic view that people's salvation is up to them, without the need or help of any transcendent being. Rather, human beings have the capacity and sole responsibility, themselves, of bringing about a better world. Communism professes no moral absolutes that would guide the societal conduct of its people. Therefore, it is easy to accept brutal ends as justifying the means. Communism exists with man as a faithful pawn of a powerful government, who has little personal freedom to become his/her own person and is thus robbed of the freedom that makes a human being human and aspiring. Under Communism, the freedom and truth that God offers, as a choice to every human being is lost for the sake of subjugation to a state manipulated by men (97-98).

Christianity, on the other hand, affirms that the universe was created and ordered by the hand and supernatural power of God the Father. It is a universe that is orderly, dependable, and predictable. This God is the Alpha and the Omega, the beginning and end of all truth. Christianity goes further to state that God is a matchless power of endless love and forgiveness whose values are absolute and eternal in guiding societal conduct. Christianity is founded on the fundamental premise of love and projects that love is the equalizer of all human conduct. It is Christian love that directs the principle that the ends must justify the means. Under Christianity, freedom can be gained through a faith that gives human beings a choice. Further, "humans are crowned with glory and honor, endowed with the gift of freedom" (99).

The Christian faith evolves around the belief that there is a God who created the universe and who is able, through his omnipotent power, to do all things. While there are those who question the existence of an omnipotent God due to flagrant evil, natural catastrophes and human illnesses that are present in the world, these problems have often been the result of human's own abuse of science, knowledge and reason. God does give human beings the freedom of choice, and it is this freedom of choice buttressed by science, knowledge and reason that has allowed human beings to perpetrate all types of atrocities upon others. By the same token, human beings have accomplished outstanding works and contributions for the good of the human race by choosing to do what is good, right and just with intelligence. These outstanding works of good and right produce freedom. Beyond this, there are the unanswered mysteries of God's creation that have to be accepted on faith. But for the Christian, historical faith has produced freedom, alleviated burdens, and removed obstacles. (107).

History has shown that manifestations of evil, whether they be ideologies, institutions or persons, will fail. The failure of Communism has already been discussed. Add to that colonialism, segregation, the Stalins, Hitlers, Mussolinis and Napoleons. They too have failed. There is a law of morality present in the world that continues to show that, in the long run, only good will prevail, and as stated by Dr. King: "The power of the sword cannot conquer the power of the spirit. "Ultimately, the passion of the masses for justice will revolt in the name of freedom and bring a halt to oppression and injustice". And this passion of the masses for justice is no less than the historical God who created the universe, working in his own time, through his people as instruments, to bring freedom (109-110).

What about fear? Everybody's freedom is affected in some way or the other by fear. Dr. King felt that, "Normal fear protects us. Abnormal fear paralyzes us. Normal fear motivates us to improve our individual and collective welfare; abnormal fear constantly poisons and distorts our inner lives. To live in fear can become a prison. How can fear be mastered? There appear to be at least four solutions: Number one is confrontation or giving the fear a microscopic and honest appraisal, or reality check. The second is calling on courage. Courage is that quality of the human personality that stands up to obstacles, real and imaginary, in defiant revolt and declare that the person is larger than the problem. The third is using the freedom of love towards others. Love diminishes, if not eradicates, fear. The fourth is faith. Faith is an attitude toward living that gives human beings a hope and assurance that they are not alone when confronting the trials, burdens, uncertainties and catastrophes that will surely come to every life.

It appears, again, that love is a weapon of revolt and freedom. In terms of a modern day focus on global fear, it seems that hate founded upon fear is the driving force that keeps wars and rumors of wars ongoing. Out of fear of one another, world powers create larger and more deadly arsenals of missiles, nuclear weapons and other war machinery. These weapons force others to comply out of fear but cannot substitute for the brotherly love that will be the only long term and lasting solution. This is true because love gives freedom to life. Love empowers the best in human nature to shine through for self and others (116-117).

The enigmatic presence of evil in the lives of human beings and the effort to remove and or overcome that evil remains the daily challenge of every life. Human reliance on reason and science has failed to rid the world of such evils as greed, murder, poverty and war. As lives are crushed under the burden of these evils, the so-called age of reason, where man is in charge, has become an age of anxiety and terror. The best intentions of altruistic humanism have also failed. Further, the resigned submission of waiting on God with prayer will not do. God will no more do everything for humans than humans are able to do everything for themselves. But, rather, it is God and human beings working together with God giving no more power nor intervening no more than humans have the will, through faith, to accept. It is humans working in obedience, through faith, and God working through omnipotence and love that holds the keys to freedom from the shackles of evil. Dr. King identifies two types of faith that are necessary in the revolt against evil; the first is "Mind's faith, which is a belief that God exists. The second is heart's faith wherein the individual effects surrender of self to God. Both of these working together enables God to do for people what they cannot do for themselves. Therein, they become new creatures endowed with a freedom to do good for others (117-124).

There is a vast chasm existing in America between the magnificent progress and advances that have been made in the scientific and technological domain versus the halting and grudging progress made in the moral and spiritual domain. The people of God must be in vigilant revolt with the objective being to close and then eradicate this chasm in the name of peace and freedom for all. Again, and unfortunately, it appears that the American church does not really perform its role in society. Why is there "A white church and a Negro church? How can segregation exist in the true Body of Christ?" These are two questions frequently raised by Dr. King. All human kind came into existence through one blood and one flesh. God created only one man and one woman. People were made to co-exist as one. The church has a significant role to play in bringing the walls of segregation and discrimination to a close, beginning with its own congregation. Americans (every American) have a birthright of freedom and they are obligated to protest until the playing field of opportunity is level and equal for everyone in every domain. Again, love for one another is the ultimate weapon of power that will eradicate racism and issue in justice and freedom (100-101).

After studying numerous philosophical concepts and ideologies, with the intent of gaining some insight into the best approach to deal with the indignities and oppression of racism, Dr. King happened upon Mahatma Gandhi's philosophy of nonviolent protest. Dr. King's particular view was to find a protest strategy that dealt with "The whole man, not only his soul but also his body, not only his spiritual well being but also his material well being. Religion must address the total needs of a person—the spiritual and the social. Dr. King found the answer in studying what Gandhi had accomplished against the British Crown using nonviolence within the concept of *Satyagraha*. *Satya* is truth that equals love while *graha* is force. Combined the word means truth-force or love-force. A closer examination *Satyagraha* revealed to Dr. King that this philosophy would bring together the love ethic of Christianity and the nonviolence ethic practiced by Gandhi and his followers. Dr. King saw in the power of this combined thrust the potent weapon needed to liberate the oppressed to freedom (151–152). Nonviolence produces a new self-respect on the part of the oppressed and pricks the attitude of justice in the oppressor causing a change for reconciliation and solidarity. For a time, the impression of this force was intellectual but would be used in live action during the Montgomery boycott struggle.

Dr. King's work as a civil rights champion resulted in great personal suffering: bombings of his home, daily threats to himself and family, an almost fatal stabbing, betrayal, and false accusations, His personal sufferings served as a catalyst and foundation for the context of many of his ideas and thoughts. However, seeing himself as a chosen instrument of God to do the work that he was doing, he looked at difficulties as opportunities to strengthen his Christian commitment and bring him closer to God. Dr. King's firm belief was that "Unearned suffering is redemptive" (154).

Dr. King speaks quite pointedly of mission, burden, and their relationship to freedom and revolt when he states that "We are gravely mistaken to think that religion protects us from the pain and agony of moral existence. Life is not a euphoria of unalloyed comfort and untroubled ease. Christianity has always insisted that the cross we bear precede the crown we wear. To be a Christian, one must take up his cross, with all its difficulties and agonizing and tension packed content, and carry it until that very cross leaves its mark upon us and redeems us to that more excellent way which comes only through suffering" (24-25).

Garrow in Albert and Hoffman, eds., *We Shall Overcome* (1990), stated that the more excellent way referred to here is the freedom of *agape* love. One can conclude, therefore, that Dr. King, though burdened and at times fearful for his life, accepted the role that destiny and history had placed on his shoulders, and he was willing to embrace it to the end, whatever that end might be. He saw the end as redemptive, enhancing, and liberating (19). Indeed, according to Richard King in Albert and Hoffman, eds., (1990), Dr. King was speaking of freedom of the whole man as a condition of being and making decisions about the world: "The capacity to deliberate, decide and respond" (139). Richard King identifies two important types of freedom expressed in the actions and pronouncements of Dr. King. The first of these is the freedom that is the "Corporate experience of deliverance from oppression by God's action in history as sacred and secular." Freedom was seen as sacred because it was ordained and given to humans by God. Freedom was seen as secular because it carried the meaning of what every American aspired to and what the founding heritage of the American republic envisioned from its beginnings (138). However, the history of America as seen by Dr. King, showed a courageous pursuit and desire for freedom by white America, who, at the same time, invoked a protracted and, at times, violent denial of the same freedom to black Americans. The "One nation under God with liberty and justice for all" is the paradox that Dr. King was fighting to reconcile into an enduring just co-existence of brotherhood and freedom. His idea of a **beloved community** was the name that gathered these visions into one entity.

His next book, *Why We Can't Wait* (1963), brings into broad focus the concepts of freedom for whites and freedom for blacks.

WHY WE CAN'T WAIT

The introduction of *Why We Can't Wait* (1963) portrays the life of a young black boy and a black girl. They have no name, age, or address. They have no other description, except that one lives in Harlem, the North, and the other lives in rural Alabama, the South. They appear to be symbolic of the historical past and the foretold future that have been a plague upon the lives of black Americans since being brought to America in chains. The two black youngsters are on the threshold of reliving a life similar to that of their parents, grandparents, aunts, uncles, other relatives and ancestors. It has been a life of oppression—where the ancestors of these two youngsters have been asked to wait a little longer for justice and freedom. However, the black boy and girl stand up in revolt with a determination to fight for their future. Thus, the boy and girl joined their Negro comrades fighting for their future in Birmingham, 1963.

The purpose of this book is to explain why wait-time had run out. The background of the book is the true historical events that took place in Birmingham, Alabama and nearly one thousand other cities during the summer of 1963—events that caused a black revolt. Dr. King wrote the book as a descriptive and detailed essay in order to identify, explore, address and explain what happened during that "special summer" of the civil rights struggle, and to explain the effectiveness of nonviolent direct action as a weapon of protest.

Why Birmingham? Why 1963? Negroes had suffered over three hundred years of indignities based on race by 1963. During those three centuries, they had petitioned, protested, and rebelled about their human condition as American citizens; however, these protests were not taken seriously by US presidents, elected officials, or by the Supreme Court. Civil rights laws, including the 1954 school desegregation decision were not enforced and were, therefore, ignored by many school systems in the country, and especially in the South. The spirit of "with all deliberate speed" as directed by the Supreme Court school decision ended up, due to legal segregationist maneuverings, being "with all deliberate delay." School systems and municipalities came up with their own time line for implementation, which in the majority of cases nullified the Supreme Court ruling. This blatant refusal on the part of white America to obey a just and fair ruling handed down by the highest court of the land made it clear to Negroes that their rights would continue to be unprotected and ignored–that they would continue to be treated less than equal in every domain. A frustration and disappointment began taking place that took nine years, 1954-1963, to erupt into open revolt and rebellion.

Other issues that motivated the summer of 1963 were the frequent reminders to Negroes that the U.S. government was willing to send their military forces to the farthest corners of the world to defend and die for the peace and freedom of other (at the time, it was Vietnam) peoples while doing little to guarantee the civil rights and freedom of twenty million of its own citizens. Negroes recognized this stance as gross hypocrisy. Then, during this era, there was the independence being won from colonial oppression by numerous countries in Africa and Asia. Thus, American Negroes were witnesses to freedom and independence in the land of their ancestry, while they were being handed a few crumbs of tokenism or nothing at all. In America, African representatives were voting on world issues in the United Nations while many Negroes could not exercise their citizenship right to vote in their local and state elections, or in many places, sit at a lunch counter. Further, 1963 was the one-hundredth year of the signing of the Emancipation Proclamation by President Lincoln, but the promised freedom and justice were still a dream. Economic exploitation and the ability to make a decent living as compared to other ethnic groups in America was still a myth. Therefore, the summer of 1963 was the hour of revolution for the Negro masses. Dr. King made it explicitly clear that Freedom had been delayed and denied too long.

The principal weapon of revolt used to confront and overcome the systemic racism of 1963 was militant nonviolence. Martin Luther King, Jr. referred to nonviolence as "The Sword That Heals" (27). Even the evil of slavery needed to be forgiven.

Slavery had been used to keep the Negro in bondage physically and psychologically. Families were purposefully separated, scattered, and destroyed. Any defiance of the slave codes resulted in severe punishment or death. The culture of white America towards Negroes after slavery was "separate and unequal." When Negroes were finally freed in 1863, the majority of them were set adrift without money, belongings, property, family, or sponsors. This treatment was oppressive, mean spirited, terrifying, and different than that afforded any other ethnic group that came to America. Early settlers from Europe were afforded sponsors, money, land, and civil rights. This aftermath of slavery treatment followed Negroes from the proverbial cradle to the grave. This second and third class citizen status still existed in 1963. Negroes were victimized and exploited with impunity in both the South and the North. However, the assumption on the part of most whites during these long intervening post slavery years was that Negroes were happy and satisfied. In truth, Negroes had learned to play a survival game and were never satisfied. The best that Negroes could get in response to their demands was tokenism and promises; but tokenism was an end in itself and was a white strategy to end the process of protest and pressure leveled at segregation and discrimination (31-32).

Previous attempts (pre-1963) at bringing about justice for Negroes had failed. Booker T. Washington had advocated doing the best you could with what you had. W.E. B. DuBois had spoken about educating the talented tenth, and Marcus Garvey was sold on the idea of returning to Africa as a means of dignity and self-respect. Then, there were the entrenched legal battles of the National Association for the Advancement of Colored People (NAACP), relying on the Constitution and the federal courts to fight segregation. However, when a case was won in the courts (and applauded by all), implementation ran into one roadblock after the other, and each roadblock represented a denial of freedom and justice. Finally, the Black Muslims came onto the stage with a philosophy of separation of the races in America. Their doctrine was that freedom should be pursued by any means necessary. In light of these unsuccessful attempts to bring about liberation of Negroes, the ultimate weapon for change, as Dr. King saw it, would be nonviolent direct action.

Nonviolent action allowed Negroes the freedom of militant revolt without using violent force. According to Dr. King, militant nonviolent protest had a proven record of success. Indeed, nonviolence was against the old dogma of fighting violence with violence; rather, it was based on the foundation of fighting violence with love, moral force, and attempts at reconciliation. The weapons of the soldiers of nonviolence were "their heart, their conscience, their courage, and their sense of justice" (39). Therefore, nonviolence would liberate the oppressed to a new personhood, dignity and self-respect, while at the same time neutralizing the weapons of violence used previously by the oppressor. Nonviolence was a two–edged sword, then, in that it gave freedom to both the oppressed and the oppressor. Birmingham would be the most valid test of the effectiveness of militant nonviolence.

The Birmingham of 1963 was reminiscent of a police state regards to segregation. Everything adhered to total separation of Negroes and whites. Dr. King paints a vivid picture of historical racism in Birmingham: schools were still segregated. Negroes were not allowed in public parks that their taxes helped pay for. All the local stores were segregated. Negroes could not eat at lunch counters in white establishments. Churches were segregated. the Metropolitan Opera could not perform in Birmingham due to the use of black performers and musicians. The NAACP was outlawed in the State of Alabama as a "foreign corporation." Jobs held by Negroes were the most menial. Negroes were unable to register to vote. Police brutality against Negroes was legendary and done with impunity. Whites who saw the injustice dared not speak out for fear of retaliation. They remained silent for fear of social, political and economic reprisals (Garrow 1986:232). The good people remained silent (47–50). Birmingham was seen, therefore, as the fortress of segregation that it was, and the decision was made that a major protest and victory there would set the direction for freedom and justice throughout the nation. The Negro civil rights fighters were not to be turned aside by the formidable racist presence of the Commissioner of Public Safety, (police and fire departments) Theophilus G. "Bull" Connor (Fairclough 1995:17).

Dr. King and his close advisors were prepared to go jail in Birmingham as part of their struggle for freedom. Participants in the protest were required to sign a Ten Commandments pledge card, which stated: "I hereby pledge myself–my person and body to the nonviolent movement. Therefore I will keep the following Ten Commandments…" (63). While complaints that the timing was poor and that Dr. King and his entourage were "outsiders," the counter argument was made that no Negro could be an "outsider" any place in America when justice and equality were at stake. Further, the invocation of court injunctions, would not block the course–since court injunctions had been finally identified as another legal maneuver used by segregationists to stall, circumvent, or nullify the rights of peaceful assembly guaranteed by the Constitution.

At the outset of the Birmingham protest, Dr. King was jailed and placed in solitary confinement. A few days later, he wrote his famous *Letter From Birmingham Jail.* This letter was written in response to a statement published by eight white Birmingham clergy criticizing his leadership in the Birmingham Negro revolt. But beyond this, Ling (1998) informs us that King wanted the Birmingham strategy of non-violent direct action to bring about "such a crisis and tension that a community that has constantly refused to negotiate is forced to confront the issue... Since freedom is never voluntarily given up by the oppressor" (18).

Letter From Birmingham Jail contains some of Dr. King's most fundamental themes of protest. Ten of those key points will be highlighted here:

- The fight for freedom and justice in America has no boundaries. Wherever there is oppression and the need for aid that is where the true Christian should be.

- Campaigns of nonviolent direct-action follow four basic steps: collection of the facts to determine whether injustices exist; negotiation; self-purification; and direct action (78).

- Waiting had taken its toll after 340 years of Negro patience. Third World countries around the globe were gaining their independence, while Negroes were still struggling for the civil right to sit at a lunch counter.

- In the name of freedom, people have a right to disobey unjust laws. "Any law that uplifts human personality is just. Any law that degrades human personality is unjust. All segregation statutes are unjust because segregation distorts the soul and damages the personality" (82).

- The injustice of segregation must be exposed, brought into the open, shown to be morally wrong and healed. While violence may at times result during the quest for human rights, the presence of violence is no reason to curtail the pursuit of just ends.

- The influence of the Negro church played a key role in keeping the participants of the freedom summer of 1963 nonviolent. Love was the defining attitude that gave direction to the movement.

- "Oppressed people cannot remained oppressed forever. The yearning for freedom eventually manifests itself, and that is what has happened to the Negro struggle of 1963" (87).

- The label of being an extremist for justice can be applied to some of the greatest champions and defenders of Christian values, namely: the Prophet Amos, the Apostle Paul, John Bunyan, Abraham Lincoln, Thomas Jefferson, and Jesus Christ, himself (88). Creative extremism made a difference in Birmingham, and Dr. King appears to be saying that the world needs more role models, such as those mentioned here, who are willing to embrace the struggle and pay the price for the moral courage required to be an extremist for change.

- The Christian Church everywhere must stand up and be counted when issues of fairness, freedom, and justice are at stake. During the Birmingham struggle, the Church, too often, was silent and acted with an attitude that was unbiblical. (91–92).

- Negroes were in America before the good ship Mayflower landed the first Pilgrims from Europe; the latter had come in the search of freedom. Negroes, likewise, have searched for freedom and will achieve freedom in Birmingham and all over the country because the goal of America has always been human liberation. In the words of Dr. King: "We will win our freedom because the sacred heritage of our nation and the eternal will of God are embodied in our echoing demands" (93).

It is evident that *Letter From Birmingham Jail* was written at a critical and defining moment in the civil rights struggle and the points brought out in the letter were pivotal and prophetic of the direction that the movement would take from that point on. Certainly, Dr. King felt betrayed by his fellow clergy in that they denied or did not seem to understand the truth and justice in what he was doing. In this connection, he also saw the white church as an oppressor supporting injustice. However, the Negro church helped to keep the love and reconciliation ethic before their congregations. And this saved the day time and time again. The idea of disobeying unjust laws had been a defining principle from the very beginning of the civil rights struggle and it was now taking on its boldest confrontation in Birmingham. In defending against the label of extremist, King was again calling the clergy to understand the meaning of America—protesting for freedom and justice is indeed as American as the Star Spangled Banner. And the Birmingham protest aroused the solidarity of all age levels.

On May 3, 1963, the Negro children of Birmingham joined in the protest by leaving their classrooms (without permission) to take part in the demonstrations.

Their young and valiant efforts, in the name of freedom, were met with biting police dogs, high-pressure water hoses, billy club beatings, and jail. This show of unrestrained police brutality against children and women was televised throughout America and around the world. It was a turning point in the civil rights struggle that caused every American to see the brutal truth of what Dr. King and other leaders had been protesting about (100). As a consequence, federal civil rights legislation was put back on the congressional agenda and the far reaching Civil Rights Bill of 1964 was passed.

Further, the May 3 police brutality event against children and women brought about a flurry of activity in the Justice Department of the Attorney General's office. Lawyers were dispatched to Birmingham to negotiate a settlement between white merchants and Dr. King's forces (103). A settlement was reached that brought on a campaign of retaliation and bombings by white supremacists that resulted in the deployment of 3,000 federal troops and possibly the Alabama National Guard (107).

During this time four Negro children were killed by a bomb while attending Sunday school class at the 16th Street Baptist Church. Police killed a Negro youth while another was shot dead by white terrorists as he rode a bicycle. Except for a few brave clergy, no whites from the school system or city hall attended the funerals of these youth (112-113). All of these violent acts against the Negro citizens of Birmingham only intensified their determination to stand together in defiant revolt against an evil system. Finally, even the white clergy joined Negroes in their fight for freedom, and some of them went to jail for supporting the cause.

Historically, therefore, America has a long history of racial bigotry that needs to be healed and reconciled to a new way of recognizing and affording equality to all Americans. Racism is a part of America's national culture that must be extricated before we can truly be the democratic society that we proclaim to be. The Freedom Summer of 1963 was a beginning in closing this long existing schism that has been a plague in America's midst.

Dr. King concludes this book by speculating about the future. His first premise is that American society has no right to bargain with Negroes for the extent and quality of freedom, which is already theirs. As a background, he returns to the practice of manumission, which was used by slave owners in requiring slaves to buy their freedom or the freedom of others. As a result, a slave was able to buy his physical freedom. There is a parallel in today's society when many well meaning Americans ask, "what is the Negro willing to pay for his freedom." (127). The implication is that one American can bargain with another American for freedom. This is irrational, because a people cannot be half free and half slave. The segregationists have persisted in asking the above question, and it is their intransigence that aroused the masses of 1963 as much as any civil rights leader. During this time, wise Negro leadership of differing opinions finally unified when it was a question of responding to the masses.

Other perspectives on the future put forth by Dr. King state that society for hundreds of years has done something *against* the Negro. It is time for society to do something *for* him (134). For example, the Negro must be absorbed socially as well as economically. To enable equality, the Marshall Plan concept used in Europe after World War II would be a good beginning. Another point of view would be a new Bill of Rights for the Disadvantaged for Negroes and poor whites. In accomplishing this, the federal government must enforce its rules, and organized labor and the government must be on the right side, not in the middle (137-138).

In the final analysis, the civil rights victories achieved during the freedom summer of 1963 were healing for the nation and brought with it a new degree of freedom for all Americans. The use of nonviolent revolt in solving social problems was the answer for the nation and for the world. Dr. King continued looking to the future and the healing of America in his next book.

WHERE DO WE GO FROM HERE: CHAOS OR COMMUNITY?

Where Do We Go From Here: Chaos or Community? (1968), is a review as well as an analysis of the civil rights struggle from the mid-fifties through 1968. This 1968 Kingian perspective included the Montgomery boycott, the Albany, Georgia campaign, the Selma, Alabama struggle, the Birmingham, Alabama crisis, and the Chicago, Illinois campaign. In addition, three major pieces of federal legislation are placed into perspective. These are: the 1954 Supreme Court ruling on the desegregation of public schools, the 1963 Civil Rights Bill, and the 1965 Voting rights Act. As with Dr. King's previous books, this one is also written as a detailed, historical essay, from a first person perspective. He wanted to clarify that other strategies being advocated for the civil rights struggle, such as Black Power, could co-exist with militant nonviolence. He recognized that every strategy was striving for the same goal: justice and freedom. However, he continued to believe that "nonviolent direct action... was a more reasonable, practical, and moral strategy" (Washington 1986).

Dr. King advises that the solution to future peaceful social change in America is a double lock with two keys: Negroes have one key, and whites have the other. Working together, in good faith, nonviolent change could occur (21-22). Thus, there is the choice of chaos or community.

In light of this interpretation, one of the obstacles to community would be white backlash against efforts to bring a halt to racism in America. The federal legislation that was passed (noted above) came about as a result of blatant violence against Negroes by systemic segregation. The 1954 school integration ruling addressed the deplorable "separate but equal" law that dated to 1857 and the Dred Scott decision, which was handed down by another Supreme Court. This decision legalized segregation and stated in essence that Negroes, free or slave could not claim United States citizenship; Negroes had no rights as citizens. Therefore, Negroes had no value in the eyes of mainstream white America, and, the 1963 Civil Rights Bill came about as a result of the atrocities in Birmingham, Alabama. The 1965 Voting Rights Act was passed after the tragedies in Selma, Alabama. However, laws were not always obeyed. Many white citizens welcomed the laws of change but later retreated from the day to day application of these laws, which would move the nation toward equality. This was the essence of white backlash (68-69). The status quo was hard to change in the areas of education, housing, employment, and general civil rights. The needs to implement structural change for equality to take place had brought a new type of white resistance–North and South. The prevailing feeling was that Negroes had come far enough.

The Black Power slogan and movement came into being as a result of white backlash and intransigence. Black Power was a concept that had many different interpretations, some positive and others negative. The concept developed and was supported by the Student Nonviolent Coordinating Committee (SNCC) and The Congress of Racial Equality (CORE) after James Meredith was shot as he conducted a peaceful, one man march through Mississippi protesting the discrimination at 'Ole' Miss. In truth, however, Black Power was a reaction to the white power that continued to resist justice and freedom to Negroes. White power had dominated Negroes since they came to America. Black Power was a call to manhood, self-esteem, and worthiness. The idea of Black Power, further, was to dispute the slave mentality of many Negroes, to instill pride in being black, and to give rebirth of pride in a Negro history and heritage that had made outstanding contributions to American civilization and the world. Black Power had as its vision the development of political and economic independence on the part of the Negro masses (38).

It is evident that the idea of equality to blacks and whites has never meant the same thing. To blacks, equality means co-equals. To whites, equality simply means improvement (37). Consequently, Black Power was a psychological survival word in the face of white power. Black Power was born from despair and a loss of hope by many Negroes during the fifties and sixties. It was another type of revolt in the name of long denied freedom on the part of some civil rights strategists'.

Dr. King still contended, however, strength would come when the thrust for civil rights was allied with other groups, such as the white poor, Jews, Catholics, other ethnic groups, and friendly white liberals. After all, the pressure from many whites for justice was a major factor in civil rights legislation and changes. Blacks could not have done it alone. Therefore, black paths and white paths have intersected and need each other in reaching common goals of justice and freedom. (51). America belongs to Negroes as much as any ethnic group, and the ideal is to seek a "colorless power" of equality and justice for everyone (53).

In accomplishing civil rights goals of justice and freedom, nonviolence brought about more change with less loss of life than all the violent riots of 1963. Nonviolence had reconciliation and brotherhood as its goal. Violence breeds hate; and hate generates more violence—in a never-ending spiral. On the other hand, Black Power, with its leanings to change by any means necessary had the potential of duplicating the most inhumane behavior of white society. However, the future of the Negro was to be realized out of revolt that brought about a freedom that was interlaced with love and justice. Love is the only effective counter force to hate. That is why nonviolence has made such a positive impact. The world is in need of more of this new creation and power (64).

Dr. King adds, however, that the problem of race in America is a white dilemma that has impoverished the status of the Negro, and that this dilemma can be eliminated by whites desiring the same freedom for Negroes that they desire for themselves. Thus, justice and equality for Negroes must become a priority. But white backlash or the step back from this truth has, too often, continued to be the norm. For many Americans, racism, the myth of an inferior race, has become a way of life, thinking, and existence. Slavery was a result of this mentality, and it brought about white supremacy as a part of every fabric of living including the interpretation of the Holy Bible. The Negro had no rights that whites had to respect.

Slavery, therefore, was sanctioned by the church, learned scholars, government, higher education, the military, business leaders, and publishers. Even the founding fathers, from Washington to Lincoln, were ambivalent and vacillated morally on the slavery question (68).

On January 1, 1863, when the Emancipation Proclamation went into effect, four million Negroes were set free to survive as best they could. Thus, for the Negro, freedom was founded upon famine and severe hardship. There was no program to settle them into American society other than through continued subservience and inequality. Consequently, there was no true freedom but more despair and injustice (79). to stay alive, many Negroes returned to their former slave masters.

Parallel to the Negro dilemma was the destructive treatment of the Native American Indian. Dr. King gives his views on this issue:

The poisoning of the American mind was accomplished not only by acts of discrimination and exploitation, but also by exaltation of murder as an expression of courage and initiative of the pioneer. Just as Southern culture was made to appear noble by ignoring the cruelty of slavery, the conquest of the Indian was depicted as an example of bravery and progress… these concepts of racism, and this schizophrenic duality of conduct, remain deeply rooted in American thought today. This tendency of the nation to take one step forward on the question of justice and then to take a step backward is still the pattern (80).

Dr. King elaborates further on this point regarding persons of color in America:

Our nation was born in genocide when it embraced the doctrine that the original American, the Indian, was an inferior race. Even before there were large numbers of Negroes on our shores, the scar of racial hatred had already disfigured colonial society. From the sixteenth century forward, blood flowed in battles over racial supremacy. We are perhaps the only nation, which tried as a matter of national policy to wipe out its indigenous population… Indeed, even today we have not permitted ourselves to reject or feel remorse for this shameful episode. Our literatures, our films, our drama, our folklore all exalt it (120).

It is apparent that being a person of color in America has meant being scarred by a history of ethnic exclusion and debasement, slavery, inequality, and family disorganization. The Negro family was purposefully split-up and disorganized for over three hundred years. Therefore, the human suffering of the Negro has been great—and often fatal. Thousands of Negroes and Native American Indians died for no other reason than the color of their skin.

On the question of freedom and justice for Negroes, Dr. King declared that the institutional white church, with few exceptions, remained uninvolved. The church had a duty to take the lead in bringing about integration through what can be called the unenforceable–the obedience to the laws, positive attitudes, good will, morality, and fairness. These are issues of the heart. But these are areas that cannot be enforced by legal statutes. "They concern inner attitudes, expressions of compassion which law books cannot regulate and jails cannot rectify… The ultimate solution to the race problem lies in the willingness of men to obey the unenforceable" (100). It is these issues of the heart that will bring whites and Negroes together spiritually for societal reconciliation and transformation. When this happens, there will be a new freedom, which will neutralize old obstacles such as fear, prejudice, lies, pride, stereotyping, and irrationality (101).

Another view of the dilemma of Negroes as the saga of their Americanization continues to unfold was that, after almost three hundred and fifty years of racial injustice, they are still expected to be as responsible, informed, competitive, productive, faithful, dependable, resourceful, and loyal as those Americans who have been privileged and have never experienced one day of the oppression that was suffered by Negroes. Dr. King states that "he who starts behind in a race must forever remain behind or run faster than the man in front. What a dilemma! It is a call to do the impossible… And yet, there are times when life demands the perpetual doing of the impossible. The life of our slave forebears is eternal testimony to the ability of men to achieve the impossible… The performance of our lives must go on, without self-pity or surrender; we must go forward (120-121).

It seems that the going forward that Dr. King is referring to involves helping America to become a nation where a new humanity, civilization, freedom, and justice would prevail. Negroes must join hands with poor whites and other have-nots to form coalitions and thrusts to a higher livelihood. Nonviolent pressure on the government must continue, because the record has shown that political power yields little without the crisis of confrontation and the ballot. Programs that provide parity in the job market and economic arena must become a reality. In light of their large numbers in trade unions, Negroes must come together to position themselves for the kinds of power that place them in decision making roles as these relate to hiring, wages, promotions, and supervision. Negroes must become dignified and selective consumers by not doing business with establishments that do not employ Negroes (144). Negroes must use _the ballot and develop alliances with whites to heal the hateful politics that appeal to racism to win victory at the polls (152). Professional Negroes must pursue their careers, but they must also remain active in the political arena learning and passing on to the next generation the strategies of effective social and political action (155). Thus, the Negro revolt for freedom must be built on a foundation of solidarity, faith in each other, and trust. There is liberation and strength in unity.

Indeed, the world, itself, hungers for liberation and freedom from poverty, war, and pestilence. The advances of science and technology have brought the world into an interdependent neighborhood. In connection with this line of thought, Belinda Jack (1996) writing about worldwide Negro liberation in her book *Negritude and Literary Criticism* states that "because he has more than all others the sense of revolt and the love of liberty and because he is the most oppressed, it is the liberation of all that he necessarily pursues when he labors for his own deliverance" (75). One can conclude that Ms. Jack is suggesting that the civil rights struggle in America takes on a new dimension when it is seen in the context of world impact and need.

Addressing this issue of freedom in the world, Dr. King concludes that "one of the great problems of mankind is that we suffer from a poverty of the spirit which stands in glaring contrast to our scientific and technological abundance. The richer we have become materially, the poorer we have become morally and spiritually" (171). He goes on to state concerning the internal and external state of every human: "The internal is that realm of spiritual ends expressed in art, literature, morals and religion. The external is that complex of devices, techniques, mechanisms and instrumentalities by means of which we live. Our problem today is that we have allowed the internal to become lost in the external. We have allowed the means by which we live to outdistance the ends for which we live" (171). Dr. King is saying that these phenomena must be reversed so that the spiritual and moral takes precedence over the scientific. Otherwise, "we end up with guided missiles and misguided men." When this takes place, humans everywhere will find their freedom at risk as the result of abusing the creativity of their own intelligence (172).

War and its destruction are major examples of intellectual creativity being used to destroy and imprison human beings rather than lead them to freedom. Thus, the best minds are being used for the technology of warfare rather than finding solutions to war and the resulting poverty, oppression and suffering. The devastating destructive power of modem war machinery removes even the negative good that a war can accomplish. If the nations of the world would devote as much money, time, and effort to the pursuit of peace as is spent for war and defense, there would be an unequaled reign of reconciliation and harmony in our midst (183).

Dr. King suggests that: The philosophy and strategy of nonviolence become immediately a subject for study and for serious experimentation in every field of human conflict, by no means excluding the relations between nations... It is necessary to love peace and sacrifice for it (184-185). Dr. King took on a more pronounced worldwide view of protest for freedom and peace in his last book, *The Trumpet of Conscience*.

THE TRUMPET OF CONSCIENCE

The Trumpet of Conscience (1968) was the last book written by Dr. Martin Luther King, Jr. The book consists of five talks given by Dr. King during November and December 1967, over the Canadian Broadcasting Corporation radio network as part of the Vincent Massey Lecture series. These lectures were named in honor of the late Right Honorable Vincent Massey, former Governor General of Canada. As to the overall meaning of the lectures themselves, Dr. King draws a link between slavery and the Underground Railroad, which ran from the Southern United States to Canada, providing a road to freedom and hope for escaping slaves. He points out, consequently, that there has been a historical relationship between American Negroes and Canadians for many years. Negroes were fighting for freedom then, and they are still fighting for freedom now.

The book is written in the essay genre with the typical Kingian power in the use of vocabulary, metaphor, imagery, and tone. As to themes, he addresses some that have already presented such as militant nonviolent protest and civil disobedience; new themes include the Vietnam War, black and white youth, and peace. Speaking out in strident and unrelenting protest against the war in Vietnam, Dr. King informs us that:

> "A true revolution of values will lay hands on the world order and say of war: "This way of settling differences is not just." This business of burning human beings with napalm, of filling our nation's homes with orphans and widows, of injecting poisonous drugs of hate in the veins of peoples normally humane, of sending men home from dark and bloody battlefields physically handicapped and psychologically deranged, cannot be reconciled with wisdom, justice, and love. A nation that continues year after year to spend more money on military defense than on programs of social uplift is approaching spiritual doom (Washington 1986:640).

Thus, for King, war was obsolete in solving the long-term sufferings of human beings. Due to nuclear weapons, he thought that we have moved to the brink of mutual annihilation. Speaking out against the war in Vietnam, King concluded that blacks were fighting in disproportionate numbers in a war for freedoms and justice that they did not have at home. In the name of solidarity, survival, and mutual trust, "black boys and white boys fend for one another eight thousand miles from home in a way they would never live on the same block in Detroit... Southwest Georgia or East Harlem. I could not be silent in the face of such cruel manipulation of the poor" (21).

War, therefore, for King was another form of violence that ought not to be tolerated in the name of freedom and brotherhood. He felt strongly, thus: "I speak as a child of God and brother to the suffering poor of Vietnam… I speak for the poor of America who are paying the double price of smashed hopes at home and death and corruption in Vietnam. I speak as a citizen of the world, for the world as it stands aghast at the path we have taken. I speak as an American to the leaders of my own nation. The great initiative in this war is ours. The initiative to stop must be ours" (31).

Dr. King's focus by this moment of his civil rights journey has taken on worldwide dimensions. By this time, his speaking out against the war in Vietnam has gained him many critics and cost him many friends (Washington 1986). But he continued to stand alone pursuing what he believed to be right–even at the cost of being vilified by high ranking and influential business and governmental allies, including the President.

The question Dr. King raised at the time of the writing of the book was not whether Negroes would be free but by what means. The phases of the 1950's civil rights battles as well as that of the 1955-1965 era had been fought. Revolt and rage was shown on the part of many Negroes, while the hidden bigotry on the part of many whites came to light. "It is not the white race per se that we fight but policies and ideology that leaders of that race have formulated to perpetuate oppression" (8). Negroes had been called on to be lawful while numerous white bigots continued to practice lawlessness with impunity.

Returning to the Negro revolt and riots of 1963, Dr. King identifies five elements that contributed to them and caused the impasse in race relations: "(1) *the white backlash*; (2) *pervasive discriminatory practices*; (3) *unemployment*; (4) *war in Vietnam*; (5) *urban problems and extensive migration.*" If used efficiently, the wealth, knowledge, and resources of the United States are more than adequate to eliminate the conditions that caused these problems (9).

In order to get the attention of the powers that be, Dr. King is recommending at this time that mass civil disobedience be used as a weapon. "Mass civil disobedience as a new stage of struggle can transmute the deep rage of the ghetto into a constructive and creative force. To dislocate the functioning of a city without destroying it can be longer lasting, costly to the larger society but not wantonly destructive. Finally, it is a device of social action that is more difficult for the government to quell by superior force" (15). The purpose of this broader tactic would be to compel reluctant authorities to bend as a result of the tension caused when confronted with petitions for justice.

The slogan of the Southern Christian Leadership Conference (SCLC), "To save the soul of America," and even the world, is fitting here as King states that "these are revolutionary times all over the globe and men are revolting against systems of exploitation." And if we do not act in the name of true freedom "we shall surely be dragged down the long, dark corridors of time reserved for those who possess power without compassion, might without morality and strength without sight" (33-34).

A characteristic spiritual emptiness impacted significantly the young generation of the 1960s. Unfortunately, this "spiritual emptiness" had manifested itself by being transformed into "spiritual evil." The war in Vietnam was a devastating example of the evil of the times. American lives were sacrificed for a democracy which was non-existent, and, which the American black soldier had never known in his own homeland (37).

The consciences of the young who were reared during the 60s and who saw four wars: World War II, the "cold war," the Korean war, and Vietnam realized that there was no hope for humankind using the violence of war. The nuclear bomb made them realize that world annihilation could be an instant reality. They were troubled, critical of the status quo, and revolted at the conditions in which they and people of the world had to live (38).

According to King, these young persons divided into three groups: The first group was those who attempted to adapt to the then current societal dogma–socially, economically, and politically. But they were looking for something better. The second group, the so-called radicals, was bent on changing the system from top to bottom. Their revolt was to change society by whatever means possible–from its state of current evil. They were willing to shed blood–their own, and that of their opposition. Their goal was transformation through whatever means necessary. The third group was the "hippies." These young people withdrew from society as a statement that they rejected what they saw and experienced… The hippies were complex and often times contradictory. According to King, inwardly, they sought isolation, peace, and security in non-conformism and drugs. Outwardly, their aim was peace and love, which can only be found in a community of solidarity with others. It appears that their movement was one of revolt to nihilism and escape from reality. Yet, it is clear that their dream was the dream of mankind: "Social justice and human value" (39-44).

However, there was a fourth group of young people who stirred resistance and revolt for freedom more than any of the other groups mentioned. That group was young Negroes. They used the tactics of nonviolent resistance through "sit-ins, freedom rides, kneel-ins, wade-ins and pray-ins" to prick the conscience of a nation towards transformation and in the process transformed themselves. Young Negroes stopped being imitators of white middle class values and began forging a new ethic of revolt that led whites to learn from them. Therefore, young Negroes were in the forefront of the 1960s peace movement. Their aim was the establishment of "responsible rebellion" that took on national as well as international significance. Their major focus was on the idea that injustice anywhere is a threat to freedom everywhere (45–47). Concerning the latter idea, Dr. King also felt strongly that our struggles and loyalties must reach beyond our local and national interests, because we live in an interdependent world where the loss of the contributions of one person diminishes the freedom of every other person. Consequently, he urged that "we must work urgently with all peoples to shape a New World" (50).

The principal means that Dr. King saw of accomplishing peaceful revolt in search of freedom on a world scale was nonviolent civil disobedience. The use of nonviolent civil disobedience had made impressive inroads against entrenched racial segregation in the Southern United States. The goal of protracted civil disobedience is to create tension and disruption to normal municipal order; this disruption can only be tolerated for a short period without relief. The strategy forces demands to be negotiated. Birmingham (1963) and Selma (1965), Alabama were two notable examples where the strategy literally brought these two cities to a standstill and resulted in changes in the name of justice and freedom at both the local and national levels. (54).

At the time of the writing of this book, Dr. King's vision of America had taken on revolutionary tones. He believed beyond a doubt that the civil rights revolution must continue to mount momentum against the oppression created by institutions, because ultimately it was institutions, not individuals that controlled jobs, wealth and equal opportunity. As an example, the Jim Crow laws segregating Negroes were put into effect by institutions and existed for some two hundred and fifty years, and the residual effects of those laws, on many fronts, still drive the momentum of America today. Thus, it was the institutional injustice and racial oppression from many different fronts that gave cause to and energized the Negro revolt of the 50s and 60s. Included in this view of necessary targets were the institutions of congress and government themselves. At the time of the writing of this book, plans had been set in motion to orchestrate a massive civil disobedience campaign in the name of the Poor People's March on Washington, DC. This was to have taken place in the summer of 1968 (60-61).

This initiative which was to follow the strategy of the Birmingham campaign of 1963, using non-violent direct action, had as its goal to place pressure on the federal government to withdraw from the war in Vietnam and to redirect these billions of dollars to the War on Poverty and other much needed programs of liberation for the American poor.

Dr. King advised that the study of peace and the implications of using nonviolence in all areas of human conflict be given serious consideration on an international scale. The philosophy and strategies of nonviolence should be studied as diligently as the strategies of modern warfare (68). The state of worldwide poverty in India, Africa, Asia, Latin America, and certainly here in America, provided overwhelming evidence that the priority of the civilized world should be on the elimination of poverty and its oppressive consequences more than anything else. Peace on earth demanded that we see every human being as a neighbor: "No individual can live alone; no nation can live alone, and as long as we try, the more we are going to have war in this world" (68).

Peace will come when means and ends are just. Just means will result in just ends. "This is saying that, in the final analysis, means and ends must cohere because the end is pre-existent in the means, and ultimately destructive means cannot bring about constructive ends" (71).

In the pursuit of peace, the power and need for the love ethic must be fully understood. Dr. King explains three kinds of love: *"Eros"* is aesthetic, romantic love. The yearning of the soul for the realm of the divine. An expression of romance. Then there is *"philos"* or the love between personal friends. The kind of love you have for those whom you get along well **with.** The third type of love is *"agape."* This is a love that is more than just romance or friendship. It is understanding, creative, redemptive goodwill toward all men that seeks nothing in return. "Theologians would say that it is the love of God operating in the human heart. Its ultimate expression is that you love all people, including your enemies, because God loves and created them. It is the kind of love that causes you to "love your enemies and pray for those who despitefully use you and persecute you" (Matthew 5:44), (72-73).

Dr. King felt that the privilege to love was a freedom that must not be lost no matter how bitter the burdens. It is an *"agape"* love born and refined by revolt that will endure. Thus, he writes, "We will wear you down by our capacity to suffer and one day we will win our freedom for ourselves. We will so appeal to your heart and conscience that we will win you in the process, and our victory will be a double victory" because our love will have transformed you, the oppressor, and liberated us, the oppressed (75). It appears that Dr. King is saying that peace thrives, lives, and maintains on love—and love alone.

Peace will come when hate gives way to loving every neighbor and understanding that all human life is sacred and that we are chosen by the God of creation to bring a halt to oppressing and killing one another (74).

Finally, peace on earth will come when we accept the ultimate morality of the universe and the facts that we have cosmic help as we search for freedom. In spite of civil rights betrayals and disappointments, the dream must be kept alive. Hope must be continually reborn so that brotherhood and freedom in a worldwide **beloved community** will come about and that we will not study, nor prepare for war anymore. And when that time comes, "it will be a glorious day; the morning stars will sing together, and the sons of God will shout for joy" (78).

SUMMARY AND INTERPRETATION

Martin Luther King Jr. learned the importance of social activism and protest for civil rights and justice from two of his early mentors. His father was King's "in-house" mentor. Then, When King went off to college, there was Dr. Benjamin Mays, the President of Morehouse College. These two men had an enduring influence on the life of young King. They figure prominently in his writings and speeches on the issues of revolt and freedom. The five books written by King and used in this research were all written using an essay type presentation. The text in two of the books, *Strength to Love* and *The Trumpet of Conscience* is presented in a sermonic and oratory format. The overall essay style allowed King to go directly to the reader or listener with his ideas, views, and interpretations as well as suggestions and recommendations for change. As to audience, it seems to me that King was writing and speaking to the people of America–to Afro-Americans, Jews, Gentiles, Hispanics, Asians, institutions, people in authority, and especially the government of the United States. But at the same time, recognizing his global views on oppression, justice, and freedom, he was writing and speaking to the world.

King's writings took place over a period of thirteen years. According to Harlan (1990), writing in Albert and Hoffman, eds., this situation in time should be divided into two periods: first there is the period from 1955-1965. This period is identified with the pursuit of traditional civil rights goals, such as school desegregation, voting rights, public access. Then, secondly, there is the period from 1965-1968 in which he attempted to form "a new coalition to fight the twin scourges of war and poverty"

(64). In carefully examining King's writings, one can see this development of new focus as identified here. By 1968, according to his writings and speeches, King was advocating a redefinition of American government that would seriously address the issues of race, the arms race, and poverty.

King's first book, *Stride Toward Freedom* (1958), is a personal, detailed, first-person documentary. The book is written in essay prose using a tone that is direct and descriptive; it is structured around eleven chapters that carry the story from the beginning of the Montgomery boycott to its conclusion three hundred eighty-two (382) days later. One can see in the unfolding of the book not only the evolution and confrontational struggles of the boycott but also the developing mindset and growth of Dr. King's personal journey towards revolt and fight for freedom and justice on behalf of all Americans. But beyond Montgomery and America, Dr. King's vision and struggle were for a universal human inclusiveness of all classes, races, religions, the haves, and the have-nots, where the secular and the spiritual would come together in the name of international brotherhood. In order to accomplish this, his strategy of choice was militant nonviolence based on love.

Strength to Love (1963), is a book of fifteen selected sermons of Dr. King, which contain his penetrating and theologically inspired beliefs concerning justice, goodness, human equality and the elimination of social evils. Further, the book of sermons contain the basic tenets of his thoughts on revolt, nonviolence and freedom. It is also evident that Dr. King is evaluating his civil rights leadership in terms of its theological definitions. Dr. King uses the essay, throughout, to boldly express his ideas and interpretations. His developing beliefs, it appears, was that theology must walk step by step with social change. Further, he began to develop a critical point of view and raise questions as to what the role of the church should be vis-a-vis the ongoing struggle for human rights in America. King strongly condemned the white church for its silence and abandonment of its roles of speaking out against injustice and oppression. Regarding this point, silence was seen as consent and approval. For King, it appears that the ultimate goal of both theology and the church was the redemption and reconciliation of all human beings into what he envisioned as the **"Beloved Community"**, or a transformed society where harmony, trust, peace, justice, and good will prevailed.

The purpose of *Why We Can't Wait* (1964), was to explain why waiting and patience had run out as black Americans had already waited for over two hundred and fifty years for justice and freedom. The background of the book is the true historical events that took place in Birmingham, Alabama and nearly one thousand other cities during the summer of 1963–events that caused a black revolt. Dr. King wanted to identify, explore, address and explain what happened during that "special summer" of the civil rights struggle. Again, his choice of literary genres for writing was the essay. The structure of the book is built around the eight chapters that includes one chapter looking beyond Birmingham to the future. The tone of the book paints a brilliant and factual picture of the social, political, economical, racial and religious postures of 1963 Birmingham. While incarcerated, Dr. King wrote his famous *Letter From Birmingham Jail* in which he responded to the criticism of fellow white clergy, and to the world, by explaining the meaning of Birmingham and the total civil rights protest. 1963 was eight years after King had begun his crusade of civil rights leadership. Again, based on the tone of this book, it is evident that his courage and spiritual boldness had taken on new dimensions of growth and willingness to challenge the power structure. To mount a charge against Birmingham was tantamount to the biblical story of the youthful David volunteering to fight the nine foot giant Goliath. Civil rights scholars have said that Birmingham was the most racist and segregated city in America (Bennett 1968; Branch 1988; Garrow 1986, 1989; Harding 1996, et al). Everything was segregated and no mingling of the races was allowed. Negroes were seen as persons of no value and they were abused and killed with impunity. However, King felt that if Birmingham could be defeated, the civil rights campaigns would win a major battle against racism and oppression. Thus, he and his staff implemented a master plan of civil disobedience. The Battle of Birmingham was brutal and deadly, but King's forces were victorious. The vile ugliness and brutality of Birmingham were shown to the world via television. The national government in Washington made changes, and Birmingham took a turn for the better in race relations that continue to this day. In retrospect, the 1963 civil rights victory in Birmingham was healing for the nation and brought with it a new degree of freedom for all Americans.

Where Do We Go From Here: Chaos or Community? (1967), is a review as well as an analysis of the civil rights struggle from the mid-fifties through 1968. This 1968 Kingian perspective included the Montgomery boycott, the Albany, Georgia campaign, the Selma, Alabama struggle, the Birmingham, Alabama crisis, and the Chicago, Illinois campaign. In addition, three major pieces of federal legislation are placed into perspective. These were: the 1954 Supreme Court ruling on the desegregation of public schools, the 1963 Civil Rights Bill, and the 1965 Voting rights Act. As with Dr. King's previous books, this one was also written in the style of a detailed, historical essay, from a first person perspective. There are six chapters that provide the structure for content in which he addresses the national, the global, and future imperatives regarding reconciliation. The relevant question and purpose of the book is presented in the title. King had been on the battlefield and in the trenches of the civil rights struggle now for some thirteen years. He had seen victories; he had seen defeats. There was still a bitter and vast racial divide in America between blacks and whites. The pros and cons of Black Power strategies for revolt and freedom versus nonviolence strategies were closely examined. Further, the problem of racial oppression and exploitation of blacks by whites throughout the world is brought into sharp focus. In 1968, which was near the end of his earthly life, he felt that America had reached a defining moment and the time to make a choice: "Was there going to be 'liberty and justice for all' American citizens or was there going to be ongoing civil rights confrontations?" "Was there going to be more abandoned promises, poor enforcement of laws and white backlash or faithful pursuit of equality and justice for all Americans?" He felt that the time for a definitive choice of direction had come. Concerning this choice of direction, King elaborated on four key areas of racial inequality that needed immediate correction: Education, Employment, Civil Rights, and Housing. In the final analysis, would it be "Chaos or Community?" King's hope continued in quest of the **beloved community,** which, as he saw it, could best be realized through nonviolence and reconciliation.

The Trumpet of Conscience (1968), was the last book written by Dr. Martin Luther King, Jr. The book consists of five talks given by Dr. King during November and December 1967, over the Canadian Broadcasting Corporation radio network as part of the Vincent Massey Lecture series. The book is written in essay with a clear, powerful, and intellectual rhetoric that has been typical of the writing style used by King. This writing style uses a vocabulary that is rich in detail, metaphor, and the choice of the right word and example. The book addresses in ever expanding terms such themes as nonviolent protest, civil disobedience, the Vietnam War, wealth and poverty, black and white youth, and peace. Dr. King's focus by this moment of his civil rights journey has taken on worldwide dimensions, theologically, socially, and politically. The book is a bold and fearless emptying of Dr. King 's own conscience regarding key issues (listed above) that have been foundational to the civil rights struggle as well as exposition into new territory such as the meaning of the youth movement, wealth and poverty, and the Vietnam War. These last two issues, wealth and poverty and the Vietnam war weighed especially heavy on his conscience, and he spoke out boldly in order to give them interpretation, even at the risk of losing former influential allies. Certainly, Dr. King knew that there was sufficient wealth in America to eliminate both urban and rural poverty. But the war in Vietnam had caused a redirection of the War on Poverty funds away from programs to help the poor. Vincent Harding informs us in Albert and Hoffman eds., that the war was diverting some thirty billion dollars per year (161). Looking back after more than thirty years, *The Trumpet of Conscience* has been a prophetic book whose themes of nonviolent protest, revolutionary civil disobedience, the pursuit of world peace, the obsolescence of war, and the elimination of world poverty have become much sought after realities during our lifetimes.

In conclusion, Dr. Martin Luther King Jr. was called upon by the forces of destiny to be the spokesperson and provide leadership in the struggle for justice and freedom for Negro Americans. King did not turn away from this difficult calling but embraced it as his mission and opportunity to make a difference for America and for the world. Long-standing historical discrimination and segregation against Negroes were the catalyst springboards that energized his reasons and purposes in the struggle for justice and freedom. The evolution of his leadership saw a continual growth of wisdom, boldness, and courage. Certainly, he had enemies and opposition, but he believed in the truth of his cause and refused being deterred. His writings are testimony of his evolution as he proceeds from recording the Montgomery bus boycott to the revolutionary civil disobedience and the transformation of the American government that he was advocating in 1968, the last year of his life. He was a person uniquely prepared for the role that he was called to fulfill. Because of him, America and the world have seen an example of love for freedom and brotherhood that calls us all to do likewise. His life and legacy represent the best in our human search for survival and truth. For these reasons, Americans and people of the world, of all persuasions and backgrounds, honor his memory.

A COMPARATIVE CRITIQUE OF NOBEL PRIZE ACCEPTANCE SPEECHES ALBERT CAMUS AND DR. MARTIN LUTHER KING JR.

Acceptance speeches by Nobel laureates are times to give thanks and appreciation for having been chosen for this distinguished honor from among the very best in a vocational field and calling. The experience must be humbling. However, it is also a time for the laureates to give a personal testimony before the world, concerning their values, reasons for actions, intellectual influences, likes and dislikes, burning passions, hopes, dreams, and visions for the future. To go a step farther, the speech is an opportunity for them to define the meaning of their ambitions and life work.

The thoughts of Camus and King were similar as they addressed numerous social and political issues such as: brotherhood, optimism, nihilism, the meaning of civilization, faith in human kind, and thanks to others. Following is a comparative analysis of what they had to say regarding the key words and themes noted above:

Brotherhood–Camus speaks of his art in his speech, "To me art is not a solitary delight. It is a means of stirring the greatest number of men by providing them with a privileged image of our common joys and woes. Hence, it forces the artist not to isolate himself; it subjects him to the humblest and most universal truth." This "universal truth" according to Camus, establishes him as no more than others, a servant to all others and living in community with all others. Likewise, Dr. King expresses the same feeling in saying that, "all the people of the world will have to discover a way to live together in peace, and thereby transform this pending cosmic elegy into a creative psalm of brotherhood... The foundation of such a method is love." For Camus brotherhood is using your talents to serve others. For King, it is the love ethic that will bring humans together in brotherhood.

Human Rights–Dr. King accepted the Nobel Prize in the name of human rights: "I accept the Nobel Prize for Peace at a moment when twenty-two million Negroes in the United States of America are engaged in a creative battle to end the long night of racial injustice." This injustice made Dr. King a martyr. Camus' point of view stated that "All the armies of tyranny and their millions of men cannot people his (the artist's) solitude... But the silence of an unknown prisoner subjected to humiliations at the other end of the world is enough to tear the writer from exile." It seems that both men shared a similar viewpoint regarding human rights, which is that when there is one person in chains in the world, we are all in chains. Further, they appear to be saying that it is a betrayal against humanity to remain silent when freedom is denied.

Optimism and Nihilism–Even though faced with a world that inflicted tyranny and oppression, often with impunity, Camus and King had great faith and hope that people could make the world better. Camus states strongly that to exist in a nihilistic state of rejection and despair offered no solution to the trials, tribulations and atrocities of the Second World War, but that Europeans "strove to find some form of legitimacy. We had to fashion for ourselves an art of living in times of catastrophe in order to be reborn before fighting openly against the death instinct at work in our history." While trying to establish hope amidst despair, Dr. King issued a similar challenge: "I accept this award today with an abiding faith in America and an audacious faith in the future of mankind." Both men knew that human beings played a significant role in mustering the moral courage to create the alliances of solidarity that would bring about optimism, hope, and peace to a world yet to come.

The Meaning of Civilization–Albert Camus and Dr. King, due to university training, were both excellent students of philosophy, the humanities, and social ethics. They had thought deeply on the meaning of civilization. According to the World Book Dictionary, (1978), civilization means: to change from being savage and ignorant to having good laws and customs. It means an advanced stage in social development. It means freedom from barbarity and atrocity. It reflects polite behavior, courtesy and consideration, good breeding, civility, refinement, enlightenment and justice. It holds up the sacredness of human life (377). The composite writings of Camus and Dr. King reflect that too many human beings (not all) demonstrate a severe lack of these civilizing attributes that is the reason there is racism, wars, torture, legalized murder, ethnic cleansing and persecution. This is what King was talking about when he states, "I refuse to accept the idea that the 'isness' of man's present nature makes him morally incapable of reaching up for the eternal 'oughtness' that forever confronts him." This idea of a more civilized world was likewise, a dream of Albert Camus. He was concerned that some had turned the beauty of human intelligence into an agent of hatred and oppression.

Significant Others–Albert Camus and Dr. King were both humble men with a mission, using their gifts and talents, to make the world a better place to live. However, neither took credit for change, but on the contrary, held up the countless thousands without whom their work would have been impossible. In Camus' Nobel speech, he concludes with: "I should like to receive it as a tribute paid to all those who, sharing the same fight, have received no reward, but on the contrary have known only woe and persecution." Dr. King adds to this by acknowledging: "I accept this prize on behalf of all men who love peace and brotherhood. I say, I come, as a trustee… You honor the ground crew without whose labor and sacrifice the jet flight to freedom could never have left the earth. Most of these people will never make the headlines and their names will not appear in *Who's Who*."

SUMMARY

This chapter was divided into three sections. In the first section, I examined the major works of Camus, both fictional and expository, as well as the relevant scholarly discussions of his life and work. In the second section, I considered the key works written by King, his career, and the scholarly treatment that these have received. Finally, I focused on the two authors' Nobel speeches as uniquely self-conscious expressions of their points of view on themes and issues that find common ground in their writings. Throughout my analysis I have concentrated primarily on the themes of revolt and freedom in their works while attempting to respect the ways in which their very different relations to literature affected the presentation of these themes.

The writings of Camus reflect the serious problems of the human condition during his times. Camus presented these problems to the reader in a variety of literary forms which included: the novel, short story, essay, philosophical essay, and the play. I have pointed out previously in this research that Camus was skillful in choosing the particular literary form for his thoughts based on the particular content and the response that he desired from the reader. The problems that he was most concerned with in his writings were those of the human condition as these reflected the value of life and happiness. In his writings, the solutions that he gave to problems of oppression were the solidarity of revolt and a moral humanism that had peace and freedom as their goals. Similarly, the revolt for freedom on the part of Dr. Martin Luther King Jr., was also done in the name of justice, equality, human dignity, and solidarity. His books were presented to the reader using the literary form of the essay. The content of King's writings focused on the civil and human rights of Americans, especially Afro-Americans, as well as the people of the world. Both men were in accord that neither nihilism nor violence would bring long range solutions to the social, economic, and political problems of the world, now or in the future. However, it appears that they were suggesting that healing and peace for future generations would come about as a result of solidarity, human reconciliation, equality, justice, and caring—one person for the other. They thought, further, that peace would be difficult to achieve until these concepts and ideas became the main agenda of the nations of the world.

The words of Robert Sutton in his book *Human Existence and Theodicy: A Comparison of Jesus and Albert Camus* (1992), seem to capture the thinking of both Camus and King as we have examined them comparatively: "The battle of the kingdom takes place daily. Jesus and Camus exhort us to respond to the challenges of finite existence, not as "men of violence," but as humane advocates of human happiness and liberty, armed with the virtues of intelligence, courage, compassion, dialogue, generosity and the resolute will to deny nothing" (169).

Let us take a closer look at the literary forms that were used by Camus to present his writings and thoughts to the reading public. These included the novel, the short story, plays, and essays. Camus' early schooling and university education was in the French tradition of humanities and philosophy, where students who succeed have been exposed to a rigorous curriculum involving the French literary masters and European philosophers. He used the influence of this rich background to carve a niche for himself in journalism. From his journalistic exposure, he stepped out into the deeper waters of short stories and essays. Thi::. lead to *The Stranger*, which has become an all time classic novel. From there, his professional career as a writer began. Camus is recognized as a classical stylist whose mastery and use of the French language are unsurpassed. He used this power of language style and its nuances to write successfully in several different literary genres. It is evident that he planned each one of his works with the fore thought and care of an accomplished architect. His mission as a writer was to continually "engage" the reader, confront the reader's sensibilities, and move the reader to action in the name of what is good, right, and just. Based on the wide appeal of his writings as well as Nobel Prize recognition, he accomplished this mission in a superb manner.

The essay was one of Camus' literary genres of choice. *The Myth of Sisyphus* and *The Rebel* (already discussed in this study), according to Ellison (1990), "are crucial to an understanding of Camus' thought and both are important in the evolution of the history of ideas in our century." Camus used Sisyphus as a symbolic answer to the nihilism, despair, hopelessness, and death of the forties—the war years. Sisyphus offered to a suffering people an image of hope and stubborn survival against seemingly insurmountable circumstances. Sisyphus embodied a role model and image that were desperately needed at the time and represented a positive attitude towards life when one is faced with the dilemma of life's most extreme absurdities. It was this positive attitude and scorn towards the hardships and vicissitudes of life that pushed Sisyphus into the winner's circle rather than that of a loser.

The Rebel was Camus' philosophical and penetrating treatise on the meaning of human rebellion and freedom. It gave the parameters around which civilized human beings were to live and find their co-existence in the name of what is civil and tolerable versus what is uncivil and intolerable. With the atrocities of World War II still fresh in his mind, Camus embarked upon a stinging denunciation of the ideological barbarity committed by some Marxist and totalitarian nations during the war in the name of social, economical, and political progress. He concludes that there are certain human values that are inviolate and demand respect by everybody. And when tyranny violates these values, the course of protest is collective revolt for freedom.

While King was not categorized as a professional writer, and while he wrote only in the essay genre, his books, articles, speeches, papers, and sermons have captured, clarified and presented the human condition of Afro-Americans with a poignancy and accuracy that have not been witnessed since W.E.B. Du Bois wrote *The Souls of Black Folk* in 1903. In fact, King was still addressing the same issues of injustice and inequality that Du Bois challenged in his book. The composite of King's writing output, while confined to civil rights and humanitarian issues, are no less vital to American literature and the meaning of America than the works of any mainline author. It seems fair to say that it was both Dr. King's leadership in the American civil rights struggle as well as his writings that caused him to be chosen for Nobel Prize for peace in 1965, at the age of 36—a very young laureate.

The five books written by King, which have been presented in this research, are a testimony that capture the pathos, past, present, and future, of what it means to be a black human being in America, and indeed, what it means to be a black human being in the world. His concern for justice and equality went beyond the shores of America. But in addition to documenting and elucidating the problems caused by skin color, he also offered what appear to be researched, thought through, and reasonable solutions. And King was nobody's consensus advocate when it came to tough decisions. Rather, he was a person who had the courage to stand for the truths that he believed in—even when he had to stand alone. This was evident in his disputation of the "Black Power" slogan, the very unpopular position that he took on Vietnam, and his unrelenting advocacy of militant nonviolent direct action as the most effective means of overcoming the oppression of systemic racism.

In concluding this chapter, I wish to present several issues comparing the two men in the area of influences that affected their literary output. In the first place, their upbringing and life experiences prominently influenced their writings. Camus was reared in poverty with one parent. His meager existence lasted through his teenage years. He also knew the poverty of serious illness when he contacted tuberculosis at seventeen. At the time of this disease, in the thirties, tuberculosis was often fatal. In addition to his own and his family's miserable plight, Camus also witnessed, in Algeria, bigotry, injustice and oppression practiced by the French colonialists against the native Arabs. As has been previously reported, these early influences had a life long impact on his writings and his search for justice and freedom. As a journalist, novelist, playwright and essayist, Camus employed his writer versatility, using various literary forms, to bring to the attention of the world the call for a humanism involving justice and freedom. His writings and his art were his major means of activism and protest.

Martin Luther King Jr., while raised in a protective middle class Negro family with both parents, grew up in the world of Southern racial discrimination, injustice, and oppression against black people. King knew that there was no protection against American racism if you were black. The color of your skin set you apart and destined you for inequality. King had been a victim and had witnessed the oppression of black people as an everyday occurrence. When the time came, he marched with his feet and his pen to struggle against the evils of second class citizenship. In fact, both he and Camus experienced and knew the meaning of bigotry and discrimination–Camus as the result of being born in a colonial territory, Algeria, and King as the result of being born black in America. Just as Camus, King was a masterful essayist and this was the genre that he used for his writings. Just as Camus, his call to the people of the world was for nonviolence, justice, and freedom for all human beings.

Interestingly, Camus and King had similar educational background influences. They were both superior scholars who had been mentored in their formative years by key educational personnel–Camus by Louis Germain and Jean Grenier and King by Benjamin Mays and Modecai Johnson. In addition, both men had similar educational preparation in the humanities, ethics, and philosophy. This background comes through in the writings and thought of both men and has been presented in this research. Their style of writing, use of language, ideas, examples, and illustrations attest to the intellectual level from which they approached their writing tasks.

CHAPTER THREE

METHODOLOGY

Restatement of the Problem

1. A Comparison of the Concepts of Revolt and Freedom in the Thinking of Albert Camus and Dr. Martin Luther King, Jr.

2. Explanation of Methodology and why Chosen.

METHODOLOGY IS THE PARTICULAR FRAMEWORK SELECTED IN WHICH to place data so that it can be interpreted and analyzed more clearly (Leedy 1997). The Methodology that will be used in this study will be a comparative analysis of areas of common grounds between two writers. The focus on common ground will be from two perspectives: first of all the common ground that identify parallel or similar social, historical, professional, and political experiences in the lives of these men will be discussed. Secondly, a comparative literary analysis will be made comparing their concepts of freedom and revolt. This second common ground perspective has already been presented in Chapter Two. However, additional analysis will be included in this chapter. A third area of common ground in the literary domain was the comparison of how the two men used the essay genre to present ideas and concepts.

Concerning social and historical experiences, ten areas of common grounds have been identified. Two significant areas of contrast have also been identified. The review of literature has not shown any comparative study made between Camus and Dr. King. Therefore, this study will be exploring, analyzing, and developing new information to fill the gap in the field of comparative literature. Hopefully, it will lay the foundation for further research in the field.

A comparative analysis of Camus and Dr. King will be made in light of specific common grounds dealing with social, professional, political and historical issues. The following have been identified:

COMMON GROUNDS

1. The writing of both men strongly addressed the problem of historical and current injustice in the world and the need to put an end to it.

   - Camus: Colonialism, German Occupation in France and Africa, Communist oppression, the death penalty, and racism.

   - King: Racism, segregation, the Ku Klux Klan, The White Citizen's Council, the oppression of racial discrimination (Negroes and Native Americans), poverty.

2. The writings of both men use revolt and freedom as catalysts for their writings and thought. Their vision is a just and humane society where people can be reconciled.

3. Both men are Nobel Laureates chosen for the composite impact of their work.
   - Camus 1957, for literature.
   - King, 1964, for peace.

4. Both men were the best in their Nobel category and professions at the time of their selections.

5. Both men lived during similar historical moments and world problems.
   - Camus: 1913-1960 World War II, The Korean War, the War for Independence in Algeria, racism in Algeria, Francisco Franco oppression in Spain, Stalinist oppression in Europe.

- King: World War II, the Korean War, the Vietnamese War, racism in the USA.

6. Both men were members of organizations that were founded for purposes of combating and eliminating oppression, injustice and exploitation.
    - Camus: The French Resistance, editor of the underground newspaper *The Combat* (anti-war, anti-German) during War II.
    - King: The Montgomery Improvement Association and The Southern Christian Leadership Conference.

7. Both men suffered unexpected death at an early age while at the height of their careers and while still in the process of working for justice, freedom and peace.
    - Camus, January 4, 1960 at age 46 in an automobile accident.
    - King, April 4, 1968 at age 39 by assassination.

8. Both men blacklisted for their social and political activism.
    - Camus for his militant journalism, criticism, and editorial activism (both in Algeria and France).
    - King for leading boycotts, marches, political activism and speeches.

9. Both men transcended bitterness and the use of violence as a means of correcting social, political, and economic evils.

10. Both men were from countries where ethnic groups had been exploited and oppressed.
    - Camus: Algerian-French.
    - King: African-American.

MAJOR CONTRASTS

1. The domain of religion:
    - Camus has been labeled as both an atheistic and agnostic moralist.
    - King is identified as a Christian and theologian of the first order.

2. The problem of pain and suffering:
    - Camus believed that God does not help or alleviate our pain and suffering even when the result of a good cause.

    - King believed that pain and suffering for righteousness and innocence are redemptive and perfecting.

The purpose of the comparison and contrast methodology is to give a very close and analytical examination of Camus and Dr. King using the areas that have been identified. What commonalties are evident in their works, lives and thinking? What is the message that they have left for these times and future generations concerning the truth, justice, and the human reconciliation that are so desperately needed by the people of the world today?

Historically, comparative literature, due to its large nature and content, has been accommodating to different methodologies as long as the writer has shown it to be appropriate for a particular project. The methodology is inherent in the name "Comparative." The idea of comparing writings dates to ancient times of the Old and New Testament (Prawer 1973). According to Bassnett (1993), comparative literature acquired its name as early 1816 as a result of a series of French anthologies used in teaching literature. The German version of the term appeared in 1854 and the earliest English usage appeared in 1848.

This methodology is popular not only in literature but is a very common approach used in other studies, such as: history, law, medicine, politics, education, business, economics, etc. (Remak, 1978). Comparison and contrast enables the researcher to determine what something is and what something is not. An accepted point of view among writing critics is that the true essence of a work is brought out when it is compared with a similar work or contrasted with some other work (Prawer, 1973).

Another interpretation of comparative literature is given by Remak (1971) when he states that a comparative literature study does not have to be comparative on every page nor even in every chapter, but the overall intent, emphasis, and execution must be comparative. The assaying of intent, emphasis, and execution requires both objective and subjective judgment. No rigid rules should be set down beyond these criteria (13).

According to Remak in Stallknecht and Frenz, eds., (1971), there is no methodology used in comparative literature study that is a priority, necessary or peculiar to the field. The same basic guidelines apply throughout—finding information, choosing from sources, and making an interpretation of what is there. However, translation studies do require an expertise that will enable the researcher to interpret accurately different cultures, histories and traditions along with source text translation. Also, knowledge of translation theory is required, since no two cultures are the same. While this study is not in the domain of translation studies, there is the need for the researcher to interpret accurately cultures, histories and traditions.

From a more global perspective, Bassnett (1993) continues that: "Implicit to comparative literature outside of Europe and the United States is the need to start with the home culture and to look outwards, rather than to start with the European model of literary excellence and to look inwards" (38). It seems that the key point here is that Western models do not fit nor complement Third World models during the current post-colonialism era and that an awareness of literature and traditions other than one's own adds to and enriches the background from which comparisons can be made and the truths and follies of the human condition analyzed.

NOTE: Please see the expanded information on comparative literature found in the Program Summary.

The Theoretical Context of the discipline of comparative studies in literature is to compare and contrast two or more authors relative to their background and influences, their ideas, point of view, imagery, detail, tone, writing style, genre, use of language, themes, treatment of character or approaches to solutions of problems, needs, concerns of the human condition, or other phenomena (Roberts 1978). The two writers being compared in this research are Albert Camus and Martin Luther King, Jr. The major themes that were investigated in this research were freedom and revolt. In considering his composite writings, Camus has presented these themes through short stories, novels, plays, and essays. In utilizing these genre he reflects his humanistic views of compassion, justice, and freedom. Dr. King, on the other hand has presented his writings, ideas, and interpretations using the essay genre. Camus was an accomplished professional writer while Dr. King was a seminary trained Baptist preacher who was writing so that the world could be informed and understand the American civil rights struggle for freedom.

Methodology Limitations involved the choosing of two authors for comparison rather than using the common grounds to examine the views and thinking of other authors whose writings reflected similar issues. Much has been written about these two men and closure for this particular report had to be established at some point. However, there will be opportunity to continue this research at a future time.

3. Explanation of Data (the facts) Collection Procedures
Data collection for this project was based on general comparative literature procedures. The literary areas as well as twelve other specific areas that I chose to compare and contrast the two authors have been researched and referenced. Primary and secondary data sources were found and recorded from numerous libraries, the Internet, and my own private library at home. Sources used were texts, anthologies, indexes, abstracts, encyclopedia, thesaurus, dictionaries, magazines, and scholarly journals.

4. Explanation of Data, Presentation and Interpretation
The purpose of *Common Grounds* is to research and select those similarities and differences, which form the basis of the problem. Otherwise, there will be inconsistent or non-existent grounds upon which comparison or contrast can be made. The issue, therefore, is to compare idea with idea, style with style, point of view with point of view as well as other appropriate phenomena. The key issue is to identify the common elements, which give the comparison central unifying ideas and focus for presentation, explanation and interpretation (Roberts 1978).

CHAPTER FOUR

FINDINGS AND RESULTS

FINDINGS AND RESULTS FOR CHAPTER FOUR WERE BASED on the comparative analysis and interpretation of the concepts of freedom and revolt as well as a comparison of the utilization of the essay by Camus and King. Also, the comparing of the twelve common ground issues of Chapter Three were accomplished. These comparisons have presented new information and knowledge of Camus and King. Further, these comparisons have presented new ways of thinking about and understanding their individual and combined messages to the people of the world. The common grounds representing social, historical, professional, and political issues were interpreted first.

The Common Grounds were presented in the order that was already given in Chapter Three:

THE WRITING OF BOTH MEN STRONGLY ADDRESSED THE PROBLEM OF HISTORICAL AND CURRENT INJUSTICE IN THE WORLD AND THE NEED TO END IT.

The findings for the above common ground statement will now be reported:

ALBERT CAMUS

Camus was a living witness to the human suffering and injustice of his time. He was a witness to the ravages of the Civil War in Spain during the thirties; he saw and had first hand knowledge concerning the atrocities of World War II in France and other European countries during the forties. Likewise, he was a witness to war and racist colonialism in his own country during the fifties, against the Arabs as well as the poor whites. He would say about Frenchmen born in Algeria, "We are the Jews of France"—since they were discriminated against in Paris (Todd 1996: 329-30). Camus took up his pen in revolt against war, the Holocaust, summary executions, concentration camps, and disregard for life. Thus, his age was one of moral confusion, rebellion, suffering, and the search for a more humane world and meaningful existence.

Camus entered the freedom struggle using his writing as a vehicle to strike blows against totalitarianism, Holocaust, summary executions, concentration camps, murder, war, and disregard for life. He exemplified great moral courage in seeking positive solutions to problems of injustice at a time when many others had become victims of gloom and hopelessness. While he agreed that the lives of many, during his time, had entered the domain of the absurd, he did not adhere to the premise that one must remain engrossed in absurdist ideology as a final solution to life's dilemmas. Camus believed that the job of human beings, and certainly writers, was to change the inhumanity of existence into one where there was civility and optimism. He used his writings as a means of confronting societal injustice and oppression and to inspire people towards change and transformation. Thus, in order to express his thinking on these issues, he wrote successfully using several different literary genres. These included the novel, the short story, the essay, and the play. In his writings, the human solidarity found in team effort was one of the major means that Camus identified as being successful against the many faces of injustice. Therefore, he took special aim at Nazi and Marxist oppression and executions as evils against which human beings must fight an entrenched battle.

Camus warns that in addressing the problems of historical and current injustice, humans must be careful that they do not deify themselves and become a part of the very problems that they are fighting. In this regard, the human struggle against the problems of injustice, means and ends must have humane limits in order that they will not duplicate the wrongs of the oppressor.

Finally, on this common ground, both Camus and King felt adamantly that we must study war no more. They believed that war and its destruction are major examples of intellectual creativity being used to destroy and imprison human beings rather than lead them to freedom. Thus, too often, the best minds were being used for the technology of warfare rather than finding solutions to war and the resulting poverty, injustice, oppression and suffering. The devastating destructive power of modern war machinery removed even the negative good (deterring an aggressive nation) that a war can accomplish. They thought, further, that if the nations of the world would devote as much money, time, and effort to the pursuit of peace and justice as is spent for war and defense, there would be an unequaled reign of reconciliation and harmony in the world.

DR. MARTIN LUTHER KING JR.

As an Afro-American, Dr. King answered the call of conscience to enter the struggle against historical and current injustice as a goal of his life. More than one hundred years after the Emancipation Proclamation (1863). Dr. King entered the civil rights struggle to address issues of injustice. He played a major role in waging a struggle against segregated busing in Montgomery, Alabama. The Montgomery boycott, which was led by Dr. King, was a catalyst in the subsequent unfolding of the entire civil rights movement, and he was instrumental in persuading the United States Supreme Court to hand down a judgment that segregation in public transportation was unconstitutional. The historical victory won in Montgomery provided better racial relations and reconciliation for both Negroes and whites. The victory against injustice in Montgomery was won as a result of a solidarity, struggle, and sacrifice that had worldwide impact, especially for Third World nations. Dr. King's leading of the Montgomery struggle confronted America with the need to redefine the meaning of democracy for all citizens. He was instrumental in strategizing the Southern and Northern campaigns against injustices in the work place, education, social life, economics, fair housing, voting rights, and the courts system.

The American Negro has shown a remarkable resiliency against overwhelming injustice, from slavery to Jim Crow laws and segregation, to the nefarious idea of "separate but equal." Fights and struggles with such organizations as the Ku Klux Klan and White Citizen Councils intensified during the fifties and sixties; yet, Negroes still made positive contributions to America in every area of living. Injustices brought about by institutional racism were blatant in the South and more hidden in the North, but Dr. King exposed the problems throughout America from the point of view that Negroes could not be "outsiders" but were "insiders" anywhere in America where justice and equality were at stake. For the Negro, the fight for equality has been a struggle to keep hope alive in the midst of the absurdity of having to live out a life of being a second class American.

No ethnic group migrating to America has had to live and tolerate the abuses and injustices suffered by the American Negro. There is no question about the fact that the American Negro is as much American as anyone, and has been here since 1619. This date predates the arrival of many other ethnic nationalities. The American Negroes have paid the costs of citizenship in blood, sweat, tears, and death. And through it all, they have remained faithful to homeland America. The willingness of children to join the fight for civil rights and justice in 1963 highlighted the fact that the oppression of segregation had no age limit, that racism touches every Afro-American heart, and that freedom is still the vision.

Beyond America, Dr. King envisioned a universal inclusiveness of all classes, races, religions, among the haves and have nots, where the dream of international brotherhood would become a reality. Dr. King believed that we are all mutually interdependent and that injustice to any person diminishes every other person. Historically, a zealous champion leading the fight against injustice has often opened the way to victory. Examples include: Moses, Gandhi, Frederick Douglass, Harriet Tubman, Abraham Lincoln, Dr. Martin Luther King, Jr. (and more recently, Nelson Mandela).

The visions of the future of Dr. King stated that, due to long standing institutional injustices, America had done much *against* Negroes and, so, should be willing to do something *for* them in the area of equalizing opportunities. However, white backlash against Negro progress and opportunity was one of the sure obstacles to the full integration of the Negro into American society. Therefore, it can be concluded that the problem of racism in America is a white problem. Racism was started, supported, and maintained by white society. It is white society that must be instrumental in dismantling and eliminating the system of racial injustices in America.

The Native American Indian has been another victim of the injustices caused by the posture of white superiority in America. In the America of today, the majority of Native American Indians live in disgraceful conditions of poverty on reservations and in dilapidated shanty towns, taking whatever handouts church groups and mission workers can procure for them. They are truly the forgotten Americans.

SUMMARY

The findings of **common ground number one** substantiates that the problem of historical and current injustice in the world was a major theme in the writings of both Camus and King. While the two men viewed the terrain from different

103

perspectives—Camus from one of humanistic agnosticism and King from that of a devout Christian—they both came together concerning the need to fight against societal evils such as: oppression, poverty, murder, colonialism, exploitation of the poor, political tyranny, and war. This being the case, they were both in search of ways and means to heal and reconcile these problems for the good of human kind everywhere.

THE WRITINGS OF BOTH MEN USE REVOLT AND FREEDOM AS CATALYSTS FOR THEIR WRITINGS AND THOUGHT. THEIR VISION IS A JUST AND HUMANE SOCIETY WHERE PEOPLE CAN BE RECONCILED.

The findings for the above common ground statement will now be reported. **NOTE: This particular common ground deals with both the social and historical as well as the literary comparison in Camus' and King's writings.**

ALBERT CAMUS

Before he graduated from the University of Algiers, Camus had already given evidence of a burning passion in search of truth by writing essays concerning revolt and freedom. This was during the 1930s and early 1940s. Later, as he developed into a more accomplished writer, Camus expanded his use of literary genres by employing the novel, philosophical essay, short story, and play to present his protest to the reader. French writers, as a result of World War II, had witnessed the failure of the critical issues of their lives. This included: social progress, science, democracy, reason, and ultimately, the failure of people. Consequently, there was a loss, or certainly a lessening, of faith in traditional Christian beliefs. Therefore, the literature of this period was one of revolt that turned to human beings as the solution to the atrocities and oppressions thrust upon an uncertain human condition. Camus believed that the job of the writer was to be a witness of the times searching for freedom and justice in the midst of chaos.

In the evolution of Camus' works, we can see two distinct types of revolt. The first is metaphysical revolt, or revolt against life conditions—the reality and nature of existence vis-a. vis God and the world. The second is historical or collective revolt or revolt against the injustices and oppression meted out by other human beings. Camus addresses revolt in the former domain in his book, *The Stranger* (1942), which was written in Algeria, 1939-1940. In the book he portrayed the uncertain and death threatening atmosphere of the times. The main character, Meursault, embodies in his personality the estrangement, absurdity, and detachment from life and meaning felt by many persons at the time as a result of the grave uncertainties brought on by World War II. Historical revolt is addressed in *The Just Assassins* 1950), and *The Rebel* (1951).

Camus instructs us that to live a life of the absurd will not produce the freedom of a meaningful life that every person is seeking. The absurd links forces with violence, death, and nihilism rather than with love, hope, and positive living. Therefore, the absurd must be faced with courage, understanding and overcome with constant commitment and dedication to a winning response to life's dilemmas. The *Myth of Sisyphus* (1942) is Camus' answer to the double inhibitors of the absurd and nihilism. Camus uses the essay to present his thoughts and interpretations regarding the absurd. Sisyphus revolts against the absurdity of his condition as an example of what humans can do to triumph over severe hardship and threat of death. Sisyphus does not see nihilism as a viable option to solve his problem. He finds happiness and freedom, using an attitude of defiance, in the midst of chaos. His message to humans everywhere is to do the same, that is, to look for solutions leading to survival rather than bemoaning hardship and adversity. Therefore, the burden of this metaphysical revolt and the opportunity for victory are placed squarely on the shoulders of human beings. Reliance on doctrines, religious or otherwise, causes inertia and superstition. It is humans alone that must bear the responsibility for their lives as they continue to live out its value The second type of revolt is historical and collective. This type of revolt can be described as a total force, as a total group effort for a more just order and freedom. It originated in the feeling of human solidarity and dignity. Historical revolt is concerned with the inhumanity of war, intolerance of others, colonialism, political tyranny, totalitarianism, and any other ideological evil that is used to inflict suffering upon human beings. This type of revolt is a call to transform and civilize the inhumanity of the world into a new image of what humans can be. It is an effort to bring out the best in human beings and to subdue the worst. The effectiveness of this total team effort is found in *The Plague* (1947), which is an allegory of the struggle of the French underground freedom fighters against Nazism. It is through the humanism of collective revolt that humans prevail against the plague. As pointed out by Germaine Brée (1964), the plague "symbolizes any force which cuts off human beings from the living breath of life: The physical joy of moving freely on this earth, the inner joy of love, the freedom to plan our tomorrows" (128). It appears, further, that Camus is saying that while suffering and death will bring assault upon people as to their who? why? what? and where? it is the solidarity of collective revolt that sets to flight the plagues of the world, whatever type it might be, and replaces it with a relative freedom, justice, and semblance of order and happiness.

Camus states further that the role of the artist was to be a witness and be a combatant for freedom, even though the costs at times would be heavy; but if humans cannot refer to a common value recognized by all as existing in each other, then human beings are incomprehensible to one another *(The Rebel:* 23). As Camus sees it, the true rebel "opposes the principle of justice which he sees in himself to that of injustice which he sees being applied in the world" (24). Rebellion refutes the idea that one person is superior over another. The true rebel for justice will not tolerate racism, ethnic favoritism, abuse, or cleansing because these contradict a fundamental premise of rebellion, which declares that all humanity should have equality and freedom (14).

So, then, what is a rebel? Rebels are those persons who call a halt to the limits to which they will allow their humanity to be oppressed and transgressed upon. Rebels insist upon loyalty to certain aspects of value existing in their lives and they are willing to support these to the death. However, there are still two means that revolt can destroy: by deifying the self and committing suicide, and by pursuing absolute assent and taking the right to murder. Camus' thought on this point is that "even though faced with mutilated justice, the rebel can never be an ally to generalized injustice" (102).

In both periods of Camus' literary works, the idea of limits is maintained. The first concerns the limits to metaphysical freedom. The second concerns limits to historical freedom. Total and absolute freedom in either domain lead to lifestyles of nihilism that bring on destruction to others and to self. *Caligula* (1938) and *The Misunderstanding* (1942) and *The Just Assassins* (1950) are good examples of this concept that were documented earlier in this research report.

Just as men rallied to a collective revolt against *The Plague* (1947), Camus calls us all to be partners in the stubborn, weary, and unglamorous struggle of mankind against all types of oppression, working individually or collectively. Further, everyone is called upon to respond to a spirit of comradeship in the service of human survival that will mark the limits of the plague's dehumanizing power. This vital force in search of solidarity, justice, reconciliation, and freedom seemed to be Camus' vision of the future.

DR. MARTIN LUTHER KING JR.

As an Afro-American who grew up in the South, Dr. King experienced and was a witness to a long history of racial inequality, discrimination, oppression, and terror. Writing in *Stride Toward Freedom* (1958), he notes that "the ultimate tragedy of segregation is that it not only harms one physically but injures one spiritually. It scars the soul and degrades the personality. It inflicts the segregated with a sense of inferiority, while confirming the segregator in a false estimate of his own superiority" (22). Thus, since the human beings are created to breathe free, segregation is a prelude to revolt in any society at any time.

King uses the essay genre to record his writings on freedom and revolt. This particular genre allows him the liberty to present his thoughts, definitions, and interpretations regarding the social, economical, political, and theological issues of the civil rights and human rights struggle directly to the reader in uncomplicated language.

The arrest of Rosa Parks for refusing to give up her seat on a bus to a white man was the catalyst action that started the Negro revolt. It began on December 1, 1955, in Montgomery, Alabama. Mrs. Parks was making a statement of revolt for her own freedom as well as for All-American Negroes, who had suffered the humiliation of historical racial indignities.

The Montgomery public transportation system was an ongoing major insult to the values of self-esteem and dignity of Negro customers, who had to get up and surrender their seats to white passengers as well as stand over unoccupied "white only" seats when there was not a single white passenger on the bus. Negroes who did not comply were arrested and taken to jail.

As a result of Mrs. Parks' arrest, a public transportation boycott was put into action by Negroes that lasted for 382 days. Negro passengers comprised 80% of the passengers using public transportation. Participants in the boycott included yardmen, domestics, businessmen, doctors, students, lawyers, preachers, and college professors. On the first day of the boycott, December 5, 1955, the buses were empty of Negro passengers. The reality of empty buses continued. It was a mass demonstration of a people willing to sacrifice and suffer for their freedom and dignity.

The Montgomery Improvement Association was founded to organize and strategize the boycott and give leadership to the conditions of protest. Dr. Martin Luther King, Jr. was elected president of this organization. As a result of Dr. King's persuasive and unyielding leadership for justice, on January 30, 1956, his home was bombed while his wife, daughter, and a church friend were inside. It appeared that retaliatory violence was imminent, but in a calming speech to the gathered crowd, Dr. King admonished them that "we must love our white brothers… this is what we must live by… no matter what they do to us; we must make them know that we love them. We must meet hate with love" (117). This stance of *agape* love was central and foundational to Dr. King's Christian beliefs. It was also a survival strategy.

Agape love is defined as the "understanding good will for all men" (p. 86). It is a love that is disinterested and expects no good thing in return but only hostility and persecution. It is love for the enemy-neighbor. In taking this position, Dr. King raised the love ethic to a new level, wherein love itself was a dimension of revolt and freedom. More explicitly, the power of love enabled, simultaneously, a revolt and freedom that cleansed and liberated the emotions and attitudes from meanness, hate, spitefulness, resentment and revenge, Thus, the power to choose to love your enemy is a means of liberation of the highest order—spiritually, emotionally, and metaphysically.

The church was called upon to accept its spiritual role and responsibility of leadership. Dr. King points out that "in the final analysis, racism is not a political but a moral issue. Racism denies the meaning of Christianity and the oneness and equality of all persons in Christ. The matter of one person being superior and another being inferior because of race is contrary to biblical teaching and doctrine (182-186). Yet, there are still those persons who call themselves Christians, even clergy, who practice exclusion and bigotry. *The Letter From Birmingham Jail* addressed this point.

Wealth should be used globally, by every nation, to alleviate the suffering and violence often associated with a life of poverty. The need is overwhelming "to feed the poor, clothe the naked, heal the sick" and provide shelter for the homeless (70). It appears that Dr. King is saying here that wealth can be used as another instrument of revolt in freeing humans from lives of oppression due to poverty.

Local, state, and the federal government must continue to play a decisive role in making changes for justice and equality for all Americans. Further, American labor must provide equal training and job opportunity for all employees, because economic inequality keeps the Negro in second place when on the average he makes only 65% of every dollar that whites make. Yet, Negroes must pay the same price for goods and services as whites with one third less money. Without question, this economic disparity results in creating living conditions that give advantage and privilege to white Americans while ignoring the inequality against Negroes.

Why We Can't Wait (1963) presents in its opening pages a portrayal of a young black boy in Harlem, New York, and a young black girl in rural Alabama. They appear to be symbolic of the historical dilemma of the past and the foretold future that has been a plague upon the lives of black Americans since being brought to America in the chains of oppression… They will enter the struggle at an early age, because the sufferings of their foreparents have also been their suffering, and they, just as the children of Birmingham in 1963, feel that they have waited long enough. As stated by Dr. King, they will learn that freedom that is delayed will ultimately be freedom that is denied. So, they are ready, at an early age, to put on the full armor of revolt, demanding their freedom and full access to the bountiful opportunities that are part of the American heritage.

The Birmingham, Alabama revolt of 1963 happened because civil laws, including the 1954 school desegregation decision, were not enforced and were therefore ignored by many school systems in the nation, especially the South. School systems and municipalities came up with their own timelines for implementation, which in the majority of cases, nullified the Supreme Court ruling. White America's blatant refusal, in many cases, to obey a just and fair ruling handed down by the highest court of the land made it clear to Negroes that their rights and value as human beings and citizens would continue to be unprotected and ignored. A frustration and disappointment (already present from many years past) began taking place that took nine years, 1954-1963, to erupt into open revolt and rebellion.

Nonviolent action allowed Negroes the freedom of militant revolt without using violent force. Nonviolent means of protest had a proven record of success, and it was based on the foundation of fighting violence with love, moral force, and attempts at reconciliation. Nonviolence was seen as having the potential to liberate the oppressed to a new personhood, dignity, and self respect, while at the same time neutralizing the weapons of violence used previously by the oppressor. Nonviolence was a two-edged sword, then, in that it gave freedom to both the oppressed and the oppressor.

The key players in the civil rights struggle of the fifties and sixties had a long track record of creative extremism. The Negro church was in the very midst of the struggle and played a major part in keeping the civil rights movement nonviolent. Preachers who put their lives and/or reputations on the line included: The Rev. Martin Luther King, Jr., Rev. Fred Shuttlesworth, Rev. Ralph Abernathy, Rev. Jesse Jackson, and Rev. Robert Graetz. These freedom fighters followed a long tradition of Negro church social activism that goes back to slaves Bishop Richard Allen (1787), Rev. Absalom Jones (1787), and Nat Turner (1830).

America has a long history of racial bigotry that needs to be healed and reconciled to a new way of recognizing and affording equality to all Americans. Segregationists can little bargain with Negroes about the conditions of freedom, as if one group has the right to draw up the terms of freedom for another. Negroes and whites working together in good faith can cause nonviolent change to occur.

White backlash has played a prominent role in American racial relations. White backlash exists when white society, from appearances, welcome laws of change but later move away from the day to day application of these laws. Civil rights laws should move the nation towards equality. However, resistance to change has been evident in several key areas that include: education, housing, bank loans, and employment.

The Black Power slogan and movement came into being as the result of white backlash and resistance. Black Power was a reaction to the white power that continued to resist justice and freedom to Negro Americans. Further, it was a call to Negro self-worth and self-respect. Its aim was to dispute the slave mentality of many Negroes, to instill pride in being black, to take pride, knowledge, and appreciation of Negro history and heritage. Finally, its purpose was to empower hope and purpose in the development of political, social and economic independence on the part of the Negro masses in America and around the world.

Dr. King was a firm believer that the strength and thrust of civil rights in America would continue to solidify when it was allied with other groups, such as the white poor, Jews, Catholics, and friendly white liberals. It was the pressure from many whites for justice that had helped bring about civil rights victories. Blacks could not have done it alone. Therefore, black paths and white paths have intersected in reaching common goals of justice and freedom. This reconciliation needed to be expanded and become an inclusive entity with the goal of "colorless power."

Dr. King never lost hope that America could become a nation where a new humanity, civilization, freedom and justice would prevail. Nonviolent pressure on the government would have to continue, because the record had shown that political power yields little without the crisis of confrontation and the ballot. Job market parity would have to become a reality. Due to their large numbers in trade unions, Negroes would have to come together to position themselves where they can make a difference in hiring, job assignments, wages, promotions, and supervision.

Negroes must continue to become selective consumers and not do business with establishments that do not hire them, or provide them with equal opportunity once hired.

Young Negroes played a major role in the Negro revolt of the 1950s and 1960s. They used the tactics of nonviolent resistance that involved freedom rides, sit-ins, kneel-ins, wade-ins, and pray-ins to prick the conscience of America towards transformation. Their aim was the establishment of an effective rebellion model that took on national as well as global significance. Their major focus was on Dr. King's idea that injustice anywhere was a threat to freedom everywhere.

Nonviolent civil disobedience was the principal means through which Dr. King saw th(' accomplishment of peaceful revolt, transformation, and reconciliation in America and on a world scale. The use of nonviolent civil disobedience had made impressive inroads against entrenched racial segregation in the Southern United States by creating tension and disruption to normal municipal order. This disruption could only be tolerated for a short period without relief. Birmingham and Selma, Alabama were two notable examples where this protracted strategy literally brought these two cities to a standstill and resulted in changes in the name of justice and freedom. Mahatma Gandhi had used the strategies of nonviolent civil disobedience in India against British colonialism during the forties, and he had led his people to victory.

SUMMARY

The findings of **common ground number two** research supports the idea that revolt and freedom were catalysts in the writings and thought of Albert Camus and Dr. Martin Luther King, Jr. The writings of Camus reflect the thought of revolt from the time of his earliest writings in the 1930s where he challenges the treatment of Arabs in Algeria, North Africa by the French colonialist settlers. He continues to address revolt and freedom in his later writings from the points of view of metaphysical and historical rebellion. He makes it clear that rebellion and freedom are two sides of the same coin. Where there is revolt, human beings are making the statement that they are weary and tired of oppression and injustice and that they are ready to stand up to fight, and even die, for their freedom. The Algerian liberation fight for freedom from French colonialism in the late 50s and early 60s as well as the struggle of the French Underground fighting for freedom from Nazi atrocities and oppression served as eye witness background for some of Camus' key writings.

Dr. Martin Luther King, Jr., likewise, fighting for the freedom of oppressed Negroes, lived in a perpetual state of revolt all of his life, as does every Negro. Due to the historical plague of racism in America, with all of its negative manifestations, revolt and the struggle for freedom are as second nature to Negroes as to any ethnic people anywhere in the world. King responded to the civil rights call in 1955 by being, coincidentally, present at a meeting of time and place that thrust him into the forefront of the Negro revolt for freedom. He remained at, the head of the struggle for thirteen years–traveling, speaking, writing, and protesting. He lived with the full knowledge that his life was at risk daily. Ultimately, in 1968, he did give his life for the cause of freedom in America and around the world. He had come to Memphis, Tennessee to lead a march protesting the unequal treatment being received by garbage workers. Economic exploitation was a priority on his agenda at this time.

BOTH MEN ARE NOBEL LAUREATES CHOSEN FOR THE COMPOSITE IMPACT OF THEIR WORK, CAMUS FOR LITERATURE (1957) AND KING FOR PEACE (1964).

The findings for the above common ground will now be reported:

ALBERT CAMUS

Albert Camus was always a bright and articulate student from elementary school through the university. His original thinking and the power of his creative expression were recognized by Professor Louis Germain, a secondary school mentor, and then by Professor Jean Grenier at the university level. Camus was endowed with a gifted intellect that was always in search of truth and justice. This was evident in his first works *Betwixt and Between*, (1937), and *Revolt in the Asturias* (1937), written while he was yet in his early twenties. Camus believed that the job of the writer was to be a witness of the times searching for truth, freedom and justice in the midst of chaos.

The Nobel Prize for literature was awarded to Camus in 1957 for his work. Camus' work was always most relevant to the moment that it was written, covering a period from the late 1930s to the late 1950s. During these years, his literary values were a protest for a more meaningful, fulfilled, and just human experience. During the first period of his writing, (1937-1945), he witnessed the presence of the absurd and nihilism as having taken hold in daily human existence. However, He was not satisfied that human beings with their unlimited potential for good, could be relegated to the dismal life of uncertainty that he saw all around him. Granting the absurd, Camus was concerned with how to live profitably with it while transforming it into a positive, lucid, and creative force brought about by revolting against the meaninglessness of the absurd and nihilism. He did not see these latter two as a place to live a life, but as an obstacle to be overcome and conquered in the search for freedom.

During the second period of his writing, (1946-1958), Camus' writing ethic called for a revolt against any and all forms of injustice that created a plague against

112

human existence and freedom. The plague, incidentally, was Camus' general label for inhuman and unjust outrages against humanity. The co-existence of justice and freedom was the front behind which the thrust for freedom sought solidarity. It was this commitment to solidarity by persons of good will—turned rebels that possessed the potential to bring an end to the plagues of the world. Of course, Camus' view was that the artist, himself, must be a rebel in search of liberation for oppressed people.

Looking further at the impact of Camus, his work gave hope to people during a period of great suffering and loss. His writings and literary leadership were lights during some of the darkest hours of French and European history. Camus was a moralist who wanted to find freedom for himself, as an artist, as well as for the people of his times.

Camus' ultimate goal was the transformation of the existing values of his times that found their expression, too often, in tyranny, injustice and war into a new set of values that would find their expression in human preservation, peace, harmony, and brotherhood.

DR. MARTIN LUTHER KING JR.

At an early age, King showed signs of superior scholarship. He attended the public elementary schools of Atlanta, and attended high school at the Atlanta University Laboratory School and Booker T. Washington High School. He was a bright and ambitious high school student who was able to skip both the 9th and 12th grades. Consequently, he entered Morehouse College at the age of fifteen. King was greatly influenced by his father who was a preacher, theologian, and social activist. Dr. Benjamin Mays, the president of Morehouse College was another person of influence in the life of Dr. Martin Luther King, Jr. Mays encouraged young King to follow his father into the ministry. He also encouraged him to strive for excellence in the academic world and the need to fight for equality on behalf of Negroes. From his father and Dr. Mays, King learned early lessons about the importance of protest for civil rights and justice. He also learned to use his intellectual gifts in concert with the power of words and ideas.

Dr. King was awarded the Nobel Prize for peace in 1964 for his participation in and leadership to the civil rights struggle in America during the fifties and sixties. This struggle had been a plague in the culture of America since Negroes were brought here as slaves in 1619. Official slavery in America lasted from 1619 to 1865; this was 246 years. After 1865, years of disenfranchisement resulting in discrimination, bigotry, Jim Crow, oppression, and lynchings were the lot of Negro Americans. This continued until 1955 when the Rosa Parks incident set into motion the Montgomery bus boycott.

Dr. King entered the picture here when he was elected to help organize the boycott, plan strategies, and give leadership to the Montgomery protest. King's leadership was informed by personal experiences while growing up in the South, his theology background, his excellent educational training at Morehouse College, Crozer Theological Seminary, and Boston University. King was an effective leader of the boycott due to his commitment to protracted militant nonviolent protest undergirded by love for the oppressor. This basic strategy put forth by King never changed, and he expounded it in all of his writings, his speeches, and his personal role model. Dr. King defended nonviolence as the most effective weapon of revolt that can be used by an oppressed people. Nonviolence involved suffering, injury, pain, and at times death, but no strategy used by any civil rights group during the fifties and sixties registered more victories, gain, and freedom for Negroes.

In reflecting on the composite impact and meaning of the work of Albert Camus and Dr. Martin Luther King Jr., I want to call attention again to their Nobel Prize acceptance speeches, where they were live, on stage, speaking for themselves. The thoughts of Camus and King are similar as they address numerous social and humanitarian issues such as: brotherhood, optimism, nihilism, the meaning of civilization, faith in human kind, and thanks to significant others. An analysis and discussion of these speeches was presented at the end of Chapter Two of this research report.

SUMMARY

In summary, the findings of **common ground number three** support the fact that Camus and King were chosen for the composite impact of their work. With the above inclusion of **significant others,** both men have addressed several relevant issues that will continue to be paramount in the lives and thinking of rational and well meaning people in the free world. Moreover, Camus and King recognized the importance of human solidarity working in the name of good in order to bring about justice and freedom in society. This is the impact that they wanted their works to have, and according to the secondary sources in this research report, it is, indeed, the impact that their work has had in the past and will continue to have in the future.

BOTH MEN WERE THE BEST IN THEIR NOBEL CATEGORY AND PROFESSIONS AT THE TIME OF THEIR SELECTIONS.

The findings for the above common ground will now be reported:

ALBERT CAMUS

Authors' success and reputation can be determined by the broad audience of people who choose to read their works. Gallimard Publishing, Paris, the publisher of Camus' works has stated that his publications continue to appear at the top of the sales list. In addition, sales data shows that two of his books, *The Stranger* and *The Plague* are all time best sellers. His works continue to be read by persons of all races, sexes, ages, classes and persuasions. The research states clearly that Camus provided readers around the world with a moral perspective from which to view life. Further, Camus was able to impart to generations, past and present, a voice of hope and optimism in the face of gloom, doubt, and anxiety. This is due to the fact that Camus felt artists must be witnesses of freedom and that their writings should reflect an awareness and concern about the desperate state of human beings who were living during his times. Otherwise, he thought it would be difficult for artists to justify themselves. Thus, it appears that Camus is saying that the power of the pen was to be used to confront and help transform an oppressive society that was saturated with pain and suffering. Evil motives and actions abounded on all sides. Therefore, those who had been called to write had to give people a ray of hope that took them beyond the despair of their present moments.

DR. MARTIN LUTHER KING JR.

The life, witness, and role model of Dr. King have lifted both his life and writings to world prominence. His legacy of civil rights struggle and nonviolent revolt against formidable and life threatening odds have given a message to generations of every time and place concerning the meaning of true commitment to freedom and human rights. Consequently, his niche finds him among the great theologians of all times. During the time of his advocacy, the late fifties and the sixties, he had no peer. For thirteen years, the eyes of the world were upon him. His supporters and his enemies held him in awe. Dr. King's writings, preaching, speeches, inspired the young and old, from every walk of life, with power, hope, justice, and the regulating principle of love-brotherhood. He touched the very heartstrings and consciousness of millions of people in the name of everything that is good, just, right, and decent. He was a master at combining the intellectual and the spiritual. He proclaimed the truth with unparalleled vigor, enthusiasm, and authority. Dr. King proved that a single person can change society, and for many, he became the moral conscience of his times, in America and around the world.

Today, in our times, Dr. King's legacy and unequaled impact continue. There is a national holiday observed in his honor. Streets, boulevards and highways bear his name. Libraries, office buildings, churches, and housing developments have been named after him. Seminaries conduct classes that teach the theology and thought of Dr. King. Little children memorize his speeches for contests. Preachers strive to imitate his moving and oratorical preaching and pulpit style. There is a major center of King Research in Atlanta, Georgia. Numerous college and university libraries have secured archives, research, and artifacts on the life of Dr. King. His legacy and theology in the world of ideas and lifestyles of people are far from finished. Certainly, the difficult and destructive times in which we are living today warrant a fresh look at the teachings of Dr. King in the areas of nonviolence and brotherhood.

SUMMARY

Albert Camus was awarded the Nobel Prize for Literature in 1957 for his composite writings, "Which brings to light the problems which weigh on the consciences of men during our times." The success of his writings, from generation to generation, speak for themselves. Fifty years later, his writings continue to be among the most widely read of any writer of the Twentieth Century. At least two of his books have been on the best seller list for over forty five years. He remains one of the most discussed authors in Twentieth Century French Literature classes. In the domain of Twentieth Century world literature, he is, likewise, at the top of the list of preferred authors.

Additional popularity of Camus' works have come about as a result of the fall of the Communist powers in Eastern Europe. During his lifetime, Camus was a staunch and bitter opponent of Communist totalitarianism and predicted its demise. This stance brought criticism from many literary friends who were supporters of the Communist Party in France. The passage of time has vindicated the truth of his views and earned new interest and respect for his writings. Thus, in the Twenty-first Century, the meaning of his works continue to give moral examples to the world.

Dr. Martin Luther King, Jr. was awarded the Nobel Prize for Peace in 1964 for his leadership in the American civil rights struggle that had as its goal the obtaining of freedom for twenty two million American Negro citizens who had been denied their equal rights for over three hundred and fifty years. He has given a legacy to generations, past and present, concerning the meaning of true commitment to freedom and human rights. He was an inspiration to the young and old from every walk of life. He infused the lives of people of all races with hope, power, justice, and brotherhood, because he represented the excellency of the best in human nature.

Consequently, the respect and recognition given to Dr. King during his lifetime and since his death have been overwhelming and attest to the value that people place upon the meaning of his life and work. In memory of his work, various tributes of all types, from around the world, have been established. He is the idol of many from all races, ages, religions, professions, and socio-economic groups.

In conclusion, Albert Camus and Dr. Martin Luther King, Jr. are on **common ground number four** concerning their being the best in their professions when chosen for their respective Nobel awards. The quality and durability of their messages, achievements, and legacies have stood the test of time and support this conclusion. Right thinking people of the world continue to lift them up, and they continue to gain prominence with the passing of each new generation.

BOTH MEN LIVED DURING SIMILAR HISTORICAL MOMENTS AND WORLD PROBLEMS.

Camus: 1913-1960, World War II, The Korean War, the War of Independence in Algeria, racism in Algeria, Franco oppression in Spain, Communist oppression in Eastern Europe.

King: 1929-1968, World War II, the Korean War, the Vietnamese War, Racism in the USA The findings for the above common ground statement will now be reported:

While Camus and King were sixteen years apart in age, during their lifetimes, they both lived through similar historical moments and world problems, such as: political oppression, poverty, war, and totalitarianism. Their views on these issues are similar, and these similarities are reflected in their writings. Camus speaks out against political, economical, and social oppression in *Caligula, The Plague* and *The Rebel*. Having lived through a lifetime of political oppression as an Afro-American, all of Dr. King's books deplore political, economical, and social oppression. Camus and his family were products of an impoverished livelihood, with no father and an illiterate mother who provided for the family from the wages of a cleaning woman. He was a witness to poverty during his childhood and adolescence and was well acquainted with the tyranny of being poor. Further, he knew the poverty of illness as a result of his lifetime struggle with tuberculosis. Dr. King addresses the issue of people condemned to poverty in his introduction to *Why We Can't Wait*. He views wealth as an asset that should be used for the alleviation and elimination of poverty in America and in the world. In <u>The Trumpet of Conscience</u>, King addresses the issue of the fair distribution of wealth to eliminate poverty in America and the world. Both men had been eye witnesses to the oppression of poverty and wanted to see it alleviated.

ALBERT CAMUS

The difficult circumstances of the age to which Albert Camus was born began coming to life during his early childhood. Camus was reared in poverty and his father was killed in 1918, during the First World War. Camus was only five years old. Then, during the Second World War, 1939-1945, Camus had witnessed and had knowledge of some 70 million men, women and children who had been displaced, sent to another country, or killed. The human suffering and pain of these years created the context for some of his works.

The Korean War, 1950-1953, is included here only as a historical event that took place during the lives of both Camus and King. Considering their anti-war positions, it could be argued that they were aware of the devastation and casualties caused by this war. But historically, both America and France were just returning to a degree of normalcy after World War II. Korea was another chapter added on to World War II, the "Cold War" between America and Russia and the war in Vietnam that involved both the United States and France. This long period of wars had certainly taken its toll, especially on the young. Specifically, concerning the war in Korea, it was one of the most bloody in history, with about one million South Korean civilians killed and several million made homeless. 580,000 United Nations and South Korean troops and about 1,600,000 Communist troops were killed, wounded, or reported missing. The war was fought between Communist North Korea and democracy oriented South Korea. North Korea was supported by China and the Soviet Union. South Korea was supported by the United Nations forces from America, Australia, Belgium, Canada, Colombia, Ethiopia, France, Great Britain, Greece, Luxembourg, The Netherlands, New Zealand, the Philippines, South Africa, Thailand, and Turkey (Source: The World Book Encyclopedia, 1999, Volume K: 377-384).

On another front of hostility, the French settled in Algeria in 1830. The local Arabs never accepted French colonial rule. Consequently, there was struggle over governance between the French and the native Arabs of Algeria that lasted from

1832 to 1962. Unrest among the Arabs was due to poor living conditions, racial discrimination, unemployment, resentment against French rule, the refusal of the French to give the Algerians representation in government, and the loss of land and inheritance to French take over. In 1954, the discontent of the Arab Algerians erupted into a widespread revolt. The Algerian rebel forces used guerrilla tactics to sabotage the French military as well as the colonial infrastructure. The French retaliated with concentration camps, destruction of orchards and croplands, and torture of the Arab leaders. In 1958, General Charles de Gaulle, the president of France, prepared a new constitution that gave a five year reform plan and more local control to the Algerian people. It also provided improved economic opportunities, social conditions, and the beginning of self-rule. However, the fighting continued, and by the end of 1961, some 140,000 Algerian rebels and 20,500 French troops had been killed in the fighting. Also, 3,000 Europeans and 20,000 Muslims had been killed or reported missing. Negotiations to discuss Algerian independence resumed in 1961, and one year later, in 1962, France granted Algeria independence. An official cease-fire took place in 1964. In the meantime, the European population had fled Algeria. Others left after the granting of independence. The struggle for independence, self-rule, and a measure of freedom for the Algerian people had been long, torturous, and costly. But, human beings have, historically, been willing to pay the price and die for the causes of freedom for themselves and others. (The World book Encyclopedia, 1999, Volume A: 364-365).

While Camus deeply regretted the bloodshed and atrocities taking place in his homeland, he never took a firm stand in favor of the French or against the native Algerians. Due to his world renown, this stance caused censure from both sides. His hope, however, was that there would be a negotiated settlement between the two factions that would see joint rule and a partnership between the French and Arabs. But the long years of hostilities, suffering, racism, and distrust prevented this from occurring during his life time.

However, according to Roger Quillot (1962) writing in Brée, eds., as early as 1939 and still in his early twenties, young Camus, while on assignment as a reporter for the *Alger Republican,* did a lengthy article on the severe hardship and famine existing among the overpopulated Kabyle or Arab mountain dwellers. He appealed to the French authorities to address this severe human suffering that he had witnessed. His much repeated pleas for justice were ignored by the powers in charge. Camus informed the French authorities:

I think I can state that at least fifty percent of the population sustains itself on herbs and roots while waiting for assistance from administrative charity in the form of distribution of grain… At dawn in Tizi-Ouzou I saw children in rags fight the Kabyle dogs over the contents of a garbage can. To my questions people answered, "It's like that every morning" (41).

Camus stated further that unemployment was high and that wages were insulting. He compared the working conditions of the Kabyle as bordering on slavery and the insensitivity of the French settlers as inhumane. Conditions similar to these between the native Arabs and the colonialist French existed for over one hundred years prior to open rebellion on the part of the Arabs in 1945 and again in 1954. This uprising was brutally repressed by the French. During the ensuing years, no attempt at reconciliation could be agreed upon by both factions. Camus, himself, went to Algeria in 1956 in an attempt to bring a halt to the mutual violence by the French and Arabs. He only met hostility and had to be escorted away by armed guards. So up to the time of his untimely death, Camus had worked and hoped for a federation where the French and Arabs could co-exist in peace. Again, Quillot in Brée (1962), informs us that Camus was "passionately devoted to justice but careful of preserving human lives; a rebel, but restrained in his revolt; lucid and disdainful of the procedures of base polemics; and finally, close to men and the world in which they live, love, and suffer… "(46-47). The Algerian independence of July 1962, two years after his death and after seven years of fighting, was not, in the final analysis, what Camus had hoped for; but at least a solution had been reached that brought the internal war and bloodshed to an end.

Camus raised his pen and voice against the violent oppression of the Franco dictatorship in Spain during the late thirties. In order to help bring an end to the violence of World War II in France, he worked as a writer in the French Resistance underground against Nazism. Further, Camus was an outspoken critic of the violence being caused by Communist totalitarianism and political oppression in Eastern Europe during and after the war years. Then, while Camus deplored the colonial war in Algeria, no doubt, he also deplored the eight year colonial war in Vietnam, 1946-1954, being fought between the French and the Vietminh. This was yet another colonial war of independence that had been draining human and financial resources from the French and the Vietnamese. The French finally withdrew after a bitter defeat at the hands of the communist Vietminh.

DR. MARTIN LUTHER KING JR.

For Dr. King, war was obsolete in solving the long term sufferings of human beings. Due to nuclear weapons, he thought that we had moved to the brink of mutual annihilation. Regarding American involvement in the war in Vietnam, 1964-1968, he found that Blacks were fighting in disproportionate numbers in a war for freedom and justice that they did not have at home. In the name of solidarity, survival, and mutual trust, black boys and white boys were fending for one another eight thousand miles from home in a way "they would never live on the same block in Detroit, Southwest Georgia or East Harlem. King spoke out concerning the Vietnam War: "I could not be silent in the face of such cruel manipulation of the poor" *(The Trumpet of Conscience:* 21). King spoke out concerning the Vietnam War in a way that clarified his position regarding any war.

War, therefore, for King was another form of violence that ought not to be tolerated in the name of freedom and brotherhood. He felt strongly, thus:

> "I speak as a child of God and brother to the suffering poor of Vietnam… I speak for the poor of America who are paying the double price of smashed hopes at home and death and corruption in Vietnam. I speak as a citizen of the world, for the world as it stands aghast at the path we have taken. I speak as an American to the leaders of my own nation. The great initiative in this war is ours. The initiative to stop must be ours" *(The Trumpet of Conscience:* 31).

Another issue that was a driving force in Dr. King's outspoken views against war was the frequent reminder to Negro Americans that the US government was willing to send their military forces to the farthest corners of the world to defend and die for the peace and freedom of other (at the time, it was Vietnam) peoples while doing little to guarantee the civil rights and freedom of twenty-two million of its own citizens at home in America. This was viewed as gross hypocrisy that was costing the lives of many Negro soldiers.

Further, the Vietnam War was costing millions of dollars and human resources that could be better used to alleviate the poverty and social problems in America. The war cost America over 150 billion dollars. 58,000 young Americans were killed–disproportionately Afro American. 300,000 American troops were wounded. Many others were permanently incapacitated due to contact with the chemical warfare agents used by America in clearing Vietnamese jungles and wooded areas (The World Book Encyclopedia, 1999, Volume V: 370-377).

Finally, Dr. King projects that it was fear that manipulated the world's machinery of war. Out of fear of one another, world powers were creating larger and more deadly arsenals of missiles, nuclear weapons and other war machinery. These weapons forced others to comply out of fear but could not substitute for the brotherly love that would be the only long term and lasting solution. This was true because love gives freedom to life. Love empowers the best in human nature to shine through for self and others. Love says that we are each other's keeper rather than each other's death threat.

SUMMARY

The findings of **common ground number five** research supports that Camus and King lived during similar historical moments and world problems. Both men were witnesses to the grievous consequences of several wars, which resulted in the death, exploitation, oppression, and displacement of people. These wars included the Second World War, The "Cold War" between America and Russia, the Korean War, the war in Algeria, and the Vietnamese War that involved both the French and America. Both men deplored the political and economical victimization caused by colonialism. Both men were outspoken advocates of justice and freedom for colonialized people, and they stood up and spoke out in every way possible for those who had been victimized into poverty.

BOTH MEN WERE MEMBERS OF ORGANIZATIONS THAT WERE FOUNDED FOR PURPOSES OF COMBATING AND ELIMINATING OPPRESSION, INJUSTICE, AND EXPLOITATION.

The findings for the above common ground statement will now be reported:

ALBERT CAMUS

Camus participated in the French Resistance movement from 1942 until the end of the war in 1945. This underground liberation group fought against Nazism in France and assisted the Allies in bringing victory to that country in 1945. Camus was also the editor of the clandestine press *Combat* until 1947. This news organ gave the French people truthful news rather than the propaganda provided by the Nazis. Camus deplored the torture executions, and concentration camps that had snuffed out the lives of so many Europeans by the Nazis. One of Camus' closest friends was executed; and working with the French underground, he was at risk of being caught and executed himself.

While Camus was not a member of any political organization after resigning from the Algerian Communist Party in 1935, he was very political in his writings. His long editorship of "Combat", during the war and after, was political involvement at the most dangerous level. In writing *The Just Assassins* (1950), Camus explored the meaning and implications of political and ideological rebellion against oppressive political regimes. And of course, his far reaching philosophical essay, *The Rebel* (1951) caused a literal political storm when it was read by other writers and politicians. He was intellectually ostracized, rebuked, and expelled from the company of his fellows and friends. There was a rupture between him and Jean-Paul Sartre that was never reconciled. Camus went into literary seclusion for about six years as a result of the severe exclusion that he suffered as a result of his essay. So, rather than belong to political organizations, per se, Camus did his politicizing through his writings.

DR. MARTIN LUTHER KING JR.

Dr. King was one of the founding members of the Montgomery (Alabama) Improvement Association (1955). The purpose of this association was to give leadership to the bus boycott of segregated busing in that city. Further, the association had the goals of bringing an end to the inhumane, indignant, and disrespectful treatment given to Negroes on the public transportation of Montgomery. As the first president of the association, Dr. King was at daily risk of being jailed, beaten, or killed. The other organization that Dr. King helped found for the purpose of combating and eliminating oppression, injustice, and exploitation was the Southern Christian Leadership Conference (1957). This organization was founded by a group of pastors who joined ranks to fight the evils of racist tyranny and exploitation throughout the South. In addition to being a member and giving leadership to these organizations, King promoted these organizations to the reading and listening public with his writings, speeches and sermons.

SUMMARY

The findings of **common ground number six** research supports that both men were members of organizations that were founded for purposes of combating and eliminating oppression, injustice, and exploitation. Camus was a principal figure in the French underground movement and further exercised his political muscle with his writings. Dr. King was involved and played a key role in both the Montgomery Improvement Association and the Southern Christian Leadership Association. Both men used the power of their writing to get their ideas to the public.

BOTH MEN SUFFERED UNEXPECTED DEATH AT AN EARLY AGE, AT THE HEIGHT OF THEIR CAREERS, WHILE STILL IN THE PROCESS OF WORKING FOR JUSTICE, FREEDOM, AND PEACE.

- Camus in 1960 at the age of 46 in an automobile accident.
- King in 1968 at the age of 39 by assassination.

The findings of the above common ground statement will now be reported:

ALBERT CAMUS

Camus was killed on January 4, 1960 while returning to Paris from a Christmas vacation at his villa in Lourmarin, Southeastern France. He had a train ticket to take the train, but accepted a return trip by automobile with his friend and publisher Michel Gallimard. Gallimard was returning to Paris from vacation with his wife and daughter. Eighty miles outside of Paris, the Gallimard automobile blew a tire, went out of control and struck two trees. Camus was killed instantly from massive head and neck injuries. Michel Gallimard also died later from the injuries that he received in the accident. The wife and daughter, riding in the rear seat, were not injured. In consideration of his writings on the absurd, it is ironic that the manner of Camus death was the absurd personified–a brilliant writer struck down by an absurd and freakish accident. He would have arrived back in Paris safely had he used the train ticket found in his pocket (Lottman 1979; Discovering Authors 1996). Camus' personal briefcase was found at the scene of the fatal accident. Inside the briefcase were 144 handwritten pages of an incomplete novel that he was in the process of writing. The novel to be entitled *The First Man* was to be an. autobiographical novel of his poverty-stricken childhood, adolescence, and fatherless family in Algeria. Wilkinson (1995) states that "while the novel remains unfinished that much of the text possesses Camus' characteristic lucidity and sensuality, clearly demonstrating that his best writing was yet to come before his tragic and untimely death at the age of 47" (1).

Up to the time of his death, Camus' thoughts never left his native land of North Africa. He was forever preoccupied about the conditions of justice, freedom and peace in the land of his birth. Some critics are of the opinion that Camus would have addressed the "Algerian Issue" in this book. Camus had given the novel the title *Le Premier Homme* or *The First Man*. He had not written anything since 1957, and many were awaiting this new work. His wife Francine, who died in 1979, would not allow the partly finished work to be published. However, after the wife's death, and with much personal transcription, Camus' daughter, Catherine, finally allowed publication of the unfinished novel in 1994. More than 100,000 copies were sold worldwide during the first several months after publication (King 1995). The daughter, Catherine, in an interview with Wilkinson (1995) above, informs us also that the novel was to include a very endearing and realistic portrait of Camus' loving, half-deaf and illiterate mother as well as his respected mentor, Louis Germain. Christine goes on to say that Camus wanted "to write something to explain who he was, and how he was different from the age that had been conferred upon him" (3). According to Cook (1999), the novel was to be divided into two parts, the first "Recherche du pere" (Search of the father) and the second "Le fils ou le premier homme" (The son or the first man). So, Camus, even after his death, was still riding a wave of unprecedented popularity as a writer; and that popularity continues even to today.

DR. MARTIN LUTHER KING JR.

Dr. Martin Luther King, Jr. was killed by an assassin's bullet as he stood on the balcony of the Lorraine Motel in Memphis, Tennessee, April 4, 1968. King had come to Memphis to lead a protest on behalf of local garbage collectors, who were fighting for better wages and working conditions. From Montgomery to Memphis, Dr. King was ever defining his own personal view of what he was ordained to proclaim regarding the concepts of love, justice, freedom, and brotherhood. To the end, he had seen the vocation of his ministry as a spiritual force for social change. Dr. King was a known champion of the poor and those who were considered to be the least. He had told an audience of more that 2,000 in a sermon the evening of April 3rd, at the Mason Temple in Memphis that he was beyond the point of being fearful of death, and even possibly that he had reached the point in his faith journey, just as the Apostle Paul, that he considered death to be gain. The words of his last sermon are prophetic: "It really doesn't matter what happens now. I've been to the mountaintop, and I have looked over into the Promised Land. I'm not worrying about anything. I'm not fearing any man. Mine eyes have seen the glory of the coming of the Lord." The next day, April 4, 1968, at approximately six o'clock in the evening, Dr. King was assassinated. His dream was to be a soldier for justice and freedom. That was what he wanted to be remembered for–that he had been a faithful servant and had answered his calling with all of his heart, soul, mind, and strength–that he had fought the good fight, even to giving his life. Finally, Dr. King had proven that the commitment and leadership of a single person can change the world.

SUMMARY

The findings of **common ground number seven** research substantiates that both Camus and King suffered unexpected death at an early age while at the height of their careers. Both men were in the process, according to their vocations, of working for justice, freedom and peace. Camus was in the midst of writing a major novel that probably would have shed light on his thought concerning the meaning of his poverty stricken beginnings and his family. One can also rationally assume at this point that Camus would have also addressed the issue of *a* peaceful and equal co-existence between the French and Algerians in his native land; and finally, due to Camus' humanitarian and moral views, there may have been some additional clarification on his views of Christianity. As for Dr. King, he was in the midst of leading a major protest in Memphis with additional plans to lead a "Poor People's March" to Washington, DC to highlight the issue of poverty among blacks and poor whites. The march would have taken place during the summer of 1968 and would have had as a goal the use of massive civil disobedience, to disrupt the operations of the federal government. The devastating civil disobedience that took place in Seattle, Washington, December 1-3, 1999, against the World Trade Organization is an example of what may have happened in the nation's capitol.

BOTH MEN BLACKLISTED FOR THEIR SOCIAL AND POLITICAL ACTIVISM.

Camus for his militant journalism, criticism, and editorial activism (in Algeria and France) King for leading boycotts, marches, political activism and speeches.

The findings for the above common ground will now be reported:

ALBERT CAMUS

While reporting for the socialist newspaper Alger-Republicain, Camus was censured for his editorial criticism of the brutal manner in which the French were discriminating against and subjugating the Arab mountain people. The French closed down the newspaper. In 1940, he was expelled from Algeria by the French government. He went to Paris where he began working for the newspaper, *Paris-Soir*.

Camus actively participated in the French Resistance against the Nazis, and during that time, he was the principal writer and editor for the underground newspaper, *Combat*. The newspaper was highly critical of Nazi occupation and atrocities in France, and, as such, was on the seek and destroy list of the German Gestapo. In other words, he was committed to the point of putting his life at risk for the causes of justice and freedom.

Camus was a staunch foe of Communism and totalitarianism and his opposition manifested itself in several ways. He refused to visit the Spain of Francisco Franco. He came under heavy criticism and censure from West European Communists for his support of the protesters in the 1953 East Berlin rioting. This rioting was a result of Russian Communist oppression and the strangling regulations and treatment meted out to the German citizens of that section of the city.

Camus was a friend of the insurgents in the 1956 uprising in Hungary that resulted from severe oppression of the Hungarian people by the Russian Communists. He made an appeal to other European writers to petition the United Nations to intervene. The UN did not respond, and he withdrew his support of the UN. Camus actions were highly criticized by the French Communist Party.

The greatest censure received by camus was in 1951 with the publication of his famous treatise on human rights, metaphysical, social and artistic revolt, *The Rebel*. The long essay was highly critical of the Communist Party and totalitarianism. Consequently, camus was ostracized and censured by fellow French intellectuals from both the right wing and left wing–writers, philosophers, and historians. Also, as a result of *The Rebel*, there was a split with his long-time friend and fellow writer, Jean-Paul Sartre. For Camus, this split was painful, and it was never healed.

DR. MARTIN LUTHER KING JR.

Because he was at the center of protest for change and transformation, Dr. King was a target of criticism and censure from the time that he became president of the Montgomery Improve ment Association in 1955. In the white community, he was the target of the Ku Klux Klan, who bombed his home in 1956, and who maintained an ongoing telephone harassment crunpaign. He was a target of the White Citizen's Council. He was the target of police departments, which trumped up charges to get him jailed. He was a target of the white clergy who accused him of being an outside agitator. He responded to all of them in his famous *Letter From Birmingham Jail*.

The Federal Bureau of Investigation (FBI) carried on a protracted effort of character assassination against Dr. King. He was accused of being a communist. His telephones were tapped, and his hotel rooms were illegally wired for electronic monitoring. News leaks to the media by the FBI attempted to malign his personal and sexual integrity. As to assassination, according to Melanson (1989), "the specter of assassination was all too familiar to King. FBI files catalogued no fewer than 50 threats against his life. In addition to threats from white hate groups and violence-prone individuals, King was well aware that the FBI was, as he put it, "out to break me" (2).

Dr. King was also accused by other Negro civil rights groups as being too intellectual and too tame to bring about changes in a hateful American racist culture. Four of these groups were the Congress of Racial Equality (Floyd McKissick), the Black Muslims (Malcolm X), the Student Nonviolent Coordinating Committee (Stokeley Carmichael), and the Black Panthers (Bobby Seale). It is my view that while these organizations had different approaches to solving the civil rights problems, their goal was the same: To free Negro Americans from years of oppression. Continuing this line of thinking, Carson (1998) quotes Malcolm X as saying: "If capitalistic Kennedy and communistic Krushchev can find something in common on which to form a United Front despite their tremendous ideological differences, it is a disgrace for Negro leaders not to be able to submerge our 'minor' differences in order to seek a common solution to a common problem posed by a common enemy" (45). At the height of the Vietnam War, King was heavily censured by both blacks and whites for his speeches and writings that criticized United States involvement in the war. He categorized the involvement of the United States as colonial racism, where American soldiers, especially blacks, were fighting and dying for a democracy that many did not have at home. His unyielding criticism of the Vietnam War caused a severe breech between him and the US government, as well as President Lyndon Johnson.

SUMMARY

The findings of **common ground number eight** research supports that both men were censured and put out of favor by significant others for their social and political activism. Both Camus and King, from their early professional years to the time of their deaths, were outspoken critics of social, political, and ethnic oppression. While this caused criticism and censure, they were never deterred from protesting injustice and seeking freedom from societal evils.

BOTH MEN TRANSCENDED BITTERNESS AND THE USE OF VIOLENCE AS A MEANS OF CORRECTING SOCIAL, POLITICAL, AND ECONOMIC EVILS.

The findings for the above common ground will now be reported:

ALBERT CAMUS

Camus did not believe in violence as a means of settling discord, disagreements, grievances, and arguments–between persons, between institutions, between ethnic groups or between nations. He believed that violence was counter productive and caused misunderstanding to escalate, cause more violence and not lead to reconciliation, or in any case, make it more difficult. Camus had a very keen respect and regard for human life. He did not believe in the violence of ethnic hatred, racism, or political assassinations as means of settling differences or seeking solutions to problems. During the Algerian crisis between the French and Arabs, he used the editorial pages of French newspapers to recommend peace plans that would bring a halt to the violence in his native land. Further, he traveled to Algeria in January of 1956 in an attempt to bring about a truce in the hostilities. His trip was unsuccessful, however, due to the deeply entrenched fear, distrust, and hatred coming from both camps.

Camus deplored the violence of economic exploitation by one group of another. Therefore, he took strong issue with the manner that the French colonialists took advantage of the Arab workers. Camus was definitely against war as a means of settling disputes. He takes the violence of war and its side effects to task with his thoughts in *The Plague* (1947). He had seen the ravages of war and, beyond a doubt, had concluded that it was inhumane and far below the dignity and intelligence of civilized human beings.

In regard to Vietnam, Camus had also seen the French government and military involved in a bitter and deadly colonial war against the Communist led Vietminh and Ho Chi Minh. This war lasted eight years. The French military finally withdrew after a devastating defeat by the Vietminh at the battle of Dien Bien Phu in 1954. This was another blow against colonialist oppression by a people seeking freedom. Beyond a doubt, recovering from World War II, and fighting in two colonial wars–one in Algeria and the other in Vietnam–had drained the French government, the military, and the people. Wars had not solved any problems for the French, but had left them in social, political, and economic disarray. *The Rebel* in 1951 had addressed the issue human civility, the value and meaning of human life and a stem condemnation of totalitarianism. As a result, Camus was bitterly attacked from all sides, even though France was involved in two colonial wars. It is possible that Camus' six year writer silence, 1951-1957, could have been born from this renunciation and confusion about so called rational human beings concept of truth and right. Evidently, he needed a time to regroup.

Camus saw capital punishment as another form of violence that has been legalized by today's civil codes. He was against capital punishment as a deterrent to crime and rather pointed out the capriciousness of capital punishment in *The Stranger* (1941) where the main character is sentenced to die not so much for the crime of murder as for the disrespect of and non conformity to societal norms.

Camus did not succumb to negative attitudes that result in the violence of nihilism and the absurd. He explored these points in three of his works: *The Myth of Sisyphus* (1942), *The Misunderstanding* (1944), and *Caligula* (1945). He concluded that nihilism and the absurd neither solve problems nor give the positive directions that are necessary for happiness in human survival. Therefore, they are not viable options.

Philip Thody (1962) states that "Camus infinitely preferred the attitude of Gandhi, whom he described as 'the greatest man of our time' to that of any orthodox Communist or violent nationalist. It was Gandhi, he later said, who showed that it was possible to fight for one's people without ever losing the world's respect, and whose policy of passive resistance he would undoubtedly have liked to see applied by the Algerian nationalists" (200).

DR. MARTIN LUTHER KING JR.

Dr. King did not believe in violence as a means of settling discord, disagreements, grievances, and arguments–between persons, between institutions, between ethnic groups, or between nations. Dr. King felt strongly that violence does not bring about, love, hope, and reconciliation–the common denominators that all peoples strive for.

Dr. King was a proponent of Mahatma Gandhi's theory of nonviolence. He believed in suffering and sacrifice in order to achieve reconciliation with opponents. To avoid violence, Dr. King believed in returning good for evil, rather than fight violence with violence. He felt that the law of violent revenge hinders freedom in society and deepens cleavages between people rather than bring them together. Dr. King used the power of love as a viable force for social reform and large scale societal transformation, because he felt that love was the only effective counter force to hate.

Dr. King taught his followers to avoid external physical violence as well as internal violence of the spirit. His position was that either type of violence created more problems than it solved, and that violence never brings permanent peace.

War, for Dr. King, was another form of violence that ought not be tolerated in the name of freedom, brotherhood, and civilized society. The war in Vietnam was a devastating example of the evil and violence of the times that brought people, especially the young, to the realization that world annihilation could be an instant reality through the use of nuclear weapons. These weapons were ready for use at anytime by the Americans or the Communist backed forces. Nonviolence, on the other hand, produces a new self-respect on the part of the oppressed and pricks the attitude of justice in the oppressor causing a change for reconciliation and solidarity. Nonviolence has brought about more change with less loss of life than all the violent riots of the past, because nonviolence has reconciliation and brotherhood as its goal.

Finally, Dr. King felt that the study of using nonviolence in all areas of human conflict must be given the same diligent consideration as studying the strategies of modem warfare.

SUMMARY

The findings of **common ground number nine** research supports that both Camus and King transcended the use of violence as a means of correcting social, political, and economic evils. Neither Albert Camus nor Dr. Martin Luther King Jr. believed in violence as a means of settling discord, disagreements, grievances and arguments—between persons, between institutions, between ethnic groups or between nations. Both men had a great respect for the value of human life and took strong stands against any evil or violence that would hinder the exercise of freedom for any individual. Camus was concerned about the violence in his native Algeria between the French and Arabs. Internal terrorism, strife, and even torture had gone on already for over one hundred years.

Dr. Martin Luther King Jr. started his civil rights struggle with the strategy of nonviolence. From his first involvement with the boycott in Montgomery, Alabama, to Albany, Georgia, to Selma, Alabama, To Birmingham, Alabama, to Washington, DC, to New York, to Cleveland, to Chicago, to the fateful rendezvous at Memphis, Tennessee. His major course of action was militant nonviolence. This was his weapon of choice due to the fact that he felt it was the only way that an oppressed people could neutralize and win over the methods, guns, and hatred of the oppressor. In his own personal living, Dr. King harbored no bitterness or violence towards the people and institutions against which he was struggling. He was a warrior for justice, peace and freedom.

BOTH MEN WERE FROM COUNTRIES WHERE ETHNIC GROUPS WERE EXPLOITED AND OPPRESSED.

The findings for the above common ground will now be reported:

ALBERT CAMUS

The writings of Camus reflect the thoughts of revolt and freedom from the time of his earliest writings in the 1930s, where he challenges the treatment of Arabs in Algeria, by the French colonialist settlers. The French settled in Algeria in 1830. The local Arabs never accepted French Colonial rule. Consequently, there was struggle over governance between the French and the native Arabs of Algeria that lasted from 1832 to 1962. Arabs were not allowed to hold any public office. Unrest among the Arabs was due to poor living conditions, humiliation, discrimination, unemployment, resentment against French rule, the loss of land and inheritance. In 1954, the discontent of the Arab Algerians erupted into widespread revolt. The Algerian rebel forces used guerrilla tactics to sabotage and terrorize the French military, civilians and the colonial infrastructure. It was not until 1964 that the Algerian crisis was settled and the hostilities ceased. The Algerians were granted independence by the French. However, the Algerian natives had paid the price in blood for their freedom.

To restate another point from the literature, evidently the Arab natives were not the only persons suffering discrimination as a result of French colonialism. In mainland France, Camus makes the observation that the French born in Algeria are looked upon as the Jews of France (Todd 1996). This appears to mean that the Algerian French are treated as outsiders and may not have the same opportunities and access as the French born in France.

DR. MARTIN LUTHER KING JR.

The exploitation and oppression of Negroes began when they were captured in West Africa and brought to America as slaves. The practice of slavery continued from 1619 until the Emancipation Proclamation of 1863. This was for a period of two hundred and forty-four years. Freedom did not come with the Emancipation Proclamation, nor did exploitation and oppression cease. In fact, the second class citizenship, or no citizenship, for Negroes continued into the Twentieth Century as a result of the Plessy Vs Ferguson ruling of the United States Supreme Court in 1898. This ruling stated in essence that Negroes had no rights that white people had to respect. Thus, the floodgates of Jim Crowism, brutalities, murder, discrimination, and injustices were meted out against American Negroes with impunity by any white person who had the desire. Racism became an ingrained part of American culture that was still very much in effect when Dr. King came onto the civil rights scene in Montgomery in 1955. The Native American Indian's plight was no better. This long history of human exploitation, injustice, and discrimination, with all of their divisive ramifications, served as the reality and foundation for the struggle that King was called to lead.

SUMMARY

The findings of **common ground number ten** research supports that both men were from countries where ethnic groups were exploited and oppressed. In the case of Albert Camus, Algerian Arabs as well as Algerian poor whites were exploited and oppressed for over one hundred thirty-four years by French colonialism. For Dr. King American Negroes were exploited and oppressed for more than two hundred forty-four years, and the struggle continues even today. There continues to be incidents in America that are clearly motivated by race.

TWO MAJOR CONTRASTS

Ten common ground similarities between Camus and King have been documented and presented for this report. I wish now to investigate two major contrasts from which the two men viewed revolt and freedom: (1), the domain of religion, and (2), the problem of pain and suffering.

1. *The Domain of Religion:*
   - Camus has been labeled as both an atheist and an agnostic moralist.
   - King was a called-by-God preacher, theologian, and Christian.

The findings for the above contrast will now be reported:

ALBERT CAMUS

Camus embraced a humanism that called upon human beings to help each other. For him, there was no omnipotent being to help fight battles or remove obstacles. The struggle to gain freedom and justice was in the hands of human beings. Camus had had early contact with religion, both in his home and at school. However, he could not see visible benefits of the faith. His view was that the absolutes offered by religion such as: love, hope, goodness, honor, brotherhood, respect for life, and happiness had all been grossly abused, dishonored, and cast aside—and more often than not in the name of some religion that was supposed to bring about a better world. As a writer and person, Camus believed passionately in these absolutes but that it was up to human beings to bring them into reality. Therefore, he opted to deal in the concrete of feeling, experience, seeing and the tangible (Cruickshank 1978: 37). Thus, the literature of Camus' generation is one of skepticism that advocated the general rejection of customary beliefs.

Camus was of the point of view that man had arrived at that point in history where he was being confronted with injustices on every side, and the relevant question that he is raising is that if God is a good, loving, and omnipotent God, how can he allow all the evil and oppression to exist in the world and among people? Camus was convinced that it was up to him, individually, and working collectively with others, to revolt and create freedom. The time and moments that people possessed were in their hands to either make a difference or succumb to nihilism.

The Plague (1947), a book that reflected so much innocent suffering was his strongest indictment against Christianity. Camus felt that humans must continue to be the master of their own condition in the face of God, while seeking a better world founded on fraternity, justice, brotherhood, and solidarity. His faith was based on the tangible and not on the unseen hope of Christianity. Camus rejected the belief of life after death, because it was a phenomena that he was unable to know and experience. Therefore, on his terms, he could not accept after life as real.

Camus did not subscribe to a faith in the unseen, because faith is not concrete and tangible. His uncertainty did not make him an atheist. Thomas Hanna (1962) in Brée, eds., states that "although Camus is anti-Communist, he is not an anti-Christian—he is simply a non Christian" (49). During his lifetime, Camus had many friends who were devout Christians; and he respected them and held them in high esteem.

It is interesting to note that Camus' work reflected an ongoing dialogue with Christian metaphor and language. This is evident from the title of his master's thesis which was **"Christian Metaphysics and Neoplatonism,"** to the name of his last completed novel, *The Fall* (of humans from grace to universal guilt), to the name of the main character in that novel which is Jean-Baptist Clamence (John the Baptist), to the watery background (baptism) of the novel around the canals of Amsterdam, where the novel takes place, to the title of the work found after his death, *The First Man* (Adam).

While Camus did not subscribe to the statutes of Christianity, he, nonetheless, maintained an almost mystical admiration and union with the beauty, splendor, and majesty of the North African and Mediterranean outdoors and landscapes. He had a great admiration for creation. The beauty of the world appears on the brink of being a person in some of his works.

DR. MARTIN LUTHER KING JR.

Dr. King was a Christian who believed in the God of Abraham, Isaac, and Jacob, the Prophets, the Disciples, Jesus Christ, and the Holy Spirit. Dr. King believed in an omnipotent, omniscient, and omnipresent God who, through supernatural powers, worked in the lives of human beings for their good. Dr. King believed that in order to achieve integration and equality that Negroes must be inspired through faith and hope in a cause that was empowered by the Holy Spirit to bring about justice and freedom.

In his book *Strength to Love* (1963), Dr. King presents fifteen sermons that contain his penetrating and God inspired beliefs concerning love, justice, goodness, human equality, and the elimination of social evils. Further, the fifteen sermons contain the basic tenets of his thoughts on revolt, nonviolence, and freedom. His belief was that theology must walk step by step with social change.

Dr. King felt that the institutional white church in America, with few exceptions, had turned its head in silence away from a confrontation with racism. More explicitly, the white church had abandoned its duty to take the lead in areas of encouraging obedience to the laws, fairness, positive attitudes and good will towards all peoples. Dr. King referred to these important moral phenomena as "issues of the heart" that bring about societal reconciliation and transformation.

Non-conformity, according to Dr. King is the true mark of a Christian. The Christian must be willing to stand alone in revolt while seeking freedom. A higher loyalty to everything that is good, right, and just calls the Christian to conviction rather than conformity and consensus.

Dr. King believed with a passion that we must see each other as human beings first, with race, sex, origin, religion, economic status, etc., as distant seconds. Otherwise, humans become "things" that are depersonalized and devalued. Dr. King believed that to forgive those who have oppressed and transgressed upon your humanity is the purest test of Christian love. This is what Jesus did while being crucified. Forgiveness is an ongoing attitude that gives freedom of spirit, freedom of response, and freedom of feeling to the Christian.

Dr. King continued by stating that the Holy Bible was written to teach against moral and intellectual blindness. The Christian church and Christians are responsible for the continual providing of enlightenment to the world that comes from the study of the Word of God. When the truths of the Word are manifest in the hearts and thoughts of human beings, there will be an end to such inhumane acts as war, slavery, discrimination, ethnic exclusion, racism, and concentration camps.

Dr. King made it very clear that Christianity does not protect us from the pain and agony of moral existence. The Christian's life is not a steady stream of untroubled bliss. On the contrary, Christianity has always meant that difficult times and disappointments are part of the agonizing tension that comes with the territory. It is difficulty, hardship, and struggle that cause the Christian to grow into a new and better type of human being. This growth for the better will not take place when life has been an ongoing experience of easy, obstacle free living.

Finally, Dr. King believed that it is *agape* love that liberates the Christian to an internal and external freedom that non-Christians cannot understand. *Agape* love is caring for and loving (not only your friends) but those who hate and oppress you, without expecting any good thing in return.

SUMMARY

The findings of **major contrast one** research shows that the two men were, indeed, different in the domain of religion. Stated succinctly, Camus did not embrace the existence of an omnipotent being who was able to give providential help in difficulties. Albert Camus believed that the future of human beings was up to them, that there was no transcendent being, and that human life existed in terms of the reality of what could be experienced and known, and that the extent of life was what people experienced here on earth. Camus believed in the human attributes of love, brotherhood, goodness, justice, compassion, freedom, and the elimination of the evils of oppression in the world, but that these are accomplished by humans coming together in solidarity of purpose rather than their coming from any other source.

Dr. King, on the other hand, believed that there was a Supreme Being who was at the center of all life, and, was able to intervene on behalf of human kind and sustain believers through life's struggles, uncertainties, failures and disappointments. Dr. King believed that life on this earth is not the end of humans, but that there is eternal life to those who hope, have faith, and are obedient to the teachings of the God of all creation. Dr. King believed that love for other human beings is the central defining attribute that will bring reconciliation among peoples of the world; that love can overcome hate because love is the stronger force; and that it is our love for one another that will ultimately bring the freedom and justice that every human being seeks.

1. ***The problem of pain and suffering***
   - Camus believed that God does not help or alleviate our pain and suffering even when the result of a good cause.
   - King believed that pain and suffering for righteousness and innocence were redemptive and perfecting.

The findings of the above contrast will now be reported:

ALBERT CAMUS

Camus reveals God, as he does in *The Plague* (1947), as unresponsive and indifferent to the pain and sufferings of human beings—as in the case of the ten year old Orthon boy who dies in innocence while suffering a painful death from the bubonic plague. Camus does not believe that God responds to the prayers and supplications of the righteous—as seen in the prayers of Father Paneloux, the Jesuit priest in· *The Plague*. In fact, by the end of the book, Father Paneloux, himself, dies of the plague, even though he has given of himself to alleviate the suffering of others afflicted with the deadly disease. So God does not answer Paneloux' prayers for others nor does God spare the life of one of his chosen and anointed. The same is true with the character Tarrou who has given of himself as a tireless servant to help others in the local fight against the plague. He too is infected, suffers, and dies. The medical doctor Bernard Rieux takes, what appears to be position of Camus, in regards to the suffering of innocent children and good people when Rieux tells Father Paneloux that there is no way that he could ever accept the suffering of innocence by a loving God.

Camus shows the same type of indifference on the part of God in *The Misunderstanding* (1944). At the end of the play when Maria is vocally agonizing over the murder of her husband and cries out to God to help her, the old servant, who is symbolic of God, answers, "No" (254).

DR. MARTIN LUTHER KING JR.

Dr. King believed that unearned pain and suffering for righteousness and as a result of innocence are redemptive and perfecting. He believed, further, that Negroes with their historical capacity for suffering, for Christian love, understanding, and good will, may be God's instrument for bringing about peace and survival to Western civilization and the nations of the world.

Dr. King viewed personal difficulties as opportunities to strengthen Christian commitment and bring a person closer to God, and consequently make that individual a stronger person. In *The Trumpet of Conscience,* Dr. King gives what he considers the Christian view on the suffering of the righteous: "We are gravely mistaken to think that religion protects us from the pain and agony of moral existence. Life is not a euphoria of unalloyed comfort and untroubled ease. Christianity has always insisted that the cross we bear precede the crown we wear. To be a Christian, one must take up his cross, with all its difficulties and agonizing and tension packed content, and carry it until that very cross leaves its mark upon us and redeems us to that more excellent way which comes only through suffering" (24-25). So the views of these two men on suffering comes through in stark contrast as they reflect agnosticism and Christianity. However, in each case, they maintain the attitude of being servants.

SUMMARY

The findings of **major contrast two** research reveals several recurring themes regarding the problem of pain and suffering in the thought of Camus and King which will be summarized here. Camus does not see God as an omnipotent being who is concerned about the pain and suffering of human beings, whether those human beings are good or evil. He feels that God does not prevent pain or suffering, so he must allow it to happen. Camus cannot rationalize that God answers prayers when the good and innocent are overcome by disease and the calamities of nature just as those who are vessels of evil, oppression, and injustice. Dr. King, on the other hand, believed that suffering and pain causes human beings to grow from ordinary people to, in many cases, extraordinary people. King thought that an uninterrupted life of ease without obstacles, difficulties, disappointments, or hardships produces an individual who is selfish, soft, uncaring, and easily manipulated. King points out that the Bible is full of mediocre personalities, including the Prophets and the Disciples, who after extreme trial, suffering, and overcoming, became great achievers because of their faith and obedience to God.

CHAPTER FIVE

SUMMARY AND CONCLUSIONS

THIS CHAPTER WILL SUMMARIZE THE FINDINGS OF THIS study; a discussion of the findings will be presented and interpreted, and conclusions will be presented.

Restatement of the Problem:

A Comparison of the Concepts of Revolt and Freedom in the Thinking of Albert Camus and Martin Luther King, Jr.

SUMMARY OF CHAPTER ONE

Chapter One of this research has covered the following content:

1. **The Introduction** which established the historical as well as the current context of the study.

2. **The Statement of the Problem** which identified revolt and freedom as the defining comparative literature concepts through which the works of Camus and King would be interpreted. The concepts of revolt and freedom were

presented using the novel, short story, philosophical essay, drama, and essay for Camus, while these concepts were presented using the essay for King.

3. **The Purpose of the Study** was to present and comparatively examine the ideas and visions of two highly acclaimed human rights champions whose lives, work and thoughts were worthy of Nobel Prize awards. This particular comparative study of the thought of these two men has not yet been undertaken by scholars in the field. The current study proposes to address this gap in our knowledge.

4. **The Importance of the Study** was to examine and interpret the messages that Camus and King brought forth in addressing the human condition problems of their times and ours. These problems weigh negatively on the lives and consciences of humankind. These problems include oppression, tyranny, injustice, murder, racism, war, persecution, greed, and holocaust.

5. **The Basic Assumptions** of the study have addressed the components that propose to synthesize the major issues in a manner that adds clarity for the reader. Four basic assumptions were given.

6. **The Delimitation's** have been presented in order to provide the particular parameters that will guide and control the investigation. This is necessary inasmuch as ·numerous studies have been written on both men. There will be many opportunities and possibilities to continue investigation into other relevant areas in the future.

7. **The Definition of Terms** has been provided in order to define frequently used terms in the study. These definitions give consistent interpretations to key words and concepts for the reader.

SUMMARY OF CHAPTER TWO

This chapter was divided into three sections as follow:

1. The review, using primary and secondary sources, of literature pertaining to the key writings, speeches, sayings and life of Albert Camus. This review was done using a comparative analysis approach. The focus of this review has been revolt and freedom.

2. The review, using primary and secondary sources, of literature pertaining to the key writings, speeches, sayings and life of Dr. Martin Luther King, Jr. The review was done using a comparative analysis approach. The focus of this review has been revolt and freedom.

3. The Nobel Speeches given by the two men have also been critiqued and presented as important primary source references to their thought. This was done in order to show their points of view in such key areas as brotherhood, human rights, optimism and nihilism, the meaning of civilization, and the importance significant others. These are critical areas that are allied with freedom and revolt and I wanted to capture this relationship using their own words on the important occasion of the Nobel award.

Finally, in doing the literature review, I have consulted sources from the 1960s through the 1990s to inform this research report. I have endeavored to corroborate over a forty year span, using the best authorities, what has been written about these two men concerning revolt and freedom. Therefore, it appears that in responding to the difficult and uncertain human conditions of his times as an agnostic, the writings of Camus reflect a humanistic and moral revolt for freedom, peace, equality, solidarity, and brotherhood as the answer to these problems. He presents his writings to the reading public using literary genres that include, the novel, the short story, the essay, the philosophical essay, and the play. As to Dr. King, it appears that in responding to the Negro human conditions of segregation and discrimination as a Christian, the writings and activism of King reflect a revolt for freedom based on militant nonviolence. He presents his writings to the reading public using the essay. The ultimate vision of King was the coming together of people into the **beloved community**. Both men are on common ground concerning human value, justice, equality, human dignity and brotherhood. Both men were in accord that neither nihilism nor violence would bring long range solutions to the spiritual, social, economic, and political problems of the world now or in the future. However, it appears that they are suggesting that healing and peace for future generations would come about as a result of people recognizing when there are plagues in their midst and forming the fronts of solidarity to destroy them. Peace will be difficult to achieve until these concepts become the main agenda of France, America and the nations of the world.

SUMMARY OF CHAPTER THREE

The methodology used for this qualitative study was a critical comparative analysis of ten areas of common ground between the two writers. Two significant areas of contrast were also compared. The focus on common ground was from two perspectives: first of all the common ground that identified parallel or similar social, historical, professional, and political experiences in the lives of these men was discussed. Secondly, a comparative literary analysis was made comparing their concepts of freedom and revolt. A third area of common ground, in the literary domain, was the comparison of how the two men used the essay genre to present ideas and concepts. The review of literature did not show any comparative study made between Camus and King. This study has explored, analyzed, and developed new information to fill the gap in the field of comparative literature. A listing of the ten similar and two contrasting common grounds have been given previously. See pages 109-111 for this listing.

The comparison and contrast methodology was used in order to give a very close and analytical examination of Camus and Dr. King. Relevant commonalties were sought out in their works, lives, and thinking. What was the message that they left for these times and future generations concerning truth, justice, freedom, and the human reconciliation? Attributes such as these were their concern and are still begging for solutions by the people of the world today.

My perspective in this research has been to discover how comparison and contrast would best clarify and interpret the thought of these two men. Consequently, I have been able to determine what something is and what something is not. Stating again a basic premise of comparison/contrast methodology: the true essence of a writer's work and thought are brought out when they are compared with a similar work and thought or contrasted with similar work and thought. I have given points of history and background on the use of this research methodology in Chapter Three. Certainly, there are other areas that could have been involved in this research. These may be covered with future investigation.

Pursuing the theoretical context of comparative literature, I have endeavored to compare background influences, ideas, genres, point of view, detail, themes, approaches to solutions of problems, needs, and concerns of the human condition. The ultimate purpose of common grounds methodology used in this report was to select those similarities and differences, which formed the basis of the research problem.

SUMMARY OF CHAPTER FOUR

The findings and results for Chapter Four were based on the comparative analysis and interpretation of the common grounds of Chapter Three. As a result of this common ground analysis, I have presented the results and findings as factually as possible—as they were recorded in primary and secondary sources. Based on these findings, it can be stated that Camus and King had numerous common grounds in their social, educational, professional, and historical lives. These common grounds were discussed and interpreted based on literature search findings. Likewise, two major differences that were relevant to their thought and perspective have been closely examined and the findings presented. From these comparisons/contrasts and common grounds, the messages to the reader and to the world from these two men have been concluded. Additional information on these common ground findings will now be given.

SUMMARY OF COMMON GROUND FINDINGS

The findings of **common ground number one** substantiate that the problem of historical and current injustice in the world was a major theme in the writings of both Camus and King. While the two men viewed the terrain from different perspectives—Camus from one of humanistic agnosticism and King from that of a devout Christian—they both came together concerning the need to fight against societal evils such as: injustice, racism, oppression, poverty, murder, colonialism, exploitation of the poor, political tyranny, and war. This being the case, they were both in search of ways and means to heal and reconcile these problems for the good of human kind everywhere.

The findings of **common ground number two** research support the idea that revolt and freedom were catalysts in the writings and thought of Albert Camus and Dr. Martin Luther King, Jr. The writings of Camus reflect the thought of revolt from the time of his earliest writings in the 1930s where he challenges the treatment of Arabs in Algeria, North Africa by the French colonialist settlers. He continues to address revolt and freedom in his later writings from the points of view of metaphysical and historical rebellion. He makes it clear that rebellion and freedom are two sides of the same coin. Where there is revolt, human beings are making the statement that they are weary and tired of oppression and injustice and that they are ready to stand up to fight, and even die, for their freedom. The Algerian liberation fight for freedom from

French colonialism in the late 50s and early 60s as well as the struggle of the French Underground fighting for freedom from Nazi atrocities and oppression served as participatory as well as eye witness background for some of Camus' key writings.

Dr. Martin Luther King, Jr., in a like manner, fighting for the freedom of oppressed Negroes, lived in a perpetual state of revolt all of his life, as does every Afro-American. Due to the historical plague of racism in America, with all of its negative manifestations, revolt and the struggle for freedom are as second nature to Negroes as to any ethnic people anywhere in the world. King responded to the civil rights call in by being present at a meeting of time and place that thrust him into the forefront of the Negro revolt for freedom. He remained at the head of the struggle for thirteen years–traveling, speaking, writing, and protesting. He lived with the full knowledge that his life was at risk daily. Ultimately, in 1968, he did give his life for the cause of freedom in America and around the world. He had come to Memphis, Tennessee to lead a march protesting the unequal treatment being received by garbage workers.

The findings of **common ground number three** support the fact Camus and King were chosen for the composite impact of their work. Both men have addressed several relevant issues that will continue to be paramount in the lives and thinking of rational and well meaning people in the free world. Moreover, Camus and King recognized the importance of human solidarity working in the name of good in order to bring about justice and freedom in society. This is the impact that they wanted their works to have, and according to the secondary sources in this research report, it is, indeed, the impact that their work has had in the past and will continue to have in the future.

The findings of **common ground number four** are supported by research evidence concerning Camus and King being the best in their professions when they were chosen for their respective Nobel awards. Albert Camus was awarded the Nobel Prize for Literature in 1957 for his composite writings, "Which brings to light the problems which weigh on the consciences of men during our times." The success of his writings, from generation to generation, speaks for itself. Fifty years later, his writings continue to be among the most widely read of any writer of the Twentieth Century. At least two of his books have been on the best seller list for over forty-five years. He remains one of the most discussed authors in Twentieth Century French Literature classes. In the domain of twentieth Century world. literature, he is, likewise, at the top of the list of preferred authors.

Additional popularity of Camus' works have come about as a result of the fall of the Communist powers in Eastern Europe. During his lifetime, Camus was a staunch and bitter opponent of Communist totalitarianism and predicted its demise. This stance brought criticism from many literary friends who were supporters of the Communist Party in France. The passage of time has vindicated the truth of his views and earned new interest and respect for his writings.

Dr. Martin Luther King, Jr. was awarded the Nobel Prize for Peace in 1964 for his leadership in the American civil rights struggle that had as its goal the obtaining of freedom for twenty two million American Negro citizens who had been denied their equal rights for over three hundred and fifty years. He has given a legacy to generations past and present concerning the meaning of true commitment to freedom and human rights. He was an inspiration to the young and old from every walk of life. He infused the lives of people of all races with hope, power, justice, and brotherhood, because he represented the excellency of the best in human nature.

Consequently, the respect and recognition given to Dr. King during his lifetime and since his death have been overwhelming and attest to the value that people place upon the meaning of his life and work. Thirty-three countries have postage stamps with his likeness on them. In memory of his work, various tributes of all types, from around the world, have been established. He is the idol of many from all races, ages, religions, professions, and socio economic groups.

The quality and durability of the messages, achievements, and legacies of Camus and King have stood the test of time and support these conclusions. Right thinking people of the world continue to lift them up, and they continue to gain prominence with the passing of each new generation.

The findings of **common ground number five** research support that Camus and King lived during similar historical moments and world problems. Both men were witnesses to the grievous consequences of several wars, which resulted in the death, exploitation, oppression, and displacement of people. Both _men deplored the political and economical victimization caused by colonialism. Both men were outspoken advocates of justice and freedom for colonialized people, and they stood up and spoke out in every way possible for the underdog.

The findings of **common ground number six** research support that both men were members of organizations that were founded for purposes of combating and eliminating oppression, injustice, and exploitation. Camus was a principal figure in the French underground movement. Dr. King was involved and played a key role in both the Montgomery Improvement Association and the Southern Christian Leadership Association, But just as importantly, Camus and King were men of courage whose writings and positions did not always please the status quo. However, they were not allies to truth according to consensus. They dared to stand alone for what they thought to be right and just.

The findings of **common ground number seven** research substantiates that both Camus and King suffered unexpected death at an early age while at the height of their careers. Both men were in the process, according to their vocations, of working for justice, freedom and peace. Camus was in the midst of writing a major novel that probably would have shed light on his thought concerning the meaning of his poverty stricken beginnings and his family. It is also possible that Camus may have addressed his latest views on the Algerian crisis between the French and Arabs and finally, due to Camus' moral views, there may have been some additional clarification on his views of Christianity. As for Dr. King, he was in the midst of leading a major protest in Memphis with additional plans to lead a "Poor People's March" to Washington, D.C. to highlight the issue of poverty among blacks and poor whites. The march would have taken place during the summer of 1968.

The findings of **common ground number eight** research support that both men were censured and put out of favor by significant others for their literary, social, and political activism. Both Camus and King, from their early professional years to the time of their deaths, were outspoken critics of social, political, and ethnic oppression. While this caused criticism and censure, they were never deterred from protesting injustice and seeking freedom from societal evils.

The findings of **common ground number nine** research supports that both Camus and King transcended bitterness and the use of violence as a means of correcting social, political, and economic evils. Neither Albert Camus nor Dr. Martin Luther King, Jr. believed in violence as a means of settling discord, disagreements, grievances and arguments—between persons, between institutions, between ethnic groups or between nations. Both men had a great respect for the value of human life and took strong stands against any evil or violence that would hinder the exercise of freedom for any individual. Both men believed in the teachings of Mahatma Gandhi. Camus was concerned about the violence in his native Algeria between the French and Arabs. Internal terrorism, strife, and even torture had gone on already for over one hundred years. Camus' hope was for a peaceful reconciliation that supported a co-existence for both sides. Camus was a personal witness to the violence of World War II, both in North Africa and France. He raised his pen and voice against the violent oppression of the Franco dictatorship in Spain, from 1936-1939. In order to help bring an end to the violence of war in France, he worked as a participant and writer in the French Resistance underground against Nazism. Camus was an outspoken critic of the violence being caused by Communist totalitarianism and political oppression in Eastern Europe.

Dr. Martin Luther King, Jr. started his civil rights struggle with the strategy of nonviolence. From his first involvement with the boycott in Montgomery, Alabama, to Albany, Georgia, to Selma, Alabama, To Birmingham, Alabama, to Washington, DC, to New York, to Cleveland, to Chicago, to the fateful rendezvous at Memphis, Tennessee, his major course of action was militant nonviolence. This was his weapon of choice due to the fact that he felt it was the only way that an oppressed people could neutralize and win over the methods, guns, and hatred of the oppressor. In his own personal living, Dr. King harbored no bitterness or violence towards the people and institutions against which he was struggling. He was a warrior for justice, peace and freedom.

The findings of **common ground number ten** research support that both men were from countries where ethnic groups were exploited and oppressed. In the case of Albert Camus, Algerian natives were exploited and oppressed for over one hundred thirty-four years by French colonialism. As a native Algerian, Camus was sensitive to this discrimination against persons from his country. For Dr. King American Negroes were exploited and oppressed for more than two hundred forty-four years. Native American Indians have also felt the bitter sting of racism. The struggle continues even today, as there continue to be incidents in America that are clearly motivated by racism.

TWO MAJOR CONTRASTS

Ten common ground similarities between Camus and King were documented and presented for this report. There were also findings concerning two major contrasts from which the two men viewed revolt and freedom: (1), the domain of religion, and (2), the problem of pain and suffering.

The findings of **major contrast one** research shows that the two men were quite different in the domain of religion. Camus did not embrace the existence of an omnipotent being who was able to give providential help in difficulties. Albert Camus believed that the future of human beings was up to them, that there was no transcendent being, and that human life existed in terms of the reality of what could be experienced and known. Further, he believed that the extent of life was what people experienced here on earth. Camus believed in the human attributes of love, brotherhood, goodness, justice, compassion, freedom, and the elimination of the evils of oppression in the world, but that these things are accomplished by humans coming together in solidarity of purpose rather than their coming from any other source.

According to Woelfel (1975), "Camus' "church" is of course the human community. Its substance and reality are not the person of Christ but the solidarity of persons in their common life and suffering. Its catholicity is its universal extension in time and space embracing all human beings of all periods and places. Its apostles and saints are those persons everywhere who lead the revolt against the many plagues that beset man for the sake of that life which is uniquely human. Its summary of the law is those values that inhere in the solidarity of our condition and come to light through rebellion against injustice: life, dignity, freedom, knowledge, beauty, happiness" (114).

Dr. King, on the other hand, believed that there was a Supreme Being who was at the center of all life, and, was able to intervene on behalf of human kind and sustain believers through life's struggles, uncertainties, failures and disappointments. Dr. King believed that life on this earth is not the end of humans, but that there is eternal life to those who hope, have faith, and are obedient to the teachings of the God of all creation. Dr. King believed that love for other human beings is the central defining attribute that will bring reconciliation among peoples of the world; that love can overcome hate because love is the stronger force; and that it is our love for one another that will ultimately bring the freedom and justice that every human being seeks.

MAJOR CONTRASTS

The findings of **major contrast one** research supports this difference in the domain of religion in the writings of Camus and King. Basically, Camus sees human beings as the sole provider for their destiny. There is no transcendent being to assist with the problems, hardships, and difficulties of life. Camus feels that the only reality he knows in the realm of faith is what he can feel, see, and experience; he believed that it is the solidarity brought about by revolt against the plagues of the world that brings about justice and freedom.

Dr. King, following his seminary tradition, believed that there is an omnipotent God who created the universe, its inhabitants, and manages the orderly existence of the world. King believes that human beings working in solidarity with an all powerful and knowing God will bring about justice and freedom in the healing of the plagues of world. The solidarity of revolt by people of goodwill will be the means through which change occurs.

Both men were firm believers in the human attributes of love, goodness, justice, compassion, freedom, and the elimination of oppression.

The findings of **major contrast two** research reveals several recurring themes regarding the problem of pain and suffering in the thought of Camus and King which will be summarized here. Camus does not see God as an omnipotent being who is concerned about the pain anci suffering of human beings. He feels that God does not prevent pain or suffering that is inflicted by others or by natural disaster; so if he is an omnipotent being, he must allow it to happen. Camus cannot rationalize that God answers prayers when the good and innocent are overcome by disease and the calamities of nature just as those who are vessels of evil, oppression, and injustice.

Camus' view of suffering and pain, as presented by Woelfel (1975), is that the Christian attitude of acceptance of pain and suffering in the expectation of a better world yet to come is a hope that no one has ever verified as existing. In fact, Camus is bothered by the Christian tendency to accept passively the sufferings and pain of the human condition brought on by the evil of other human beings. Therefore, Christians would allow God to fight the battle of human suffering and death as seen in the incarnation, while awaiting an after life of bliss if they would just trust and obey. This Christian view of human condition reality "has all to easily provided a rationalization for passivity and fatalism in the face of injustice and death. The person… always run the risk of accepting plagues instead of resisting them, on the grounds that God has willed them, endured them, and eternally transfigured them" (121-122). Consequently, Camus sees too many Christians as allies to an attitude of letting things work themselves out, when, in fact, they are the ones who have to accomplish the working out within the context of solidarity brought on by revolt against these conditions.

Dr. King, conversely, believed that suffering and pain causes human beings to grow from ordinary people to, in many cases, extraordinary people. King thought that an uninterrupted life of ease without obstacles, difficulties, disappointments, or hardships produces an individual who is selfish, soft, uncaring, and easily manipulated. King points out that the Bible is full of mediocre personalities who after extreme trial, suffering, and overcoming became great achievers because of their faith and obedience to God. King is an example himself of a person who believed totally in the omnipotence of God as creator and sustainer of the order and beauty in the universe. However, his view, as brought out in all of his writings, · was that human beings cannot stand still and wait on God to fight every battle, but rather, human beings must do all that they can and look to God as an all knowing ally and provider who is on the side of justice and right. King does not believe the life of the Christian is one of ease and bliss. To the contrary, he has stated that: "We are gravely mistaken to think that religion protects us from the pain and agony of moral existence. Life is not a euphoria of unalloyed comfort and untroubled ease. Christianity has always insisted that the cross we bear precede the crown we wear. To be a Christian, one must take up his cross, with all its difficulties and agonizing and tension packed content, and carry it until that very cross leaves its mark upon us and redeems us to that more excellent way which comes only through suffering" *(Strength to Love* 1963: 24-25).

SUMMARY

The findings of **major contrast two** concerning pain and suffering find support in the writings of Camus and King as well as secondary sources. Camus believes that God allows pain and suffering among the innocent, and does not answer the prayers of the just nor even the spiritually anointed. Christians, too often, have an accepting attitude that allows for evil and oppression to exist without taking a stand against them. Evil and oppression do not work themselves out but must be eliminated by revolt.

Dr. King believed that innocent suffering and pain were redemptive, purifying and growth producing. He saw personal difficulties as opportunities to strengthen Christian commitment and bring a person closer to God. He believed that God is on the side of the faithful in the many hardships and difficulties of life in order to help them overcome. Dr. King, was a Baptist preacher who had earned a Ph.D. in Systematic Theology. He believed in the Creator and omnipotent God of the Bible who offered suffic, i.ent grace for every struggle to those who believed in Him. (Oates 1982; Cone 1991; Carson 1991; Smith and Zepp 1986; Branch 1988, Garrow 1986 and 1989).

CONCLUSIONS

The problem of this research was to make a comparison of the concepts of freedom and revolt in the thinking of Albert Camus and Dr. Martin Luther King, Jr. The use of common grounds was the methodology utilized to identify similarities and differences regarding these comparisons. Based on the findings of the comparisons, the conclusion of this research is that there are, indeed, numerous common grounds between the two men in the specific conceptual areas of freedom and revolt; and that that there is also common ground in several related areas.

In order to get a clear focus on where the value of this research will apply, we will return to portions of the text that explained **the purpose of the study** as well as **the importance of the study** to allow the findings to direct themselves to several human condition problems of today:

The purpose of this qualitative study was to present and comparatively examine the ideas and visions of two highly acclaimed human rights champions whose lives, work and thoughts were worthy enough for both of them to be awarded a Nobel Prize. Their impact on "Making a Difference" (Brée 1964; Bennett 1968) for the good of humanity and the world we live in is still taking shape. It was my perspective and desire to research and discover their individual message for today's generations. In addition, I believe their combined message has implications and directions that will provide the foundation for plans of action that will assist with the development of the moral courage changes among people living in a civilized society. Further, they provided answers to the problems of oppression, tyranny, racism, injustice and war— the plagues of our times, then and now. The two writers urged every human being to be actively involved in answering the challenges presented in this undertaking. In so doing, everyone can join the ranks of solidarity in helping to bring about reconciliation among all people and the lessening of suffering for all. The findings have shown what an agnostic and a Christian are telling us to do in order to humanize the world for now and the future?

This comparative study has addressed the gap in our knowledge regarding the message of these two men, and to further the impact of their thought upon ongoing attempts to resolve the problems cited in the above paragraph. Camus, on the one hand, embraced a humanism that called upon human beings to care and show compassion to each other. There was no omnipotent being to help fight battles or remove obstacles. The struggle was in the hands, individually and collectively, of human beings who were willing to join the team. The writer in good conscience, is obliged to become a team member and must confront and engage an audience or reading public with a writing ethic that called for revolt against any of the various faces of tyranny—otherwise known as the plagues of our times. (Brée 1964; Hanna 1969; O'Brien, Conor Cruise 1970; Cruickshank 1978; Lottman 1978; Thody 1989; Ellison 1990; Todd 1997, et al).

Dr. King led The Montgomery (Alabama) Improvement Association boycott of segregated busing in that city. The protest against inhumane, indignant, and disrespectful treatment given to blacks on public transportation gave rise to the call for revolt. A master plan of **militant nonviolence protest** was organized and implemented that began the civil rights movement of the 50's and 60's in the United States (Bennett 1968; Oates 1982; Cone 1991; Carson 1991; Smith and Zepp 1986; Branch 1988, Garrow 1986 and 1989. et al). This master plan was presented in a discussion of Dr. King's book *Stride Toward Freedom* was found in Chapter Two of this document. The meaning and impact of the Montgomery movement has literally touched the lives, in some manner or other, of every American (and people worldwide) during the last forty years.

Looking at the importance of this study from another point of view, neither Camus nor Dr. King believed in violence as a means of settling discord, disagreements, grievances and arguments–between persons, between institutions, between ethnic groups, or between nations. Nonviolence was identified as a strategy of protest when human freedom was being oppressed. Here in the United States, let us suppose the statutes, strategies, and principles of nonviolence had been taught to young persons and older persons who have committed senseless, multiple shootings and murder in at least ten different locations, from coast to coast. We remember some of the places: Littleton, Colorado; Jonesboro, Arkansas; Pearl, Mississippi; Giles County, Tennessee; and West Paducah, Kentucky. In November, 1999 a thirteen-year-old "role model" teenager who shot four of his classmates, at school, in Oklahoma, for no apparent reason. Then, on May 27, 2000, a twelve year student in Florida was sent home for poor conduct but returned with a pistol, shot his teacher in the face, killing him on the spot.

All of these atrocities have resulted from a confused disregard for human life, ethnic hate/racism, a loss of hope, or a nihilistic disposition towards life's difficulties, rejections, and shattered dreams. They are extensions of the acts of violence against human life that Camus and King were concerned about. If the statutes, strategies, and principles of nonviolence had been taught to these individuals, what would have been the difference? What would have happened if the assailants had at their disposal better coping mechanisms to utilize when the disappointments of life became severe? Was no reconciliation possible? Will there be others who will follow these patterns? Is there no solution available, or will all Americans, at any time and place, continue to be at risk? This research has provided some answers.

Moving now from the national to the worldwide domain, what could have served as a deterrent to the war of ethnic cleansing and the grievously inhumane atrocities and, murders that took place in Kosovo, Yugoslavia? There is civil war currently going on among ethnic groups in Africa–Angola, Sierra Leone as well as in Sri Lanka and Indonesia. What about the fifty years of hostilities and killings that has gone on between the Palestinians and Israelis? Just a few days ago, the leaders of these two countries were at Camp David, Maryland attempting to reach an agreement that would bring peace and an end to the suffering of thousands of human beings. Is the utter destruction, disruption, and terrors of war the best means to solve differences between ethnic groups and nations? Is a solution possible?

Camus and King have given us some insights and solutions to the prevention of the various types of plague that continue to confront human beings of this day and time. Based on the research findings and the prevailing themes that find common ground in the writing and thought of both men, let us review the key points that they are suggesting that we seriously consider:

1. Revolt against oppression and injustice obliges every human being to struggle, suffer, and if necessary, to die for the freedom that ought to be the birth right of every person. Revolt is seen as a force that drives people to defend what is right and just for every human being.

2. Major social change can be accomplished without violence; militant nonviolent revolt and protest has proven to be an extremely successful strategy used by oppressed people in the struggle for freedom.

3. Racism is evil, wrong, and has no place in the brotherhood of human beings; it is a grave hindrance to the freedom of both the oppressor and the oppressed.

4. Governments, agencies, and people of good will from any persuasion and walk of life must come together in solidarity to work vigilantly for human rights, dignity, equal opportunity, and justice for all peoples.

5. The dream of freedom must become a dream that can be equally shared and hoped for by all ethnic groups in the world.

6. Camus and King envisioned a dream of universal human inclusiveness of all classes, races, religions, the haves and have-nots as coming together to carry out a dream of international brotherhood where peace, harmony, and fulfillment prevailed.

7. Love, compassion, and human understanding are the principles that form the ultimate reality of life and existence for allthe human race. These principles should be taught in every home/ family and in every school—from kindergarten through university.

8. Camus and King believed that forgiving your enemies rather than retaliation is a means of diminishing hostilities among people.

9. The life of every human being is valuable. A true understanding among people requires that we see each other as human beings first, with race, sex, origin, religion, economic status as having little consequence.

10. Violence is not a successful operational means of settling differences, and it creates as many problems as solutions. Violence seldom brings lasting good will and peace among factions that are at odds; but rather, violence begets violence in a never-ending escalating cycle.

11. Acts of war in today's world is violence of the highest order. It is legalized murder proclaimed in the name of peace and civility.

12. Personal wealth must be directed to better uses and purposes by being utilized to alleviate the human suffering and oppression caused by poverty. Wealthy nations must began to share their wealth and resources with impoverished nations.

13. All life is interrelated, and whatever effects one person directly effects everyone indirectly. Everybody, therefore, is a freedom provider for everyone else.

14. The basic human instincts found in all people such as caring, valuing, justice, kindness, peace, hope, sharing, and fellowship must become the absolutes that guide day to day living.

15. Human existence can be caught up in absurdity where life does not appear to have meaning. Life can abound with the incomprehensible, the incongruous, and the unpredictable. However, life is still valuable and must be preserved at all costs.

16. Nihilism is a pessimistic approach to life that does not solve problems. Nihilism is the denial of the good, right, and just in preference to living a

life of hopelessness and despair. Nihilism should be viewed as a point of departure that is moving towards something better. Nihilism is negative and possibly a destructive human disposition that cannot be accepted as a positive end in itself.

17. The solidarity of people of good will working together against the plagues of life such as: tyranny, injustice, war, totalitarianism, racism, genocide, murder, poverty, and disease will in the long run make a difference.

18. The life mission and goal of every living person should be to make a difference in the alleviation of human pain and suffering (physical and emotional), putting whatever skills and abilities with which he/she is endowed to the service of other people.

19. The people of the world are obliged to recognize that there are common values existing and needed by all human beings. The oppression of these values is cause for revolt. These values include life, freedom, justice, love, peace, happiness, food, shelter, livelihood, and worthiness.

20. It is a betrayal against humanity to be silent when freedom and justice are being denied.

21. Revolt for justice, change, and freedom must have means and ends that are defined by limits. Otherwise, the purpose of revolt can lose its origin, exceed boundaries, and possibly end in oppression, and even murder.

In conclusion, a careful examination of these points should make it clear why the legacies of Camus and King are attractive and revered by each new generation. The reason is that these men stood for the true values of life, which are given above. And true values cannot be destroyed. The history of the world has shown that these values never die. Further, the possessors or purveyors of these values become, themselves, enduring personalities that the passing of time do not erase. I contend that it is not necessary to be a card carrying Christian to live and carry out these values: "A good man will be filled with the fruit of his deeds." Proverbs 14:14. Certainly, we need to be reminded that the spiritual is not confined to strict forms of religion and dogma, but can also be identified in certain persons, fraternities, orders, clubs, and academies whose primary focus is the transformation and the establishing among human beings everything that is good, just and liberating to life and human existence.

CHAPTER SIX

RECOMMENDATIONS

THE PURPOSE OF THIS STUDY WAS TO RESEARCH a comparison of the concepts of revolt and freedom in the thinking of Albert Camus and Dr. Martin Luther King Jr. This research was conducted using a common grounds methodology of investigation. Ten common ground similarities were identified. Research findings substantiated the existence of these ten similarities. Likewise, two common ground differences were identified that were substantiated by findings. From a literary perspective, we identified the novel, short story, philosophical essay, essay, and the play as the genre used by Camus to present his writings, thoughts and ideas to the reader. Dr. King used the essay to present his writings, thoughts, and ideas to the reader. The findings and results have shown what an agnostic and a Christian are telling us to do very similar actions in order to humanize the world for now and in the future. Twenty-one summarization points pertaining to the major themes of the writings of Camus and King were given to synthesize common ground research findings and results. Based on these findings and results, I wish now to make two sets of recommendations: The first set of recommendations will be for future research. The second set of recommendations pertains to strategies that are being used by governments, agencies, groups, and people to implement the solutions and recommendations that Camus and King advocated. The research has shown that these two men were passionately committed to bringing about a better world for human beings.

FUTURE RESEARCH RECOMMENDATIONS

1. Expand the comparative study to include other writers with similar or different views of the human condition. Each new comparative study would further clarify the meaning and implication of the thought of Camus and King. Each new study would fill the gap with fresh insights.

2. Expand the common grounds concept to include other areas of commonality or differences. Due to limitations, my study remained with the twelve areas identified in my original PDE proposal. A More expansive comparative investigation could be done on genres and elements of literature, politics, religion, colonialism, and death.

3. Conduct future research that reflects the twenty-one summarization points given for Camus and King, These points can be combined or dealt with separately. However, they can be used as points of departure for future investigation.

4. Future research could investigate the long-term impact of Camus' and King's influence and teachings relative to peace and human rights initiatives of the twenty-first Century.

5. Future research could make an in-depth investigation of how Camus and King viewed the role of women in their writings.

RECOMMENDATION FOR IMPLEMENTATION STRATEGIES

Albert Camus and Dr. Martin Luther King, Jr. were human rights champions par excellence. Their writings and thought reflect this fact. Their messages to the world direct us to examine their thought in light of some of the problems that are causing human pain and suffering at this day and time. This section of recommendations concerns what is being done by some people, groups, programs, and agencies in implementing what Camus and King were advising us to do during the forties, fifties, and sixties. This section goes a step beyond what may normally be presented as PDE, Chapter Six, Recommendations, but I wanted to connect what Camus and King are suggesting (freedom, revolt, justice, reconciliation, caring, peace, solidarity, human value, etc.) to what is actually happening, right now, to bring their visions and dreams into fruition. As the researcher for this PDE, it is my feeling that these Implementation Recommendations add completeness to this work. The following initiatives are examples of strategies and solutions that have been implemented locally, nationally, and internationally.

1. **The Vineyards Project** of Dayton, Ohio consists of paired churches (one black and one white) working together to identify means of racial reconciliation. Some of the activities of different pairings include: preacher pulpit exchange, choir exchanges, National Issues Forum discussions on critical social issues, exchange meetings in homes, taking trips together, picnics, youth activities, Habitat for Humanity work, marching together on Dr. Martin Luther King Jr. holiday, eating out together, having discussions on racial issues, etc. (Source: The Vineyard Project brochure, Jim Burton, President, Dayton, Ohio, 1999). This particular program is example of what both Camus and King said needed to be done to bring about societal transformation through the efforts of the universal church as change agents. We recall, especially, Dr. King's indictment of the white church *(Letter From Birmingham Jail)* for its non-involvement and aloofness during the civil rights struggles in America. Likewise, Camus was critical of the European church, including all denominations, for their cowardly and inhumane stand during the seizure, incarceration, and deportation to death camps of some six million Jews. His indictment of the Church is most pronounced in *The Plague*. Based on available information, programs that are similar to the *Vineyards* model have proliferated through out America and the world. This type of program represents the idea of human solidarity on the part of Camus and the "**Beloved Community**" of King. Key points #3, #4, #7, #14 and #20 from Chapter Five apply here.

2. **The Teaching Tolerance** programs for schools that are promoted by the Southern Poverty Law Center in Montgomery, Alabama. This civil rights agency also promotes a Militia Task Force, Klanwatch, Ten Ways to Fight Hate booklet, and the Responding to Hate at School booklet (Southern Poverty Law Center, Morris Dees, President, Montgomery, Alabama, 1999). Montgomery, Alabama was the city where the civil

rights revolt for freedom started in 1955. The Southern Poverty Law Center is an organization that has taken the leadership in bringing about programs of racial reconciliation in the South and throughout the USA. The Southern Poverty Law Center is the premier organization in America today that is providing leadership, doing research, keeping statistics, and publishing documents on tolerance and racial diversity. Mrs. Rosa Parks is a co-director of the Center. Key points #3, #4, #7, #14 and #20 from Chapter Five apply here.

3. **The Promise Keepers** national program, Boulder, Colorado. This program is designed to bring men from all ethnic groups together in the name of being better men, husbands and fathers. Their motto is "Break down the barriers" of race, class, persuasion, religion, and socio-economic group. I attended a Promise Keepers rally in 1996 at Three Rivers Stadium, Pittsburgh, Pennsylvania. There were over 50,000 men in attendance for the weekend. They all took the seven-point pledge to be better men, husbands, and fathers.

Men of all races held hands, sang motivating songs, worshipped, hugged, and fellowshipped with each other in ways never done before. They made promises to be better men, husbands, and fathers as well as to see people as people, and therefore, to reach beyond the barriers of race, religion, persuasion and class. (Source: The Promise Keepers, literature pack, Bill McCartney, President, Boulder, Colorado, 1999). At a time when three marriages out of four are ending in divorce and children are being poorly cared for and in many cases, living in poverty, the Promise Keepers are striving to reclaim men to be better and more responsible human beings. The end result will be the rearing of better, more compassionate, and responsible children. Key points #3, #4, #7, #14 and #20 from Chapter Five apply here.

4. **The Race and Reconciliation Collaborative** of Dayton, Ohio which is a coalition of professional groups coming together for the purpose of improving local area race relations in the 21st Century (Source: The Dayton Daily News, December 15, 1999, Section B: 1). This initiative was begun by a local judge who saw the need for an ongoing effort in the professional community to dialog and to put into place a forum with working documents that are addressed to equality of opportunity, diversity in the workplace, and reconciliation. Key points #3, #4, #7, #14 and #20 from Chapter Five apply here.

5. **Concerning Church Leaders,** the January 1999 visit of Pope John II to the United States where he spoke out against abortion, euthanasia, assisted suicide, racism, and the death penalty. (Dayton Daily News, Section C-Religion: 1, January 30, 1999). The Pope spoke out against several of the plagues existing in our day. For sure, some these are controversial, but the Pope is taking a stand from the Catholic point of view concerning what he believes to be right and just for the world. This is a far cry from what the European Catholic Church did during the deportation, incarceration, and murder of six million Jews during the Holocaust. The official church was silent, and this was one of the main arguments that Camus had against the church. Key points #3, #4, #7, #14 and #20 from Chapter Five apply here.

6. **"Millennium Generation"**–A full page article on race relations in America citing data from a Gallup Poll done in June 1997. The poll indicated that young people have a brighter view of race relations than their elders in six key areas. Quote from *The Color of Our Future* (1998) by Faria Chideya: "This generation is re-creating America's racial identity every single day. And if anybody is going to erase the color line, it's going to be them" (Dayton Daily News, February 28, 1999: 21A). As documented in the research for this PDE, American young people played a very significant role in the civil rights campaigns of the fifties and sixties. They spearheaded the sit-ins, the kneel-ins, the vote-ins, the pray-ins, the wade-ins, boycotts, demonstrations, and marches. Black and white young people, male and female, were protesting for justice, right, and peace. They were revolting for freedom, and they will continue to carry the torch for doing what is right into the new millennium; this is what Camus and King advocated. Key points #3, #4, #7, #14 and #20 from Chapter Five apply here.

7. **The Birmingham Pledge** against racial prejudice is a pledge initiated by the city's bi racial Community Affairs Committee in an effort to transform the municipality and its image from that of high pressure fire hoses, billy clubs, biting dogs, and children in jail to a humane and progressive city on the move. Educators were encouraged to have their students sign and return the pledge to the committee showing their support of racial equality. The pledge which encourages student to "Sign it. Live it" states:

THE BIRMINGHAM PLEDGE

I believe that every person has worth as an individual.
I believe that every person is entitled to dignity and respect, regardless of race or color. I believe that every thought and every act of racial prejudice is harmful; if it is my thought or act, then it is harmful to me as well as to others.

Therefore, from this day forward I will strive to eliminate racial prejudice from my thoughts and actions.
I will discourage racial prejudice by others at every opportunity.

I will treat all people with dignity and respect; and I will strive
daily to honor this pledge, knowing that the world will be a better place because of my effort. (end of pledge).
(Source: SPLC Report, June 1999, Volume 29, Number 2, p. 5, The Southern Poverty Law Center)

The pledge requires a signature, street address, city/state, and zip code. Information so far is that over 10,000 students and their teachers have signed and returned the pledge. We recall that Birmingham was the site of the bloodiest civil rights struggle in America. It happened in 1963. Since that time Birmingham has made outstanding progress in the area of race/human relations. It is fitting that this far reaching pledge against racism should emanate from that city and be sent out to all America. Points #1, #2, #3, #5, #7, #8, #9, #13, #14, #17, #19, and #20 from the implementation strategies apply here.

8. **_J'he Wright-Dunbar Prize** created by the DaCapo Foundation of Dayton, Ohio for purposes of awarding teenagers from around the world who exemplify social activism and leadership in the struggle to bring about mutual understanding and diversity. This year's awards went to teenagers from seven different countries, who came to New York on the United Nations' International Day for Tolerance to receive their prizes. The initiative is designed to commemorate the signing of the peace accords in Dayton that ended the Bosnian War in 1995. (Source: The Dayton Daily News, November 17, 1999: 1A). This international program, involving

teenagers, is again an example and model of what is taking place around the world for purposes of promoting freedom, peace, diversity, and tolerance. These young people are making a difference. Key points #3, #4, #7, #14 and #20 from Chapter Five apply here.

9. **See You at the Pole**–a national student Christian movement that began in Texas in 1990 with a church youth group who met and prayed around a flagpole. By 1998 the movement had grown to more than 3 million participants in high schools and colleges around the United States. The message of the pole is to see people as brothers and sisters not as Baptists, Methodists, Catholics, Jews, Presbyterians, or whatever. The idea is ecumenical inclusiveness. (Dayton Daily News, September 13, 1999). This is yet another example of what youth are doing to make a better world. Key points #3,#4, #7, #14 and #20 from Chapter Five apply here.

10. **The National Day of Prayer** (the first Thursday in May)–A national day of prayer and fasting in which persons of all faiths pray in their own way for peace, goodness, forgiveness, hope, courage and love towards all humanity (Source: The Dayton Daily News, May 6, 1999: 1A). The National Day of Prayer is shared by Christians and non Christians in the name of solidarity. Key points #3, #4, #7, #14 and #20 from Chapter Five apply here.

11. **Common Stride** a project in Helena, Arkansas dedicated to move from debate to deliberation, unity, and equality, and to end the black-white race divide; from literature pack distributed by Dr. Mary Olson and Naomi Cottoms, May 9, 2000, Dayton, Ohio. This is another example of initiatives and programs going on in small places in the world for the purposes of equality and reconciliation of people. Key points #3, #4,#7, #14 and #20 from Chapter Five apply here.

12. In conclusion, It is initiatives, efforts, movements, and programs such as these that are bringing people together in solidarity. And this solidarity is ecumenical crossing lines of race, gender, sex, national origin, religion, political persuasion, and socio-economic standing. The fortunate fact of the matter is that these events are gathering momentum worldwide. The reason that these events are happening is because people realize, as Camus and King pointed out so clearly, that we are all human beings who must

learn to live together and care for each other. Therefore, the voice and vision of these two men along with their passion for justice give a message for now and the future. Will the people of the world be serious about following it? I hope so. The crisis situation of killings in America and around the world has brought people to the realization that enough is enough; that life is precious, that "I am my brother's keeper", and that "I want the same peace and freedom for others as I want for myself." Camus referred to this solidarity as revolt, in the name of getting rid of the plagues of the world in search of freedom. King referred to it as establishing the **"Beloved Community"** in the name freedom, justice, and reconciliation.

A BRIEF LITERATURE REVIEW FOR COMPARATIVE LITERATURE

THE COMPARING OF NATIONAL LITERATURES CAME INTO BEING long before it became a science that follows form, methodology and protocol (Clements, 1978). The Hellenistic specialists who were versed in two literatures and wrote about them. At that time, of course, the name comparative literature had not arrived on the scene. It was just a normal and scholarly thing to do, to compare myths, heroes and tales from the then known world as an effort towards enlightenment.

The Romans and Greeks of antiquity compared poetry and oratory against one another (Prawer, 1973) as another point of reference regarding the beginnings of comparative literature. Men of letters and learning spoke with pride in being able to refer to works in several languages.

Comparative literature takes place when two or more authors are compared relative to their ideas, theories, themes, strategies, characters or approaches to solutions of problems, needs and concerns of the human condition. Comparative studies help to clarify concepts and they help one to understand better the perspectives from which two writers may choose to address issues.

Therefore, one is able better discern when comparing more than one entity in regards to its being good, original, difficult or accomplished. An even more desirable comparison is to advance across national and cultural lines. No doubt this is why Remak (1971) gives the working definition that Comparative literature is the study of literature beyond the confines of one particular country and the study of the relationships between literature on one hand and other areas of knowledge and beliefs, such as the (fine) arts, philosophy, history, the social sciences, the sciences, religion, etc. on the other. In brief, it is the comparison of one literature with another or others, and the comparison of literature with other spheres of expression (1).

The boundaries of comparative literature go beyond the perimeters of one country and one literature. Also, comparisons have worldwide dimensions that penetrate beyond the domain of just literature alone. Relationships between literature and other areas of knowledge such as, the natural sciences, philosophy, religion, social sciences, history and the fine arts. Indeed, literature is the carrier and the cultural interpreter of comparisons between these diverse phenomena (Clements 1978:5).

The realism of this interdisciplinarity of comparative writing was stated by Matthew Arnold (1857) with the idea that there is connection and illustration everywhere. No single literature or event is truly understood unless it is compared with other literatures or events (Bassnett, 1993:1).

The present study will compare the thinking of Albert Camus and Dr. Martin Luther King, Jr., as their thinking addresses the concepts of **revolt and freedom.** The vehicle used to make this comparison will be that of comparative literature.

According to Bassnett (1993), comparative literature acquired its name as early as 1816 as a result of a series of French anthologies used in the teaching of literature. The name of this anthology series was *Course de litterateur comparee.* The German version of the term first appeared in 1854 and the earliest English usage appeared in 1848. The idea of comparative literature, therefore, has been with us for many years (12).

Comparative literature gives scholars, teachers, students and readers a better and more comprehensive understanding of what a total literature imparts rather than bits and pieces from this national literature or the other (Remak 1971). Remak adds to this definition in stating that a comparative literature study does not have to be comparative on every page nor even in every chapter, but the overall intent, emphasis, and execution must be comparative. The assaying of intent, emphasis, and execution requires both objective and subjective judgement. No rigid rules should therefore be set down beyond these criteria (13).

Prawer (1973) informs us that "comparative literature" implies a study of literature, which uses comparison as its main instrument. Prawer states further:

we cannot fully appreciate the individuality of Wadsworth, his place in a tradition, or a modification of that tradition, without comparing his work, explicitly or implicitly, with that of Milton, James Thomson, and that of Shelley and Keats (2).

Comparative literature, then, makes its comparisons *across national frontiers* (2).

Indeed, it is this international perspective on literature that has truly made it comparative. The practitioners who compare literature are positioned at the very center of international literary themes, ideas, books or feelings. As such, they work between two or several literatures. Normally, they read two or more languages and are familiar with the rich bibliographic sources of the profession.

Therefore, in light of the multidimensional perspective from which the comparatist must view literature, Bemheimer (1993) makes a strong point in stating that it is important that the person has a historical basis for his/her thinking. There must be a connection that shows how the major issues have developed through the centuries to give the scholar the background necessary to evaluate current debates in their historical context. The next section on world dimensions will address the large geographical environment included in comparative literature.

WORLD DIMENSIONS

The interrelationships brought about by the world dimensions perspective of comparative literature provides another vantage point from which to view the whole. The most prominent world dimension groups are, I. Western Literature, 2. East-West and 3. World Literature. As viewed by Clements (1978), Western Literature is the bringing together of those literatures commonly taught in American or English universities. This would be: ancient Greek and Latin, English, American, French, Spanish, Portuguese, Italian, German and Russian. The tradition also includes the medieval and Renaissance stages of these literatures (23).

Given these literatures, according to the American Comparative Literature Association Report II, this world dimension would also include a broader perspective on works and authors, the tracking of motifs, themes, and types as well as a larger understanding of genres and modes. Literary criticism would also be part of this expanded package. The bottom line was to transport faculty and students beyond disciplinary boundaries into an exploration of literature with the other arts and humanities, namely, philosophy, ·history, history of ideas, linguistics, music, art and folklore. Thus, the need for breadth is at the very center of comparative literature studies (Clements 1978: 24).

The second category of literature, East-West, draws upon some of the same world dimensions as does Western Literature and includes courses being taught at such Asian universities as the University of Tokyo and the University of Hong Kong. Other universities involved include: Central Philippine University, Hebrew University of Jerusalem and the Middle East Technical University in Turkey (27). The idea of comparatism in these universities takes on a flavor and dimension that reflect their inherited culture, traditions, needs and problems as seen by their vision of the world.

Bassnett (1993) argues that. "Implicit to comparative literature outside of Europe and the United States is the need to start with the home culture and to look outwards, rather than to start with the European model of literary excellence and to look inwards" (38). The key point is that these Western models do not fit nor complement Third World models during the current post-colonialism era.

World Literature is the third dimension of comparative literature. World Literature encompasses and reflects the previous two literatures and includes those particular pieces of literature that represent global lasting values for all times. Further, it represents the best of international authors from the beginning of literary record to the present. Several titles that would enter into this category would include: *El Cid*, *A Tale of Two Cities*, *Madame Bovary*, *Moby Dick*, *and Roots*.

This awareness of literature and traditions other than one's own adds to and enriches the background from which comparisons can be made and the truths and follies of the human condition analyzed. Further, it allows the writer to draw upon the cultural point of view and visions of other nationalities as he/she practices the skills of the craft. Prawer (1973) also stresses that the reader is challenged to widen their experiences in the personal, social, economic, scientific and philosophical domains as a result of reading from World Literature. Add to this the possibilities of improved ethnic and cultural relations/interchanges, translations, human interaction, and debate.

According to Bernheimer (1995), a more broadened view of the world dimension is included in the Greene Report on Standards of comparative literature (1975), which states that, "There has also arisen a widespread and growing interest in the non-European literatures–Chinese, Japanese, Sanskrit, Arabic, and many other less familiar, as well as oral "literatures"… A new vision of *global* literature is emerging, embracing all the verbal creativity of our planet, a vision which will begin to make our comfortable European perspective parochial (30). Added to this grouping above should be African Literatures. The native languages Bantu, Swahili and Yoruba do not have very large reading publics. Therefore, African writers lean to French and English as the vehicles used to present their writings. However, their themes and concerns are based on the African heritage, visions, cultures and tradition (Clements 1978).

It appears that traditional comparatists are not prepared for the implications of this new thrust in the profession, but it cannot be ignored. Change always has the promise of honing out something better. Ahearn and Weinstein (1995) writing in *Comparative Literature in the Age of* Multiculturalism, eds., Bernheimer, alludes to there being no other defensible route to take except global inclusion. With rapid travel making the world smaller and more accessible and with the impact of Internet and the world wide web that networks the planet, we live in a global, interdependent and multicultural world on every front–education, business, economics, science, military, social, and politics.

Therefore, Ahearn and Weinstein continue, "The geopolitical activities, conflicts, and dilemmas of our times require a citizenry that has learned something about the history, aspirations, and complex reality of other peoples, and that the study of literature and other arts is a privileged entry into these matters... comparative literature is inherently pluralist, aware but not defined by Difference in all its powerful forms: language, religion, race, class, and gender" (78).

It appears, then, that comparative literature is one of our best chances to enter into global cultures in order to examine values, beliefs and aesthetics. A New Cultural Literacy may, indeed, result that will allow us a more honest intellectual appraisal of the world, and most importantly, a more honest appraisal of ourselves.

PERIODS AND MOVEMENTS

Periods and movements form a helpful structure for the study of literature. It has often been the case during the long history of ideas and intellectual pursuits that writers have, during a certain historical moment, shown unity by expressing the same thing in much the same manner across international boundaries. Thus, their literary offerings reflect the same, or similar, themes, plots, point of view, style and setting.

Clements (1978) explains that, "A literary movement will thus retain its essential identity as it crosses the continent; but it will undergo adaptations and modifications that tell us about the countries involved and even about the potential of the movement itself." the benefits to the writer, it seems, are shared beliefs and values, direction and inspiration.

The following are several of the more prominent literary movements, approximate time period and key descriptor words, dating back to the Medieval era. Source: *(World Book Encyclopedia and the World Book Dictionary,* volumes I & II, 1988)

- 500–1450   The Medieval Period   The study of man, nature and the world

- 1300–1500   The Renaissance   Rebirth, adventure, curiosity, change

- 1600–1798   Classicism   Order, rigor, balance, reason, simplicity

- The 1800's   Romanticism   Passion over reason, expression of the emotions, feelings and imagination.

- 1740–1850   Realism   Describes life as is, accurately, honestly.

- 1880–1925   Naturalism   Applies the scientific method and theory to writing. Stresses power of environmental influences.

- 1885–1915   Symbolism   Indirect suggestion to meaning, mystical, sacred, pessimistic.

- 1924–   Surrealism   Super-realism, reform of evil, explores the subconscious mind, strives for a higher reality in living.

- 1800's–1960's   Existentialism   A person is the sum total of thoughts, choices, actions and beliefs. Existence precedes essence. Freedom, responsibility, subjectivity, focus on the "now" of human existence. The person is in charge of her/his destiny.

Of course, some of these literary movements overlap and transcend a beginning or ending time. Generally, each movement disputed and divorced itself from the previous era. However, it appeared that writers were caught up in the *zeitgeist* of the historical time and added their intellectual power to the ongoing momentum. Besides influences on literature, literary movements have also impacted education, the fine arts, music, social and political thought.

While giving an examination to the research on past literary movements, and specifically to the ones recorded above, I am drawn again to look at the forces that focus on the two writers being dealt with in this doctoral project–Albert Camus and Dr. Martin Luther King, Jr. What literary movement would they be assigned to?

Based on my literature search, Camus' era would certainly have been that of existentialism. While, according to Germaine Brée (1964), Camus denied being an existentialist writer, some of his writings touch on the themes and ideology of the existentialist movement. Four of his major works, *The Myth of Sisyphus (1942)*, (the absurd) *The Stranger* (1942),(alienation, nihilism) *The Plague (*1947),(alienation, revolt) *and The Fall (1956),(guilt,* nihilism) fall into the broad definitions of the movement.

However, the true meaning of Camus' writing came from his life and experiences during World War II and the ravages of those historical times. Camus saw a world that: was bleak, uncertain, unjust, war torn, corrupt, sanctioned legal murder, approved racism, promoted political persecution and execution. It appears, therefore, that the passions behind Camus' writings were more a product of his times than the literary alignment with any particular movement.

The same can be said for Dr. Martin Luther King, Jr. Dr. King's writings emanated from his total experiences of growing up Black in America. He had experienced the full measure of indignities that any Black had to endure. No literary movement was necessary to fuel the fire. The fire had always been there. It was the segregation, discrimination, lynchings, bombings, oppression, fear, injustice, war and racism that had been tolerated so long, and, that exploded on the December evening in 1955 when Rosa Parks refused to give her bus seat to a White man. History was written. So, in the cases of both Camus and King, the right historical moment met with the right person, and the world was no longer the same. Rather than becoming a part of a movement, they were movement catalysts who gave it leadership.

LITERARY THEORY AND CRITICISM

To begin this section, it seems appropriate to define the meaning of **theory and criticism** as they are used in the domain of comparative literature.

As identified by Stallknecht and Frenz (1971) theory includes several constructs. These are: definition, structure, movements, function, style, inherent values, parallelism, canon, influence, genres and themes. From these constructs (and there could be others), comparatists draw guidelines that give explanation to operational principles and doctrine. These operational principles and doctrine provide the basis from which literary works are viewed, discussed and interpreted.

On the other hand, according to Roberts (1978), literary criticism is allied with judgment and evaluation. Criticism requires the taking of a stand, pro or con. Further, criticism makes a distinction between good and bad, right and wrong, acceptable and non-acceptable. Criticism also must decide based on a set of standards. Roberts points out these standards as follows with some of my own applications and interpretations:

1. **Truth**–Does the literary product have generalizeable and universal themes of truth? For example, in Camus' *The Stranger*, the main character, Meursault has an attitude of indifference to the needs of other people. This indifference to societal norms puts him at odds with others and even with his lawyer, who is defending him for the senseless murder of a man on a beach. Meursault is more concerned about his disturbing a beautiful beach scene by the firing of a gun than his act of violence, which takes a man's life. Likewise, he shows no remorse or grief at his mother's funeral. Meursault is symbolic of a disregard and disrespect for human condition norms that society will not tolerate. Symbolically, he is a negative character who is sentenced to death, not for killing the man on the beach, but for his long history of anti-social behavior. Meursault is a stranger to himself and to other people. The truth of Meursault is that people have a responsibility to care for one another and when we do not, we can become destructive to others and to ourselves. This is a universal and generalizeable truth.

2. **Affirmation of Life**–Affirmation of life means that human existence and people are worth caring about and writing about. The conditions of living could be deplorable or the best. Humans may abuse their conditions of living. But, however an auth<?r portrays the lives of characters, the literary product must respond positively to the universal principle that life is valuable. Life is worthy and is to be held in high esteem.(In the example above, this is where Meursault went astray) The sum total of our life strivings ought to be noble and aspiring to dignity. This is a universal and generalizeable principle to which literary criticism should adhere.

3. **Look at the Whole Picture.**–Honest and effective literary criticism does not judge a work by its parts but by the whole, from A to Z. For instance, while the structure of a work might be of poor quality, the characterization, language quality, description, plot, theme, tone, etc. may be superior. So, the work should not be declared inferior because of structure but judged in its entirety, which would probably put it into a better category. Therefore, in the world of criticism, a literary product may appear flawed, but when the sum total of the product outweighs the imperfection and renders the flaw a minor distraction, The product, in fairness, has to be judged positively. This is a generalizeable and universal principle to which literature should adhere.

4. **Vigor & Power**–A good work of literature should bring its characters alive. A good work of literature should write description so vividly that the reader can see a picture coming off of the page. A good work of literature, if it is essay prose, should be written with such intensity and compelling urgency that the reader feels the writer's yearning to be heard. The aforesaid is one meaning of vigor and power. Another meaning of vitality is that work or those works that have an endless appeal to generation after generation of readers. Such a book would be *Roots* (1976), by Alex Haley. This vigor and power is found in the composite works of both Albert Camus and Dr. Martin Luther King, Jr. There is something new to be found each time a person reads their works. It is this never ending appeal, represented by the presence of vigor and power, that keeps them on the best seller lists and their writings being used as texts in many classes, at both the secondary and college levels.

5. **Beauty**–Beauty is how a work is put together. That is, how are the relationships between unity, balance, harmony and proportion established in the work? Do the functions of the individual parts blend into the whole in a manner that demonstrate beauty? Other determinants of beauty in a literary work include such characteristics as symbolism, tone, structure, point of view and style. Any one of these qualities would provide grounds for literary criticism. However, neither of them, alone, would be strong enough to warrant the label beautiful. Thus, the inclusive and complementary power of the total work must be examined in order to adjudge the presence of beauty and use it as a criticism descriptor for the work.

6. **Subjectivism**–Personal preferences, likes and dislikes, will play a role in just about every critic's repertoire. However, these preferences must be justified based on literary evidence and able to stand on defensible grounds that are acceptable (not always agreed to) to other scholars in the field. In using these six standards of criticism, the literary critic is able to approach a work with reasonable objectivity that will bring about a fair evaluation of the strengths and imperfections of a particular work.

Taken together, theory and criticism attempt to find the truth. In the process, the literary problem is divided into its various parts so that it can be examined more easily. A one by one examination of the issues connected to the problem will allow for a more careful and comparative look at such qualities as meaning, structure, style and background influences. This separate pieces analysis lends itself to a more penetrating analysis. Then, secondly, this procedure aims at helping the analyst to develop a more accurate appreciation of literary excellence.

In using these six standards of criticism, it appears that the critic would be able to approach a work with reasonable objectivity to bring about a fair evaluation of strengths and shortcomings of a particular writer's craft.

FUTURE OF THE DISCIPLINE

As viewed from where comparative literature is today and where it needs to go moving into the Twenty-first Century, Bassnett (1993) on one hand does not appear very optimistic. Her reasons touch upon "The narrowness of the binary distinction, the unhelpfulness of the a historical approach, the complacent shortsightedness of the Literature-as-universal-civilizing force approach have all contributed to its demise."

On the positive side, however, Bassnett notes that comparative literature is alive and active but in new clothes. Globally, old methodologies are being reassessed. Old restrictive walls regarding disciplinary boundaries are crumbling. Gender and cultural studies are charging ahead at full speed. The emerging forces of translation studies are firing the profession into new dialogues. A new focus on multiculturalism is revitalizing the profession into new and fresh territory.

Continuing along this track at Brown University, Ahearn and Weinstein in Bemheimer (1993), take the position that future young scholars of comparative literature should receive a broad based education and that:

> It should be stressed that this "engaged" model of comparative literature is hospitable to virtually all varieties of literary analysis. From the textual subtleties of New Criticism and intertextuality and even psychoanalysis, on the one hand, to the new vistas created by Marxists, feminists, new historicists, students of ethnicity, race, sexual orientation on the other hand all of these approaches are compatible with the twin principles of internationalism and comparatism which gives us our identity (80).

An active and excellent example of the above thinking is taking place at Brown University via an outreach program known as "Great Books Then and Now" and "Texts and Teachers." These courses involve the interdisciplinary teaching that address many of the burning societal problems and issues of the day. The program has a global focus and is being done in conjunction with Brown's Institute for Secondary Education with input from local secondary teachers.

The exploratory courses include: sociology, religion, psychology, philosophy, politics, language and literature, and art. The classes present a "New perspective in the high school college-university spectrum of education" that will give participants a better comparative understanding in terms of beliefs, race, class, and gender, vis-a-vis themselves (83).

From my own educator point of view this is the type of initiative that needs to be replicated as often as possible. Public schools are in dire need of this type of rich cultural and intellectual interchange. My experiences with post secondary institutions (University of Dayton) in the Dayton, Ohio area doing similar outreach projects resulted in a very needed, welcomed and positive affect on both the public education and university personnel. Specifically, while working as on of the supervisors of English for the Dayton City Schools, a colleague and I wrote a proposal in conjunction with the UD English Department and received a grant from the Jennings Foundation to conduct a two week writing workshop held during two separate summers. The two workshops involved some sixty teachers grades 4-12 and took place on the UD campus. The workshop was modeled after the very popular and successful San Francisco Bay Area Writing Project. Evaluation reports from participants applauded the effort and strongly recommended that it be held every summer. Then, there was the ongoing collaboration between foreign language staffs from UD and Dayton Public School This took place over a period of five years and involved regular sharing meetings as well as classes and workshops.

"Does comparative literature want to globalize, democratize, decolonize?" (59) is the question raised by Mary Louise Pratt in Bemheimer (1993) as she surveys the future of comparative literature. She states with certainty that it is imperative that comparative literature look beyond the Western/Eurocentric view of *what is* towards a future that embraces the literatures, for example, of Asia, Africa and Latin America, that university teaching ranks be opened to women and persons of color, and, that the Third World enter into dialogue with the First. In response to reluctance to change and a desire to hold onto the status quo, Pratt proposes:

An alternative view of the kind of leadership I think comparative literature can perform today, a view that sets aside reactive categories of wariness, fear, border patrolling. These days, I like to advance a concept of comparative literature as a site for powerful intellectual renewal in the study of literature and culture. My list of particulars has six items on it, but the big picture is of comparative literature as an especially hospitable space for the cultivation of multilingualism, polyglossia, the arts of cultural mediation, deep intercultural understanding _and genuine global consciousness (62).

SUMMARY

The purpose of this brief literature review of comparative literature was to provide a historical view of the field as well as to give the present day definitions of what comparative literature studies involves. Based on this research, the domain of comparative literature includes a broad range of approaches that allows for flexibility in applying the parameters of the canon.

From the point of view of world dimensions, we also find a broader perspective on works and authors, the tracking of motifs, themes, and types as well as a larger understanding of genres and modes. Major voices in the field are stressing that traditional disciplinary boundaries be extended to involve explorations of literature with other arts and humanities such as, philosophy, history, history of ideas, religion, natural sciences, social sciences, linguistics, music, art and folklore. This trend towards discipline breadth is at the very core of current comparative literature studies.

Literary periods and movements continue to be used as a helpful means to identify writers and literary production as belonging to one school or the other based on reflection of same or similar themes, plots, point of view, style, setting, shared beliefs, values, direction and inspiration. Several major literary periods and movements include: Classicism, Romanticism, Realism, Naturalism, Surrealism, and Existentialism.

Literary theory and criticism, while used together, have different meanings. Theory involves definition, structure, movements, function, style, inherent values, parallelism, canon, influence, genres, and themes. Criticism, on the other hand, involves judgement and evaluation. The literary critic must take a stand on what he is evaluating, pro or con. There are standards that the critic uses in arriving at the conclusions for whatever is being evaluated.

In conclusion, the comparative literature practitioners of the Twenty-First Century are saying that the field, in order to reflect a global and inclusive perspective, must continue the trend that goes beyond the traditional European and American points of view and models in defining the discipline. Rather, the future trend of comparative literature is that it should be hospitable to a more interdisciplinary view of literary comparison and analysis.

BIBLIOGRAPHY

Abernathy, Donzaleigh. (1998). "Nonviolence." *The Black Awareness Journal.* Vol. XVIII 1998: 21.

"African American Intellectual Currents: An Examination & Appraisal." (1997). Study Pack and Readings From Union Institute Seminar Convened by Joseph Jordan and Sylvia Hill, Cincinnati, Ohio, November 7-11, 1997.

Albert, Peter J. and Ronald Hoffman (1990). We Shall Overcome. New York: Random House.

Ahearn, Ed and Arnold Weinstein. (1995). "The Function of Criticism at the Present Time: The Promise of Comparative Literature." in Bemheimer, Charles, ed., Comparative Literature in the Age of Multiculturalism. Baltimore: Johns Hopkins Press. (77-85).

Baker, Houston A. (1980). The Journey Back: Issues in Black Literature and Criticism Chicago: University of Chicago Press.

Baldwin, Lewis V. (1991). There is a Balm in Gilead: the Cultural Roots of Dr. Martin Luther King, Jr. Minneapolis: Fortress Press.

Bassnett, Susan. (1993). Comparative Literature: A Critical Introduction. Cambridge MA: Blackwell Publishers.

Baker, Houston A. (1980). The Journey Back: Issues in Black Literature and Criticism Chicago: University of Chicago Press.

Bennett, Lerone. (1968). <u>What Manner of Man.</u> Chicago, IL. Johnson Publishing Co.

Bernheimer, Charles. ed.(1995). <u>Comparative Literature in the Age of Multiculturalism.</u> Baltimore: Johns Hopkins university Press.

Branch, Taylor. (1988). <u>Parting the Waters.</u> New York: Simon Schuster.

Brée, Germaine. (1962). Editor. <u>A Collection of Critical Essays.</u> New Jersey. Prentice-Hall.

Brée, Germaine. (1964). <u>Camus.</u> New Brunswick: Rutgers University Press.

Brée, Germaine. (1983). <u>Twentieth Century French Literature.</u> Chicago: University of Chicago Press.

Brooks, Peter. <u>"Must We Apologize?" ed. Bernheimer (97-106).</u>

Burnier, Michel Antoine. (1968). <u>Choice of Action: The French Existentialists on the Political Front Line.</u> New York: Random House.

Bums, Stewart. (1993). "Martin Luther King Jr's Empowering Legacy." *Tikkun v8n2, Mar p. 49-53.* Cambridge: Harvard University Press.

Camus, Albert. "The Artist as a Witness to Freedom." from a speech given by Camus in 1947, translated by Bernard Frechtman.e-mailBrian:juanyen@tezcat.com.

Camus Albert. (1937). <u>Betwixt and Between.</u> Paris: Gallimard.

Camus, Albert (1937). <u>Revolt in the Asturias.</u> Paris: Gallimard.

Camus, Albert. (1942). <u>The Myth of Sisyphus.</u> Paris: Gallimard.

Camus, Albert. (1942). <u>The Stranger.</u> Paris: Gallimard.

Camus, Albert. (1944). <u>Caligula.</u> Paris. Gallimard.

Camus, Albert. (1944). <u>The Misunderstanding.</u> Paris. Gallimard.

Camus, Albert. (1947). <u>The Plague.</u> Paris: Gallimard.

Camus. Albert. (1950). <u>The Just Assassins.</u> Paris. Gallimard.

Camus, Albert. (1951). <u>The Rebel.</u> Paris. Gallimard.

Camus, Albert. (1957). <u>The Fall.</u> Paris. Gallimard.

Camus, Albert. (1994). <u>The First Man.</u> Paris. Gallimard.

Carson, Clayborn. (1991). "Martin Luther King, Jr., as Scholar: A Reexamination of His Theological Writings." *Journal of American History v78nl, Jun p 93-105.*

Carson, Clayborn. (1996). "King's Biography." A brief online biography, Martin Luther King Jr. Papers Project.

Carson, Clayborn. (1998). "A Common Solution" An essay perspective on Martin Luther King Jr. and Malcolm X. *Emerge* magazine, February 1998, pp.44-52.

Chavanes, Francois. (1990). <u>"You Have to Live Now" : Questions Addressed to Christianity in The Work of Albert Camus.</u> Paris: Cerf.

Clements, Robert J. (1978). <u>Comparative Literature as an Academic Discipline.</u> New York: The Modern Language Association of America.

Clouard, Henri. (1965). <u>French Writers of Today.</u> New York: Oxford University Press.

Comte-Sponville, Andre. (1995). <u>Camus: From the Absurd to Love.</u> Venissieux: Paroles d'Aube.

Cone, James H. (1991). <u>Martin and Malcolm and America: A Dream or a Nightmare.</u> New York: Orbis Books.

Cook, David. (1999). "The Last Camus." Book review of <u>The First Man.</u> Canada: University of Toronto.

Cruickshank, John. (1978). <u>Albert Camus and the Literature of Revolt.</u> New York: Oxford University Press.

Culler, Jonathan. "Comparative Literature, at Last!" ed. Bemheimer 117-121.

Davis, Colin. (1997) "Duras, Antelme and the Ethics of Writing." *Comparative Literature Studies,* Vol. 34, No.2, pp. 170-182.

Dayton Daily News, Section C-Religion, p. 1, January 30, 1999 Dayton Daily News, February 28, 1999, p. 21A.

Dayton Daily News, May 6, 1999, p. 1A). Dayton Daily News, September 13, 1999 Dayton Daily News, November 17, 1999, p. 1A.

Dayton Daily News, December 15, 1999, Section B, p. 1).

De Haan, Martin R. (1999). "Why Would a Good God Allow Suffering?" RBC Ministries. Grand Rapids, Michigan.

Dr. Martin Luther King Jr., <u>The Strength to Love (1963)</u>

Ellison, David R. (1990). <u>Understanding Albert Camus</u>. Columbia: University of South Carolina Press.

Erece, Alan T. (1989). "Martin Luther King, Jr. Gaining as Theologian." *National Catholic Reporter v25n12, Jan 13, p.22.*

Fairclough, Adam. (1995). <u>Martin Luther King, Jr.</u> Athens: University of Georgia Press.

Farris, Christine King. (1986). <u>Martin Luther King Jr.: His Life and Dream.</u> New York: Ginn and Co.

Fisher, William Harvey. (1977). <u>Free at Last: A Biography of Martin Luther King, Jr.</u>• Metuchen, NJ: Scarecrow Press.

Fitch, Brian T. (1995). <u>The Fall: A Matter of Guilt</u>. New York: Twayne Publishers.

Freeman, E. (1971). <u>The Theater of Albert Camus.</u> London. Methuen and Co. LTD.

Garrow, David J. (1986). <u>Bearing the Cross.</u> New York. William Morrow.

Garrow, David J. (1989). <u>Martin Luther King Jr. Civil Rights Leader. Theologian, Orator.</u> New York: Carlson Publishers.

Gates, Henry Louis. (1988). The Signifying Monkey: A Theory of Afro-American Literature Criticism.

Gossman, Lionel and Mihai I. Sparisou, eds. (1994). <u>Building a Profession: Autobiographical Perspectives on the Beginnings of Comparative Literature in the United States.</u> Albany, N.Y.: State University of New York Press.

Guerin, Jeanyves. (1993). <u>Portrait of the Artist As Citizen.</u> Paris: Editions F. Bourin Hanna, Thomas. (1962). "Albert Camus and the Christian Faith" ed. Brée. pp. 48-58.

Hanna, Thomas. (1969). <u>The Thought and Art of Albert Camus.</u> Chicago: Gateway.

Harding, Vincent. (1996). <u>Martin Luther King, Jr.: The Inconvenient Hero.</u> Maryknoll, NY: Orbis Books.

Harris, Wendell. (1996). <u>Literary Meaning: Reclaiming the Study of Literature.</u> Washington Square, New York: New York University Press.

Hermet, Joseph. (1990). <u>On Meeting Albert Camus: The Difficult Road of Freedom.</u> Paris: Beauchesne.

Higonnet, Margaret. "Comparative Literature on the Feminist Edge." ed. Bemheimer, pp. 155-164.

Holm, Patrick Colm. and Lalita Pandit. eds. (1995). <u>Literary India Comparative Studies in Aesthetics, Colonialism, and Culture.</u> Albany: State University of New York Press.

Holt, Robert T. and John T. Turner. (1970). <u>The Methodology of Comparative Research.</u> New York: Free Press.

Hopkins, Patricia Mary. (1969). "The Evolution of the Concept of Revolt in the Works of Albert Camus." University of Missouri: Columbia. *Dissertation Abstracts International.* Language and Literature. p. 3495-A, March 1970.

Hoskins, Lottie. (1968). "I Have A Dream": The Quotations of Martin Luther King, Jr., New York: Grosset and Dunlap.

Huggins, Nathan Irvin. (1987). "Charisma and Leadership." *Journal of American History v74n2, Sept p. 477-481.*

Isaac, Jeffrey C. (1992). <u>Arendt, Camus and Modem Rebellion.</u> New Haven: Yale University Press.

Jack, Belinda E. (1996). <u>Negritude and Literary Criticism: The History and Theory of "Negro African" Literature in French.</u> Westport Conn: Greenwood Press.

Kem Stephen. (1996). <u>Eyes of Love: The Gaze in English and French Culture, 1840-1900.</u> New York: New York University Press.

King, Adele (1995). "Le premier homme: Camus' Unfinished Novel." *World Literature Today. Vol.69, Number 1, Winter 1995. pp. 83-85.*

King, Coretta. (1969). <u>My Life With Martin Luther King, Jr.</u> New York: Holt Rinehart Winston.

King Luther, Jr.(1958). <u>Stride Toward Freedom.</u> New York: Harper Row.

King, Martin Luther, Jr. <u>(1964).Why We Can't Wait</u> New York: Harper Row.

King, Martin Luther, Jr. (1967). <u>Where Do We Go From Here: Chaos or Community.</u> New York: Harper Row.

King, Martin Luther, Jr. (1968). <u>The Trumpet of Conscience.</u> New York:, Martin Harper Row.

King's Legacy. (February 2, 1998. Online News Hour with Jim Lehrer Transcript. Interview with Taylor Branch–Martin Luther King Biographer.

Large, Ron. (1991). "Martin Luther King, Jr.,: <u>Ethics, Nonviolence and Moral Character."</u> *Journal of Religious Thought v48nl, Summer p. 51-63.*

Leedy, Paul D. (1997). <u>Practical Research: Planning and Design.</u> Sixth Edition. Upper Saddle River, New Jersey. Prentice-Hall.

Lehrer, Ariella J. (1990) "Martin Luther King., Instant Replay of History." *Classroom Computer Learning v10n7, Apr p 51-63*

Ling, Peter. (1998) "Martin Luther King's Half-Forgotten Dream." *History Today,* Vol. 48(4), April 1998, pp. 17-24.

Lomax, Louis E. (1963). <u>The Negro Revolt.</u> New York: the New American Library.

Lottman, Herbert. (1979). <u>Albert Camus: A Biography.</u> Garden City: New York. Doubleday.

Magill, Frank N. (1987). <u>The Nobel Prize Winners–Literature.</u> Vol. 2, 1927-1961: Pasadena, CA. Salem Press.

Mairowitz, David Zane and Korkos, Alain. (1998). <u>Introducing Camus.</u> New York: Totem Books.

Maurois, Andre. (1966) <u>From Proust to Camus: Profiles of Modern French Writers.</u>

Mares, C. J. (1989). "<u>Reading Proust: Woolf and The Painter's Perspective</u>" *Comparative Literature, V41N4, Fall,* (327-359).

Melanson, Philip. (1989). <u>The Murkin Conspiracy.</u> New York: Praeger Publishers.

Michelman, Frederic. (1995). "French and British Colonial Language Policies: A Comparative View of Their Impact on African Literature. *Research in African Literatures 1995*, v26n4, Winter p.216-225.

Michigan Citizen. (May 10-16, 1998). "Thoughts on the Black Radical Congress." p. B-1.

Miller, William Robert. (1968) <u>Martin Luther King, Jr.: His Life. Martyrdom and Meaning For The World.</u> New York,;_Weybright and Talley Publishers.

Mohammed, Rafik A., (1998). "A Call to Arms." *The Black Awareness Journal.* Vol. XVIII 1998.

Moses, Greg. (1997) <u>Revolution of Conscience: Martin Luther King, Jr., and the Philosophy of Nonviolence–Critical Perspectives.</u> New York: Guilford Press.

Oates, Stephen B. (1982). <u>Let the Trumpet Sound: The Life of Martin Luther King, Jr.</u> New York: Harper Row.

O'Brien, Conor Cruise (1970). <u>Albert Camus of Europe and Africa.</u> New York: Viking.

Parker, Emmett. (1966). <u>Albert Camus: The Artist in the Arena:</u> Madison: University of Wisconsin Press.

Poster, Mark. (1975). Existentialism and Marxism in Postwar France: From Sartre to Althusser. New York. Knopf.

Powers, Georgia Davis. (1995). <u>I Shared the Dream:</u> The Pride, Passion and Politics of the First Black Woman Senator from Kentucky. Far Hills, NJ.: New Horizon Press.

Pratt, Mary Louise. "Comparative Literature and Global Citizenship." ed. Bernheimer. pp. 58–65.

Prawer, Siegbert S. (1973). Comparative Literary Studies: An Introduction. Barnes and Noble: New York.

Quillot, Roger (1970). The Sea and Prisons: A Commentary on the Life and Thought of Albert Camus. University of AL: University of Alabama.

Remak, Henry H. H. (1971). "Comparative Literature: Its Definition and Function." in Stallknecht and Frenz, eds., Comparative Literature: Method and Perspective. Southern Illinois University Press: Carbondale and Edwardsville (1-57).

Rhein, Phillip. (1989). Albert Camus. Boston: Twayne Publishers.

Roberts, Edgar V. (1978). Thinking and Writing About Literature. Englewood Cliffs, N.J.: Prentice Hall.

Robles, Manuel. (1995). Camus: Brother of the Sun. Paris: Seuil.

Rockwell, Paula. (January 1999). "The Forgotten Teachings of Martin Luther King." Online excerpts from In Motion Magazine.

Rowland, Della. (1990). Martin Luther King, Jr.: The Dream of Peaceful Revolt. Englewood Cliffs, NJ: Simon Schuster.

Said, Edward W. Representations of the Intellectual. New York: Random House.

Seattle Times: Dr. Martin Luther King, Jr. (January 1999). "Civil Rights Timeline." Online summary of key civil rights events from 1954-1992.

Smith, Kenneth L. and Ira G. Zepp (1986). Search for the **Beloved Community**. Lanham, MD. University Press of America.

Southern Poverty Law Center, "Teaching Tolerance" literature. (1999). Morris Dees, President, Montgomery, Alabama.

SPLC Report, June 1999, Volume 29, Number 2, p. 5, The Southern Poverty Law Center.

Spleth, Janice. (1997). "Negritude and Literary Criticism: the History and Theory of Negro African American Literature." *Research in African Literature v28n2, Summer, p.195-198*

Sutton, Robert Chester. (1992). <u>Human Existence and Theodicy: A Comparison of Jesus and Albert Camus.</u> New York: P. Lang.

Stallknecht, Newton P. and Horst Frenz. (1971). eds., <u>Comparative Literature: Method and Perspective.</u> Southern Illinois University Press. Carbondale and Edwardsville.

The Promise Keepers, 1999 literature pack. Boulder, Colorado. The Vineyard Project brochure. Dayton, Ohio, 1999.

The World Book Dictionary (1978). Chicago: IL. World Book-Childcraft, Inc. The World Book Encyclopedia, Inc. (1978 &1999). Chicago: IL.

Thody, Philip. (1961). <u>Albert Camus, 1913-1960: A Study of His Work.</u> London: Hamish Hamilton.

Todd, Oliver. (1997). <u>Albert Camus: A Life.</u> Paris: Gallimard.

Washington, James Melvin. (1986). <u>A Testament of Hope: The Essential Writings of Martin Luther King. Jr.</u> New York: Harper Row.

Watley, William D. (1985). <u>Roots of Resistance: The Nonviolent Ethic of Martin Luther King Jr.</u> Valley Forge: PA, Judson Press.

Weisstein, Ulrich. (1973). <u>Comparative Literature and Literary Theory: Survey and Introduction:</u> Trans. William Riggan. Bloomington: Indiana University Press.

Weisstein, Ulrich. (1989). "Lasciati ogni speranza: Comparative Literature in Search of Lost Definitions." *Yearbook of Comparative and General Literature 37.*

Wilkinson, Russell. (1995). "Solitaire et Solidaire." talks to Catherine Camus about her father and <u>The First Man:</u> The Internet. Spike@hedweb.com.

Willhoite, Fred. (1968). <u>Beyond Nihilism:</u> Albert Camus' Contribution to Political Thought.

Baton Rouge: The University of Louisiana Press.

Williams, John A. (1971). <u>The King that God Didn't Save.</u> New York: Simon Schuster.

Woelfel, James W. (1975). <u>Camus: A Theological Perspective:</u> New York: Abingdon Press. Wyatt, Christopher Scott. (1998). "Albert Camus: Biography." tameri@lightspeed.net.

Xenon Entertainment Group. (1993). *Dr. Martin Luther King, Jr.: A Historical Perspective.* (video recording). Santa Monica, CA.

CPSIA information can be obtained
at www.ICGtesting.com
Printed in the USA
LVHW010047081019
633404LV00001B/246

9 781949 981087